EXPERIENCING SHAKESPEARE

Charles H. Frey

EXPERIENCING SHAKESPEARE
Essays on Text, Classroom, and Performance

University of Missouri Press
Columbia, 1988

Library of Congress Cataloging-in-Publication Data

Frey, Charles H.
   Experiencing Shakespeare: essays on text, classroom, and
performance/Charles H. Frey.
   p. cm.
   Includes index.
   ISBN 0-8262-0653-0 (alk. paper)
      Shakespeare, William, 1564-1616—Criticism and
interpretation. 2. Shakespeare, William, 1564-1616—Study and
teaching. 3. Shakespeare, William, 1564-1616—Dramatic
                     production. I. Title.
                     PR2976.F66 1988
                     822.3'3—dc19

To the dreamers

Preface

This is a collection of free-standing essays on Shakespeare. About half of them appear in scattered publications, some of them not readily accessible. The essays date from 1975 to 1985, and, in presenting them chronologically and (with minor exceptions) as originally worded, it is my purpose to expose some vectors in a critic's developing approaches to and assessments of Shakespearean criticism over the past decade. To me this is in part an exposure of mistakes and vulnerabilities (perhaps not wholly atypical ones) as well as, I hope, an exposure of insights and growth. While I imagine that each essay may have an interest of its own, I want to believe as well that the connective order suggests one track or trajectory in developments of recent literary scholarship and teaching that happen to center on Shakespeare.

In part, these essays evolve from relatively self-enclosed concerns with interpretation and performance toward more self-reflexive concern for the institutional contexts, processes, and productions constituting the very display or presentation of Shakespeare in our culture. More particularly, retrospective interpretations of post-play concepts and of structures of meaning find themselves challenged by a desire to observe and account for how the plays unfold in our present, temporal-affective time. Ever stronger, too, is the motivating desire to consider how our era's own evaluative explications fit into varied histories of interpreting, staging, editing, and teaching the socio-historical construction known as "Shakespeare." Not without some loss in coherence and brightness, measured by one standard at least, my focus shifts from the text, the play-animal itself, swimming in a sea of barely examined assumptions, to that assumptive sea itself and its powers to nourish and to dissolve, institutionally, the textual life it harbors.

The main line of change, as I see it, swerves away from some of the paler formalisms attendant on a New Critical professional training and away from a view of Shakespeare as chief exponent for teaching a liberal, humane ideology. Reflected in the first four chapters is an ethos of interpretation that searches beyond consensus among diverse critics, all assumed ready to learn, grow, and contribute to the enrichment of our cultural heritage through their study and teaching of Shakespeare. In writing on *As You Like It, The Winter's Tale,* and *The Tempest,* I sought to reconcile and to harmonize disturbing relativities in interpretive views toward a working "fellowship," but I also sought increasingly to place and to respect the disruptiveness of the plays, their varied theatrical and textual lives, their historical contingency, their capacity to reflect and to stimulate precisely those divergent aims of social groups that a conservative or universalist or essentialist criticism might wish to ignore, or to suppress.

Why would a critic and teacher stop seeing Shakespeare primarily as a stage against confusion and start seeing Shakespeare as a confusion of reaction against democratic ideals and a scourge and skeptic against hierarchical and patriarchal views, a mind against itself, a playwright covertly subverting accepted denotation in language, thought, feeling, and art, to unaccepted detonation? Added to the pressures of political critiques from feminists (which dawned for me through family-making) and from materialists and representatives of third worlds (one of which I taught in for a time) have been more seemingly intrinsic pressures generated from years of reading and watching and teaching Shakespeare. Early to crumble was my inherited view that Shakespeare's greatest works were tragedies extolling *man's* nobility of character tested in suffering. Not only did the tragedies and histories, as repeatedly studied and as responded to by hundreds of students, pointedly question such nobility, but also the curve of Shakespeare's development seemed to lead through the antinobilisms of late tragedies and problem plays and romances to the increasingly shrewd and satiric nauseas of the post-*Tempest* plays constituting Shakespeare's post-romance. At the same time, I became much more intensely aware of modern editorial, theatrical, and filmic packagings of Shakespeare that huddle us cheerfully along in various Bardolatrous throngs. And, despite the presence of many critical groups— feminists, new historicists, deconstructionists, Marxists, textual de-collationists, performance-study advocates, and so on—I did not, until recently, perceive significant alteration in style or content of papers at key professional meetings of Shakespeare scholars, an indication that teaching Shakespeare in America remained pretty much business as usual. My attention and energy have been drawn, as a result, more and more to questioning the very conditions by which the traditional teaching and criticism of Shakespeare maintain themselves.

Taken collectively, the following essays amount, I hope, to an argument against collective stasis, atemporal unity, or proud consistency in a Shakespearean's work. The argument favors, on the other hand, critical self-exploration, exploration of what Shakespearean teachers and critics think they have been doing, what they really are doing, and what fear and desire their doings may reflect. What stage, always, are we passing through with Shakespeare? What stage is coming?

In the past few years, British leftist critiques of the Shakespeare industry and of allegedly repressive teachings of Shakespeare have increased in number and sharpened in cogency. There have been few voices in concert evident in North America, probably in part because a differing class structure and a semi-noxious tradition of excessive individualism allow teacherly goals of student self-empowerment and critical awareness to supplant needs for genuine political and collective action among student groups with interests in common, *even* in the humanities. The five chapters that conclude this volume seem to me to reflect a kind of restless skepticism, a doubtful yearning for confidence in political stance, and an argument for an ungentle Will. But, finally, after trying on the notions of immodest, free-minded theater (Chapter 7, 1981), of fair-minded editing and intergenerational scholarly reciprocity (Chapter 8, 1982), of openness to Shakespeare's sexual sadness (Chapter 9, 1983), of a need for teaching Shakespeare more dialogically (Chapter 10, 1984), and of the painful irresolutions that might be exemplified in such dialogue (Chapter 11, 1985), I wonder ever more curiously whether "teaching Shakespeare" can be other than a love that must undo us all. A few more thoughts on this subject appear in the Afterword.

I apologize for varieties of lapse, if not blindness, in these pieces. I do not wish to cover up certain of their more questionable features, because where some take umbrage others may take heart and vice versa. Also, to leave my fear and anger and unfinishedness in plain sight may encourage some others to drop protections or masks of universal logic, incessant rigor, and objective certainty. Not that a communal sense of logic or persuasiveness is *all* bad. Nor that disagreements and even dislikes should be warded off. Far from it. Yet I would hope for myself to suffer some unaccustomed feeling and fooling, if not gladly, yet at least gadly.

I find that interpreting or teaching Shakespeare comprehends so much of the contentious traffic on our particular cultural crossroads, that the enterprise seems in some respects crazy-making. And I won't pretend that it does not seem so. These essays are what I made of each moment, each stage, roughly each year, as a Shakespearean during the last decade. At each stage I believed in and felt a strength in my perception and response. And as the times have changed and I have changed, so Shakespeare has seemed to me to change as well. I know, of course, that other readers will have experienced their own interpretations or teachings of Shakespeare in terms vastly different from my terms. All the more reason for us to communicate.

C. H. F.
June 1987

Acknowledgments

For their help and encouragement in discussing my ideas or reading drafts of chapters herein, I am grateful to many, particularly my students, and including my colleagues Charles Altieri, Joanne Altieri, Paul Andreas, John Andrews, Joe Barber, Edward I. Berry, Mike Bristol, Barry Gaines, Susan Green, Gayle Greene, Donald Hedrick, Eric LaGuardia, Maynard Mack, Carol Neely, Norman Rabkin, Susan Starbuck, W. R. Streitberger, and Sara van den Berg. I thank Michael Bristol, Miriam Gilbert, and Phyllis Rackin for their suggestions concerning the manuscript. Several chapters evolved from papers given at meetings of the Central Renaissance Conference, the International Shakespeare Association, the Modern Language Association, the Pacific Northwest Renaissance Conference, the Shakespeare Association of America, the Shakespeare Institute of Bridgeport University, and the University of British Columbia. I wish to thank those responsible for invitations to these meetings and those who participated in the various sessions.

I acknowledge with thanks the kind permission of the following to quote from essays first appearing in their pages: *New York Literary Forum*; *Shakespeare Quarterly*; *Shakespeare Studies*; *South Atlantic Review* (formerly *South Atlantic Bulletin*); *Studies in English Literature: 1500–1900*; *The Upstart Crow*; and *The Woman's Part: Feminist Criticism of Shakespeare*, edited by Carolyn Ruth Swift Lenz, Gayle Greene, and Carol Thomas Neely (University of Illinois Press).

Joan Cashdollar and Virginia Chappell helped to prepare the manuscript.

Contents

Abbreviations

Ado	Much Ado about Nothing
Ant.	Antony and Cleopatra
AWW	All's Well That Ends Well
AYL	As You Like It
Cym.	Cymbeline
Ham.	Hamlet
1H4	Henry IV, Part 1
2H4	Henry IV, Part 2
H5	Henry V
1H6	Henry VI, Part 1
2H6	Henry VI, Part 2
3H6	Henry VI, Part 3
H8	Henry VIII
JC	Julius Caesar
Jn.	King John
LLL	Love's Labor's Lost
Lr.	King Lear
Luc.	The Rape of Lucrece
Mac.	Macbeth
MM	Measure for Measure
MND	A Midsummer Night's Dream
MV	The Merchant of Venice
Oth.	Othello
Per.	Pericles
R2	Richard II
Rom.	Romeo and Juliet
Shr.	The Taming of the Shrew
STM	Sir Thomas More
TGV	The Two Gentlemen of Verona
Tim.	Timon of Athens
Tit.	Titus Andronicus
TN	Twelfth Night
TNK	The Two Noble Kinsmen
Tmp.	The Tempest
Tro.	Troilus and Cressida
Wiv.	The Merry Wives of Windsor
WT	The Winter's Tale

Construe my meaning,
Wrest not my method,
Good will craves favour. . . .

Canzonet No. 20, in *Canzonets to Four Voices*,
compiled by Giles Farnaby (London, 1598)

SHAKESPEAREAN INTERPRETATION
Promising Problems

I think I can promise that for years to come there will be procedural and other problems troubling the enterprise of Shakespearean interpretation, problems whose unwelcome resistance to solution we should recognize and oppose. Also, I think that there are a number of interpretive problems that appear promising as candidates for future exploration. It is to these two issues of promising problems that I wish to address myself.

Surprising as it may seem, Shakespearean interpreters, with increasing frequency, are disclaiming an intent to say anything new. One such interpreter has argued as follows:

> Critical interpretations of Shakespeare's plays are somewhat like pianistic interpretations of Beethoven's sonatas. If true to the art they elucidate, they will in each case seem much like other interpretations. The similarities will necessarily outweigh the differences; for the words and the notes are already there. The plays are Shakespeare's and the sonatas are Beethoven's, not the property of the interpreter. What is better or worse in interpretations will reside not in originalities or critical individualism, but in subtleties of tone and conception attendant upon a responsibility to attain as nearly as possible to the work of art as its author set it down.
>
> In the discussions that now follow, accordingly, there has been no attempt at novelty.[1]

Interpretive novelties, in other words, are thought to follow wrongheaded swervings from the "work as its author set it down." But where can we find the plays as Shakespeare set

1

them down? On the page? Should we write the plays out in longhand imitating the spelling, punctuation, capitalization, and penmanship of Hand D in the manuscript play of *Sir Thomas More*? Or should we seek the plays in their original form on the stage? Might we dress in Elizabethan costume and stand in the afternoon rain inside a Southwark replica of the Globe to watch an unlighted performance, hear Elizabethan pronunciation, and perhaps have our pockets picked? Or are the plays as Shakespeare set them down a body of historically determined meanings? Should we steep ourselves in biography and other lore so as to pursue the ever-receding goal of authorial intent?

Few of us, I believe, even while granting the contributions of mature textual and historical criticism, will seek a Shakespeare of such overwhelming quaintness as these examples would yield. The words as Shakespeare set them down and the plays as he and his colleagues set them up had, in their day, contemporary meaning and full-life impact. We must give proper deference to historically conditioned meaning; yet we also seek a semblance of contemporary meaning and full-life impact whenever we change the typography of an old text or use modern lighting in a production or ask what the plays tell us about ourselves. The plays are in part the property of living interpreters who must, of necessity, view them with an endless novelty of perspective. Interpreters have discovered through the ages a sadly less than neoclassical Shakespeare, a Shakespeare of great character portraits, a Shakespeare of spectacle, a Shakespeare of dramatic poems, a myth-forging Shakespeare, and a great many other Shakespeares. Men and women peer into Shakespeare's mirrors and find through time wonderfully varied yet true images of themselves. There is no reason, I submit, to regret the turning kaleidoscope of interpretation so long as we do not take it to authorize extremes of subjectivism and relativism. Though we may disagree with them in particulars that reflect the difference between the temper of their times and the temper of ours, we often agree with such giants of interpretation as

Johnson, Coleridge, and Bradley who revealed new truths about the plays. Indeed, each age has its own job to do in discovering what seems to it most lasting and universal in Shakespeare.

If we concede that the more profound interpretations of each age will strike us as additions to and enrichments of preceding interpretation, we may conclude that current disclaimers of originality arise not from disbelief in the fact of interpretive advance but from fears of unintentionally duplicating approaches or insights of unknown contemporaries. For the Alexandrian profusion of dissertations, books, and articles interpreting Shakespeare may already be so great as to disable the individual interpreter from ascertaining whether or not a given point has been broached before. And, aside from the physical problem of reading widely enough, the problem of time lag in publication of bibliographies and of one's own work militates against guarantees of originality. Under these circumstances we can promise ourselves certain intensifying problems in the next few decades.

First is the problem of how to deal with and avoid duplicated effort. If dissertation writers and advisers, readers for presses and journals, as well as interpreters generally, will make an increasingly conscientious effort to inform themselves of known contributions to the particular subject under consideration, much repetition may be eliminated. I foresee, nonetheless, an approaching era of massive interpretive duplication, increasing charges of negligence and plagiarism, and intensified frustration until either our bibliographical resources are greatly refined or the number of publishing interpreters grows smaller.

A potential response to fears of duplication promises another problem. As some interpreters of Shakespeare may decide they are employing exhausted methods—so that their analyses of image clusters and analogues or their applications of psychology, myth, intellectual backgrounds, and the like have been anticipated—they may turn to invent startlingly new methods or even retreat from discussion of substantive content to confront questions of methodology per se. Periodically taking stock of interpretive means and ends is one thing, but a wholesale flight to realms of methodological controversy is another. I foresee in part a new and salutary methodological self-consciousness among interpreters of Shakespeare, the sort of interest in method advanced by such proceedings as the World Shakespeare Congresses.[2] I also foresee as a result of our overpopulation and overspecialization much fruitless bickering over which approaches are most valuable, some misguided claims to originality in works that merely dress up old ideas in new terminology, and an advancing chorus of calls for a moratorium on new studies, a general outcry against further interpretation. These problems may plague us until there is either a great leap forward in the art of interpretation or a great change in our culture's understanding of Shakespeare or, more likely, both.

To promise interpretive problems of the unwelcome sorts just discussed is easier than to identify problems that will prove to be interesting in the next few years. Many contemporary interpreters will pursue traditional lines of inquiry—interpreting plays in the light of sources, parallels, and the thought of the age or interpreting character, structure, authorial intent, stage history, and affective impact. Such studies may prove individually useful but collectively incoherent unless we make a determined effort to find a few organizing principles. My hope is, in part, that we will write less interpretation of the pianistic sort, in which the plays are, as it were, performed for readers, and that we will write more interpretation of the teaching sort, in which readers are encouraged toward the skill of interpreting all of Shakespeare for themselves. Interpreters should think of themselves not as performing acts upon the plays that produce disparate bits of knowledge but rather as training themselves and others toward increased appreciation of themes and procedures dominant throughout Shakespeare.

If we refer to the root idea of "interpretation," we recognize that interpreters traditionally help parties talk to each other.

The word goes back via the Latin *interpretari* to the base *per* in prepositions and preverbs associated with motion "forward" or "through." The basic idea has been that of negotiating or going between, that is, of facilitating a transaction by helping the parties to communicate clearly and completely. Ideally, an interpreter would not produce his own version of what each party said but would instantly teach the parties to understand and to speak each other's language. The Shakespearean interpreter pursues a similar goal in that he would enable one party to the transaction, that is, all readers and playgoers, to see and to respond independently. Often, of course, Shakespearean interpretation appears to be merely a matter of local and isolated gleanings from a text. A problem, for example, of rhetorical interpretation in the *First Part of Henry the Fourth* is to determine functions of the many conditional sentences. To show that Hotspur and Falstaff, particularly, are addicted to "if" clauses, to show that a common construction is "if it be not so, then I'll be hanged," and to show that "iffiness" of speech tends in the play to reflect both an imaginativeness and an uncertainty of outlook shared by rebels and tavern crowd alike might seem enough to show in a piece of interpretation. But readers of the piece might be enabled more actively to use its insights if the interpreter placed the problem of Falstaff's conditional propositions in the context of Shakespearean argumentation and especially Shakespeare's mastery of syllogistic reasoning. The consideration of *Henry the Fourth* might then lead readers to hear for themselves how Shakespeare uses rhetorical forms as motifs to reveal habits of thought in characters and even to help define the worlds of his plays. We need always to consider, in other words, how our interpretation may inform the reader's continuing relations with Shakespearean drama.

Interpreters have long marveled over the organic quality of Shakespeare's art, particularly the ways in which unobtrusive details, on examination, point germinally toward larger issues. But we still have much to do to explore the pointing itself, that middle range of meanings between gloss and essay.

In *All's Well That Ends Well,* as Parolles chides Helena for wanting to preserve her virginity, he four times uses the unobjec-
tionable expletive "marry." The editor's gloss will give a
simple equivalent: "by Mary" or "indeed." But the word
"marry" points further; it is ironically appropriate in the
mouth of Parolles, who not only favors unmarried promis-
cuity but intones with anti-Marian certainty: "there was
never virgin got till virginity was lost" (*AWW*, 1.1.131).[3] Later in
the play, Helena conceives a child, as did the Virgin Mary,
without her husband's knowledge yet without committing
adultery, so that Parolles' oath then reverberates surprisingly.
The answer to Helena's quandary has been to marry à la Mary.
The problem here is neither to expand the usual gloss on
"marry" nor to incorporate the irony into an article on *All's
Well,* but to devise an educative interpretation of how words
and action cooperate in Shakespeare's plays.

Though often neglected by Shakespearean interpreters
until recently, dramatic action, the look of things onstage,
deserves our increased attention. We need to help ourselves
and others see as well as hear the plays. Failure to visualize
each circumstance wherein the actors of *King Lear* fall to their
knees is to miss a vital demonstration of how fools and old
men crawl throughout like babes toward death. *The Winter's
Tale* contains not one but four or more statue scenes, that is,
scenes in which a quiet and still woman faces onlookers who
mistake her true nature and who witness her dramatic transformation and declaration of self. In the past few years, interpreters have shown new interest in Shakespeare's visual art:
his especially emblematic scenes, interscenic parallels and
contrasts, employment of key properties such as thrones, use
of the discovery space, orchestrations of entrances, exits, and
groupings, and patterns of changing pace, focus, and mood.
It is one of the most promising fields for future development.

Most problems of Shakespeare interpretation, if pursued in
their full dramatic context, will implicate both verbal and
visual meanings. In *Measure for Measure,* at the time when
Angelo, offstage, thinks he is executing Isabella's maidenhead

(4.2), Pompey and the Provost at the prison discuss cutting off "a woman's head" and similarities between the hangman's "turn" and the bawd's. (Cf. *Rom.*, 1.1.24–28; *Per.*, 4.6.132–33.) The play works at a deep and grisly level on the old metaphor of sexual compared to bodily dying, and it stresses grim analogies between the plot to substitute Mariana's maidenhead for Isabella's and the plot to substitute another prisoner's head for Claudio's. As Barnardine, moreover, refuses to die at Abhorson's request or "for any man's persuasion," he becomes a parody of Isabella, who refuses to yield her maidenhead at Angelo's request or even at Claudio's persuasion; when the Provost enters with Ragozine's dripping head in substitution, the parody of Isabella's bed-trick becomes especially grotesque as well as shockingly laughable.

Other images that are both visually shown and verbally discussed include the various deceptive trunks in *Cymbeline* (Iachimo's empty trunk, Cloten's headless trunk, and Cymbeline as the lopped cedar); the ring and drum of *All's Well* (as they hoop the false-oathed Bertram and Parolles into betraying themselves, both in darkness and both for want of language); speeches about and gestures of clasped hands in several plays; imagery of testing and trial in *Lear*, of multiform appetites for money, food, and sex in *Timon*, of drowning and swallowing or "kissing the Book" in *The Tempest*. Thorough investigation of such spoken and staged imageries will lead toward a better understanding of ways in which text and scene interact.

Beyond the interworkings of speech and spectacle within specific plays lie larger questions concerning themes and procedures common to all the plays. We sense that in spite of their obvious diversity the plays are strikingly similar not only in use of rhetoric, imagery, scenic construction, characterological foils, attitudes toward disorder, and the like, but also in dramatic shape and content: the opening critiques of courtly and artificial values (inherited nobility, flattered power, purchased friendships, martial pride), then the inevitable banishments, alienations, and ostracisms that purge and renew, the central search for bonds of friendship and service, the shifts from intellective openings filled with wordplay and appearance-piercing to the more flatly active final acts, and the toned-down closings that so often invite our own musing exit.

We need to help one another isolate those features of dramatic metabolism and orchestration that make the plays distinctively Shakespearean, and I think that we will in years ahead. We may, for instance, analyze much further the principle of stylistic debate that informs much of Shakespearean drama. In the comedies, men either master language or are mastered by it. In the histories and tragedies, poetic losers often confront plainer speaking and superficially more successful antagonists. And the battle of styles includes far more than idiom. In *King Lear*, Edmund allies himself with nature as free of custom or art or providential design, a nature dominated by self-interest and "lusty stealth." He denies the influence of any "divine thrusting on." He is in some ways the thing itself. But the thing itself, the natural man, not only must use his own artifice but also, eventually, must recognize his brother as a man of superior art. After Edmund whispers in scorn, "My cue is villainous melancholy, with a sigh like Tom o' Bedlam" (*Lr.*, 1.2.134), Edgar adopts part of the cue and becomes not only a nonvillainous Tom o' Bedlam but also an actor who reaches beyond nature: a "robed man of justice" at Lear's mock trial, "Child Rowland" bringing grace to the dark tower, the playmaster of Gloucester's rescue from despair (induced by illusion at Dover Cliffs), and finally a tourney knight who bluffs Edmund out of the naturalistic mode into the moral play of chivalric combat. Here Edgar explores a variety of ways in which man's life may rise in art above the beasts and prove itself more than "nothing."

A special plea remains to be made for explorations of temporal, forward-moving, truly dramatic progressions in the plays as opposed to those accounts—relatively static, spatial, and visionary—that tend to extract residual, postplay concepts. We need to note more searchingly how Shakespeare habitually first presents false or unstable sociopolitical orders and then opposes to them forms of purgative if unruly will. Often the crisis turns specifically on "election" of a leader, as in *Titus, Measure for Measure,* and *Coriolanus;* or "election" of a spouse, as in *All's Well* and *Cymbeline;* or "election" to a coveted position, as in *Othello* and *Hamlet.* These and other instances of "election," together with the many plays built on themes of jealousy and usurpation, reveal Shakespeare's intense concern with the vulnerability of authority to will and of the absolute to the attacking relative. That Shakespeare's concern may be illuminated by studies of intellectual history is undoubted, but to see how the plays set forth and solve the crisis of election is the important thing.

To a similar degree interpretation based on parallels in Sidney, Spenser, and Fletcher may help to explain why Shakespeare inevitably uses pastoral to question ideals of chastity, natural nobility, and order in nature. The movement from court to country, in Elizabethan thinking, embodies a search to define our genetic roots as either corrupt or sound. But only a study of pastoral journeys throughout the plays will enable us to make more appropriate comparisons among them, for Shakespeare's drama is pastoral not only in the comedies, romances, and *Lear* but also in plays such as *Timon* and *Hamlet.* The appearance of Alcibiades with prostitutes at Timon's cave seems anomalous and forced unless connected to the negative pastoral wherein Timon, digging for roots. discovers gold, root of evil, and, as he says, the "common whore of mankind." Ophelia's flower-giving and mad songs suggest a horror of men in a state of nature who pursue the mortal lusts of which she sings and who are, unlike Hamlet perhaps, ready to "do't if they come to't." Yet she, garlanded with nettles and "dead men's fingers," drowns mermaidlike and singing, as if familiar with elements of dissolution and death. Hamlet is just then out on waters too, and he returns still thinking on mortality but now native and endued unto that element in "readiness." Yet to see him leap on Orphelia's corpse is to learn afresh that in Hamlet's world sex and death have intertwined too closely and that those "buried quick" are all buried sick. Shakespeare's pastoral, like his romance, is surprisingly pervasive, and it is less thematically than dramatically impressive. We, as interpreters, probably cannot hope to extract from the plays a body of noncontradictory propositions about pastoral and romance, but we can hope to sensitize readers and playgoers to the turns and returns in Shakespeare's dramatic use of them.

All these observations lead toward the belief that our age occupies a privileged position for combining visual and verbal interpretation toward a more comprehensive understanding of Shakespearean drama. Editorial and rhetorical studies have alerted us to many nuances of meaning that were undetected heretofore, and the study of drama in performance has blossomed apace. We are open, moreover, as no age before us, to the energy, meaning, and impact of all the plays, and so we have a remarkable opportunity to encourage on every side a more sensitive response to the full experience of Shakespeare's art. Our job, as I see it, is primarily to help others acquire an independence of interpretive skill, not necessarily to display our own. Interpreting Shakespeare differs from playing Beethoven; it more nearly resembles aiding others toward their own playing and listening. If we can assist our age toward its own informed response to Shakespeare, we will help to shape a collective interpretation at once authentic and original. If, in particular, we interpreters can overcome the divisive aspects of our specialization and competition and if we will only search together for a renewed engagement with the form and force of Shakespearean drama as we perceive it, we may yet make our small but signal contribution to the probable millennia of Shakespeare studies.

THE SWEETEST ROSE
As You Like It as Comedy of Reconciliation

Laughter has no content. Or, rather, a sense of humor that leads to laughter is its own content. Theories of humor and its mode of expression in comedy tend, therefore, as they attempt comprehensiveness, to become theories of pure form, issuing, most often, in grand generalizations concerning golden means, avoidance of absurdity or of mechanical action, and rules of right proportions. That is, we all know, in one sense, what comedy is about; its content is always the same—love, sex, death, money, class, generational conflict—just as its result is always to expose those who would alter relations that must obtain to foster the huge ongoingness of life. Yet we need comic theory, as well as endless debate about it, because although we know that a sense of humor is somehow a sense of proportion and propitiation celebrating the ongoingness, still we do not know precisely what leads to or underlies it. While some laugh, others stay aloof.

Shakespeare's comedies, however—at least such romantic ones as *Much Ado About Nothing* and *As You Like It*—are supreme among their genre in that they evoke nearly universal laughter. Audiences bring to such comedies varying tastes in humor; yet few individuals remain aloof. Why? What accounts for Shakespeare's power to take us all in? I believe that *As You Like It* delights us partly because it addresses itself so successfully to the very question of individuated versus universal tastes. The play makes us laugh sympathetically at

11

our differences while reconciling them toward common ends such as fellowship and marriage. End and source become one, moreover, in a vision of love as both a mean and means of reconciliation as well as a generative principle of differentiation. In what follows I explore only a few of the varied ways in which Shakespeare makes the substance of his comedy out of reconciling individual and universal tastes.

If the play's title is meant to suggest only an inconsequential relativism of tastes, an analogue to *Much Ado About Nothing* or to *What You Will* or to Lodge's remark in his preface to *Rosalynde*, "If you like it, so," then the play means to disarm interpretation in advance. But the title may do more than bow to quirks of individual preference. It may say not merely, "Take it as you like," but also, "This is what you, the collective audience, like." The title may thus hint that the play embraces not only relativism but also reconciliation. This sort of ambivalence between or paradoxical union of like as differentiated taste and like as comparable taste appears in the epilogue, where Rosalind charges the women in her audience to "like as much of this play as please you" but then charges that between the men and women "the play may please." Even if we allow for the pun on play, the point is made that there should be room for both individuation and sharing of the pleasure.

I dwell, perhaps too solemnly, on this point because it hints at the distinctive metabolism of this astonishingly complex drama and its equally complex effect. *As You Like It* affirms the humor of finding that one's likes, though unique to oneself, are nonetheless shared with and thus like the likes of others. So trembling and difficult is the balance maintained in this play between individuation and harmonization, between the concrete and the universal, that solemn interpretation can hardly hope to remain as gracefully poised. One is defeated before one starts. One can, however, begin by disengaging from the sorts of approaches to *As You Like It* that stress its discontinuities, its relativity of likings, at the expense of its wholeness; for this is the most persistent mistake made with the play: to find a critic-analytic play that suits, perhaps, a critic-analytic mind.

Some kinds of solemn analysis we cannot take seriously. Consider the British headmaster who published, in 1818, a volume entitled *The Progress of Human Life,* analyzing and praising Jaques's speech on the seven ages of man as if it were the final summation of human wisdom, noting, for example, how the adjectives applied to the babe "mewling and puking in the nurse's arms" so perfectly describe what the headmaster called the "imbecility" of infancy.[1] This educationist never noted the dramatic context of the speech, the "melancholy" nature of the speaker, or the satiric nature of the seven depictions; yet he felt entitled, delightfully enough, to "correct" the baseless fabric of Shakespeare's theatrical vision by imagining Shakespeare, at the last, pointing raptly to Bible pages promising a new heaven and new earth.

Others would moralize the spectacle of *As You Like It* into quaintly secular terms. Writing on the "descent to sexual realities" in Shakespeare's romantic comedy, a recent critic seeks to praise Rosalind in these terms:

Emotionally committed to femininity yet sexually experienced in both male and female attitudes, she remains witty and skeptical enough never to be trapped in an inexpedient role. She thus deserves our closest attention as the most successful model for women in Shakespeare.

And the whole play is seen as

a complex investigation of the interaction of the conscious mind with its emotional drives and the physiological equipment with which it finds itself arbitrarily endowed.[2]

Again, the play is translated out of the theater and converted into a didactic tract. Both the schoolmaster and psychological critic seem objectionably serious about *As You Like It* because they appear, almost, not to "get" the joke or, if they do, to focus on the tensions of wit and miss the resolutions of humor. They remain too intent on divisions and dissociations of the play, its analytic processes that, in the full drama, open up a space for connective metaphor and synthesis, providing the initial shock of wit amazed at life's incongruities only to move beyond into the afterglow of humor, the process of accepting and making things even.

A special mode of excessively relativistic analysis threatens the would-be director of *As You Like It*. When love, so-called, is divided among eight individualized lovers, what hope can there be for unity of focus or judgment? Was not Shakespeare working a piece of dramatic whimsy or at least purposeful ambiguity out of his source novel, such whimsy as digesting the name Saladyne and coming up with the equally oily Oliver, such ambiguity as he made inhere in most of the main characters? Is Duke Senior silly? Or wise? Is Adam comic? Or dignified? Is Touchstone truly central? Is Jaques really melancholy? Is Celia bland? Or vivacious? Is she a vital character in her own right? Or, because present but silent, like Touchstone, much of the time, more of a sardonic chorus, disengaged from the action and helping to distance it for us? Is Orlando a straight man? Or a wit in his own right? Is Rosalind gracious, a gentlelady, not particularly comic, in the style of Helena Faucit? Or maddeningly coy, in the style of Elisabeth Bergner? Or winningly insecure in the style of Vanessa Redgrave? And how is she to divide herself into Rosalind and Ganymede? How much of each role is present in her exchanges with Orlando?[3] However one resolves these questions—and in the theater they must be resolved—one must seek fidelity to the overall progress of the action. The play, after all, does move in a direction. The first scenes are scenes of emptying the stage, and the last are scenes of filling it up. What becomes scattered gathers together again. The relativism is not final.

Let us take a closer look. *As You Like It* opens with Orlando's complaints of stifling confinement. Orlando is growing physically, and the spirit of his father, as he says, "grows strong" within him; yet Oliver "stays" him at home and "bars" him the place of a brother, so that he begins to "mutiny against this servitude." To the warring verbal images of growth versus confinement, the play adds the visual images of Orlando physically grappling first with Oliver and then with Charles the Wrestler. One senses that the court is a place of opposed energies grinding against each other until that which is good can gasp free. The second scene parallels the first. Rosalind, in the position of Orlando, enters as he did on the theme of a lost (in her case, banished) father. Celia, in the position of Oliver, establishes by contrast a loving sisterly relation with Rosalind—"I could have taught my love to take thy father for mine." Celia becomes inversely analogous to Oliver when she offers all her inheritance to Rosalind. The girls then proceed to a friendly grappling of wits as they "devise sports," and the parallel between the two scenes is continued when Celia inquires of the entering LeBeau, "What's the news?" much as Oliver had inquired of the entering Charles, "What's the new news?" As protagonists of the two scenes begin to merge, so do themes. It is facetiously suggested that LeBeau thought wrestling a sport for Rosalind and Celia to engage in, and, after Orlando overthrows Charles, Rosalind and Orlando become mutual champions in the "wrestling" of their affections. The competitive closeness of the court is held before us as Duke Frederick, toward the end of the act, declares his mistrust of Rosalind and argues to Celia:

> Thou art a fool; she robs thee of thy name,
> And thou wilt show more bright and seem more virtuous
> When she is gone.
>
> (1.1.76–78)

Shakespeare's dramas, like the bulk of the world's stories, tend to originate in family quarrels, and an almost incestuous overcloseness or excessive interdependence within families is often the motivating force of his comedies and tragedies alike. Says LeBeau, "There comes an old man, and his three sons"; Celia responds, "I could match this beginning with an old tale."[4] The play itself began by referring to Sir Rowland and his three sons. *King Lear* begins, in the fashion of LeBeau's tale, with an old man and his three daughters. Sibling rivalry, in short, is a prime cause of such drama: a brother or sister (one of which most of us are) seeks not just a superior claim to parental affection but also differentiation from siblings, an independent identity and life. We remember the recurrence of biblical narratives based on brother rivalries as between Cain and Abel or Jacob and Esau or Joseph and his brothers. *As You Like It* opens with the words, "As I remember, Adam," and the play goes on to suggest an atmosphere from Genesis with its Cainlike rivalry in Adam's garden and with Orlando, who speaks of his father's "blessing" on his brother and then imitates Jacob in leaving his father's house and journeying to a land of shepherds, where he wins his bride as Jacob won Rachel. We find, in addition, overt reference to the Prodigal Son, who was also afflicted with a jealous elder brother; that is, the genial biblicality of the play's opening suggests, without any allegorical strain, a kind of primitive, mythic entanglement of siblings who first wrestle in rivalry until one or more disengages to seek a fortune and, indeed, a separate self out in the "world." In *As You Like It*, initial entanglements provide the urge for the divisions that later dominate.

The chief spectacle of the first portion, the wrestling match, presents an emblem of affairs at the "envious court." A grappling of overclose relations, in which vertical alignment, fall, or overthrow is the issue, suits the themes of brothers' displacements and of falling in love. The court is a little world of fallings and failings presided over by Fortune's wheel, a world in which men like Orlando are not being made but rather marred and men like Charles, the Duke, and Touchstone's knight swear by their nonexistent honor; a world of the "broken music" of rib breaking, in which amity cannot yet replace enmity, in which even Rosalind is counseled to wrestle with her own affections lest she fall for Orlando.

After the wrestling match, we see the central characters uncoiling, as it were, from the envious court out into a wider "world" of Arden forest, the ways of which are to be continually anatomized. In the post-Edenic Arden, explosive energies of the court context are received, absorbed, and filtered through a variety of prisms, so that a wide spectrum of human appetites and conduct is spread forth for general survey. In his speech that opens the second act, Duke Senior sets the style of Arden. His praise of life amid nature's adversities in preference to the "painted pomp" of court is done in the Arden style of confrontation and comparison. The Duke compares and converts the icy fang of biting winter's wind into tongues of talking trees. Nature, which had seemed an all-consuming swallower, turns out to be a redemptive force issuing from sermonic mouths of brooks and trees and stones. Arden encompasses both negative and positive extremes, plus the range between, and it has a habit of converting negative extremes to positive or of suggesting that the negative is but a version of the positive waiting for metamorphosis. Travelers who arrive famished convert their impressive hunger to expressive poetry and song. Even Celia, Touchstone, and Oliver find that what seems at first a bleak desert place changes its character as they revive and change theirs—to lovers. Orlando first feels in Arden the fang of hunger, the "thorny point / Of bare distress" (2.7.95–96), but soon puts poetic tongues on trees or, as Rosalind describes it, "odes upon hawthorns and elegies on brambles" (3.2.352–53). Shakespeare rather harps on the idea of Touchstone's couplet—"He that sweetest rose will find / Must find love's prick, and Rosalind" (3.2.109–10). The "prick" of love must have its innings and its outings.

Arden's wit seems at first only explosive, relativizing, analytic, marking out distances between extremes. It is a bit absurd for the Duke to speak of smiling while shrinking with cold, just as it is more than a little absurd for Jaques to moralize the herd of deer into a thousand similes of human ill-fashion. It is the habit in Arden to anatomize the body of the world and, in an excess of emotion, to overdissect and overcompare people, ideas, lives. One thinks of Jaques's seven ages of man, his seven kinds of melancholy, and Touchstone's seven types of lies. But Orlando, too, has the analytic itch, as he devises a "Rosalind of many parts" (compare Phebe marking Ganymede in "parcels"), and Rosalind herself gets constantly at apparent divisions and relativities in life:

Time travels in divers paces with divers persons. I'll tell you who Time ambles withal, who Time trots withal, who Time gallops withal, and who he stands still withal. (3.2.302–5)

No, no, Orlando, men are April when they woo, December when they wed. Maids are May when they are maids, but the sky changes when they are wives. (4.1.138–41)

A giddy excess of long pent-up energy seems to engender on every side lists, anatomies, and hyperbolic pilings-on. Silvius tells Corin:

> If thou remember'st not the slightest folly
> That ever love did make thee run into,
> Thou hast not lov'd.
> Or if thou hast not sat as I do now,
> Wearying thy hearer in thy mistress' praise
> Thou hast not lov'd.
> Or if thou hast not broke from company
> Abruptly as my passion now makes me,
> Thou hast not lov'd.
> O Phebe, Phebe, Phebe!
>
> (2.4.31–40)

Touchstones gives three answering "I remember"s, implying an equivalence between the naive and affected sentimentalism of Silvius and Touchstone's own bawdy cynicism. This sense of equivalence in opposites is caught nicely by Touchstone's later summary:

> And so from hour to hour, we ripe, and ripe,
> And then from hour to hour, we rot, and rot,
> And thereby hangs a tale.
>
> (2.7.26–28)

The distinctive metabolism of the play inheres in its special attitude toward its own constant anatomizing. The style of division, opposition, and confrontation implies, on the one hand, a witty recognition of life's incongruities. But the diversity and relativity continually dredged up are expressed, paradoxically, through unifying devices of repeated phrases, balanced structures, echoing sounds. Making things even far outweighs, in the end, an apparent relativity of preferences. This is a meaning of that wonderful exchange in which Touchstone's relativities of court and country values encounter Corin's stolid unity of view:

> *Cor.* And how like you this shepherd's life, Master Touchstone?
> *Touch.* Truly shepherd, in respect of itself, it is a good life; but in respect that it is a shepherd's life, it is naught. In respect that it is solitary, I like it very well; but in respect that it is private, it is a very vile life. . . . Hast any philosophy in thee, shepherd?
> *Cor.* No more but that I know the more one sickens the worse at ease he is; and that he that wants money, means, and content is without three good friends; that the property of rain is to wet and fire to burn; that good pasture makes fat sheep; and that a great cause of the night is lack of the sun. (3.2.11–28)

Tautologies of nature render ridiculous man's subjective quibbling over whether the glass is half full or half empty. The four pairs of lovers, in similar fashion, reveal highly diversified styles of love, but all are in love. Shakespeare's comedy builds on the fact that it makes all the difference in the world to the individual lover exactly whom he or she is getting, but it makes very little difference to society. So long as weddings and babies result, society cares almost nothing for the varieties and mix-ups of particular loves. And so the play celebrates, beyond the diversity of those who gather in Arden, the general dance of their gathering.

It is true that *As You Like It,* like all drama, is founded on conflict, and in clashing attitudes toward court and country and in clashing romantic and unromantic attitudes to love lies much of the wit of the play. But critics, more adept at discussing tensions of wit than syntheses of humor, tend to overstate the final place of conflicts in *As You Like It*. One critic would make of Arden a "bitter Arcadia" in which men and women long to escape burdens of sex roles for return to a mysterious fount of androgynous godhead. Another critic would have us see Rosalind as motivated by a "will to dominate." The play, we are told, "focuses on the mating dance of a masterful female round her captive male," and "virtually all the relationships manifest a sense of unease, of latent or open hostility."[5]

To pretend, however, that the play leaves us with satiric wit debate is as perverse as to find that its great achievement is in depicting seven ages of man. No more can the relationships and debates be fixed in static opposition than can life be fixed in seven stages. Though, as Celia says, "It is as easy to count atomies as to resolve the propositions of a lover," this is a play, finally, not about the incorrigible divergence and shifting of likings, but about the possibility of harmonizing them. As a central image of the play's opening portion is the circle of partisan spectators around the locked wrestlers, so the recurring visual image of the central portion is the circle of foresters enjoying song. All the songs are dialectical in that, on the one hand, against leisure and love they admit rough weather and faithlessness but, on the other hand, they are all occasions for merriment. That Jaques can find melancholy in the merry notes of the first song only authorizes us to find merriment in his parody that calls "fools into a circle." Despite winter, feigning friendships, and foolish loves, the songs insist, "This life is most jolly."[6] Even the song of the deer-hunters (4.2), which suggests that all men must fear the horns of cuckoldry, is a song of celebration; the burden of love's metamorphoses can be borne without laughing the life force to scorn. The only real enemy recognized in the play is divisive time, which measures the lateness of lovers for their meetings and renders life "but a flower." Still, our counsel is to "take the present time" and its gifts of renewal. Lovers can still love the spring.

When Orlando throws down Charles, Duke Frederick shouts, "No more, no more." But the awareness of more, of all the possibilities of repetition and flowering increase, dominates the play. The characters display engaging appetites for excess. All Arden is ardent, greedy for an unending more. Thus Jaques approves the song of Amiens:

> *Jaques.* More, more, I prithee more.
> *Ami.* It will make you melancholy, Monsieur Jaques.
> *Jaques.* I thank it. More, I prithee more. I can suck melancholy out
> of a song, as a weasel sucks eggs. More, I prithee more. (2.5.9–13)

The word *more* is used more often in *As You Like It* than in any other Shakespearean comedy.[7] It is as if the characters, emerging from cramped quarters of court or winter, would find, in terms of Duke Senior, "more pageants than the scene wherein they play in." Says Rosalind-Ganymede to Orlando:

> I will be more jealous of thee than a Barbary cock-pigeon over his hen, more clamorous than a parrot against rain, more new-fangled than an ape, more giddy in my desires than a monkey. (4.1.141–45)

The play seems in its overall tone to be serenely delighted with every excess. Celia, the laughing victim of Rosalind's "petitionary vehemence" to know if it's Orlando she has seen, responds:

> O wonderful, wonderful! And most wonderful wonderful!
> And yet again wonderful! and after that out of all whooping.
> (3.2.188–90)

But the play never is out of whooping.

In *As You Like It,* rhetorical figures of repetition and structural elaborations of set themes are so pervasive as to constitute a distinctive and indelible style. Rosalind, of course, loves to say the same thing in varied ways: "Is his head worth a hat? Or his chin worth a beard?" (3.2.201–2), or "What said he? How looked he? Wherein went he?" (3.2.216–17). In order to answer Rosalind "in one word" as demanded, Celia asks for "Gargantua's mouth." In truth, it is Rosalind who has, in the play, the mouth of Gargantua. No one can or would want to still her fondness for euphuistic elaboration. When Orlando politely inquires, "Who ambles Time withal?" Rosalind answers:

With a priest that lacks Latin, and a rich man that hath not the gout, for the one sleeps easily because he cannot study, and the other lives merrily because he feels no pain; the one lacking the burden of lean and wasteful learning; the other knowing no burden of heavy tedious penury. (3.2.313–18)

The special music of *As You Like It* is this habit of mildly or wildly varying a single theme: "sleeps easily"—"lives merrily," "because he cannot study," "because he feels no pain," "lacking the burden," "knowing no burden," and so on. Editors are uncertain whether to set many of the speeches as prose or verse. This is a play wherein they are variations of a single impulse, a play filled with refrains and burdens. Orlando asks Rosalind for the marks of a lover, and she replies:

A lean cheek, which you have not; a blue eye and sunken, which you have not; an unquestionable spirit, which you have not; a beard neglected, which you have not. (3.2.363–66)

Rosalind tells Phebe to take Silvius:

Cry the man mercy, love him, take his offer;
Foul is most foul, being foul to be a scoffer.
(3.5.61–62)

The refrains and burdens have a way of drawing attention to the common theme within, a way of suggesting that a tautology lurks at the base of relativity. All eight lovers, no matter how apparently diverse their natures and attitudes, are in love. A rose is a rose is a rose is a rose.

But we do not want simply to behold the unity of human desires. *As You Like It* continues to mean, "Take it as you like it, according to your individual preferences," as well as, "This is as everyone likes it; this is the common denominator that pleases all tastes." Touchstone may even mock the play's propensity to say in many ways only one thing. As he takes Audrey away, he tells William:

To have is to have: for it is a figure in rhetoric that drink, being poured out of a cup into a glass, by filling the one doth empty the other. For all your writers do consent that *ipse* is he. Now you are not *ipse*, for I am he.
    Wil. Which he sir?
    Touch. He sir that must marry this woman. Therefore you clown, abandon—which is in the vulgar leave—the society—which in the boorish is company—of this female—which in the common is woman. . . . I will bandy with thee in faction; I will o'er-run thee with policy; I will kill thee a hundred and fifty ways. (5.1.39–56)

Elegant, empty variation may bespeak a monochromatic mind. Again we have Touchstone closing the scene with a stutter: "Trip Audrey, trip Audrey. I attend, I attend" (5.1.62).

Even Rosalind's love of elaboration flows from her singleness of purpose. Cupid, she says, was "begot of thought, conceived of spleen and born of madness." Her force of elaborative imagination stems from fecund love and is a way of defining such love. She opens up a space for desires to play in, a space in which to metamorphose the close wrestling into broad measures of the dance. Her expansive energies lift the mind of the play from obsessive focus on a single envious space to the variety and spaciousness, yet also the connectedness, of diverse lives. As she says of her own intellect:

The wiser, the waywarder. Make the doors upon a woman's wit and it will out at the casement; shut that, and 'twill out at the keyhole; stop that, 'twill fly with the smoke out at the chimney. (4.1.152–56)

No wonder that Rosalind is Shakespeare's most talkative woman. Beatrice, in comparison, speaks some 2,400 words, a mere 11 percent of her play; and Viola is in much the same position. Helena and Portia rise to the totals of 3,600 and 4,600, respectively. Even Cleopatra in her infinite variety only speaks 4,700 words, less than 20 percent of her play's total. But Rosalind speaks some 5,700 words, almost 27 percent of all those in the play. (She speaks, moreover, in excess of 1,300 different words. It is not surprising that Orlando seems a trifle bland in comparison with his relatively restricted stock of 700.)[8] Rosalind needs to speak enough and waywardly enough to turn the polarities of the play in a circle. As Ganymede she tells Orlando:

> I will weep for nothing, like Diana in the fountain, and I will do that when you are disposed to be merry. I will laugh like a hyen, and that when thou art inclined to sleep. (4.1.145–48)

Rosalind teaches Orlando to see that what seems arbitrary in love may betoken the constant pressure of love's impulse and its desire to respond to the kaleidoscopic amplitude of life.

Once the relativity of liking and the liking of relativity are well established in the play, then the underlying unity of human nature is adduced:

> *Phebe.* Good shepherd, tell this youth what 'tis to love.
> *Sil.* It is to be all made of sighs and tears, and so am I for Phebe.
> *Phebe.* And I for Ganymede.
> *Orl.* And I for Rosalind.
> *Ros.* And I for no woman. (5.2.82–86)

Diverse lovers chant a single verse. Shakespeare hints at this natural perspective in his overlapping use of names in the play: two Fredericks, two Olivers, two Jaques. All are convertible—psychically, religiously. One's analogues abound. A clown, Touchstone, meets a clown, Corin, and another clown, William. An apparently hypothetical "old religious uncle" materializes as an "old religious man" in Arden forest. Those critics who take too seriously the wit of the play, its patterns of opposition, confrontation, and relativity, are like those who might throw up their hands in surprise on meeting their double, but never extend their arms for a humorous embrace. Difference remains more real, more precious than sameness; the shocks of wit overpower the sympathies of humor. The final pleasure of *As You Like It* does not reside simply in the space opened up for metaphors and behaviors of incongruity, but rather in a harmonization of disparate impulses, in strangers' meetings becoming lovers' matings. As our perspectives open out, we become aware of hidden sympathies and correspondences. "Then," said Aristotle, describing one source of comedic pleasure:

since that which is according to nature is pleasant, and kindred things are natural to each other, all things akin to one and like one are pleasant to one, as a rule—as man to man, horse to horse, youth to youth; whence the proverbs: "Mate delights mate"; "Like to like"; . . . and so forth.[9]

This is the view that makes earthly things even and gathers them together in order and delight. In *As You Like It*, the vertically aligned wheel of Fortune, alluded to in the first act, yields to the horizontal circle of the final dance, where likes join likes in Arden's own sanctifying circle.

If some critics, then, speak too solemnly of *As You Like It*, it is because they choose to remain in realms of incongruous wit, because they find more to say about satire, ridicule, and the unromantic than they have to say about humor, sympathy, and romance. The wheel of fortune and the odds for high and low provide ready material for the discursive intellect, but what's to say about a dance? This is not to deny that, in a variety of ways, other interpreters have recognized the basic health of the play, the way it reconciles opposing positions, assimilates disparate and relativistic views into a commonalty. We have been shown how classical and Christian perspectives are combined, how reassurance underlies the perturbation, how a comprehensive philosophy emerges from the cross-qualifyings, and how the play gives to raw energy and even outrage a transforming elegance and beauty.[10] But rarely, if ever, is enough stress given to the diachronic drive of the play as opposed to its supposedly syn-chronic structure of ideas.

Nor will it do to say that Shakespeare gives us humor, as opposed, say, to Jonsonian satire.[11] Shakespeare moves us by moving from satire to humor. There is plenty of satire in *As You Like It*. We have to accept the presence of the unromantic snip-ing at the romantic, of the thorn as well as the rose. Shake-speare added to Lodge's story the complex invectives and abrasions of Jaques and Touchstone for a reason. We need to look for the drama of the play, its going from the seemingly incommensurate and relative to the all-liked and from like as quirky preference to like as shared pleasure. The process—the dramatic process and progress of finding sympathetic com-mon denominators within apparently hopeless diversity, of finding human connection among wholly individual prefer-ences—this is the gist of it. And it is why this mild, often bland, serene, supremely gentle play finally calls forth such stunning claims from some interpreters. It works, they say, a conversion of the will; it alters perspectives; it truly changes us.[12] Does not the play indeed hint at a largeness of effect, a kind of conversion? The charmed circle of the forest offers escape and salvation. Its denizens, we recall, "have with holy bell been knoll'd to church." Its "heavenly Rosalind" was devised by "heavenly synod." She claims a religious uncle and proves she can conjure even as the god Hymen can. The forest's powers to convert an Oliver and offer a "monastic" nook to such as Duke Frederick and Jaques are not the greatest of its wonders, for Orlando becomes as much the new Adam (bearing the old) in Arden as he was Hercules at court. When he sheds his falsely romantic self-concern, when he tames the "green and gilded snake" and finds "kindness, nobler ever than revenge," then Rosalind can cease to counterfeit. After melding their Petrarchan, pastoral, fleshly, and prideful loves into versions of marriageable love, the couples to be wed are like enough, as Jaques says, to be couples "coming to the ark." Though all have chewed the "food of sweet and bitter fancy," all commit themselves to wed and thus to find a single "blessed bond." By the end of *As You Like It*, a society has matured and not only matured but also become, perhaps like the society of the audience before it, much more likable.

Shakespeare's way with *As You Like It* depends for its success on our regaining a measure of confidence in life's beneficent wholeness. We enter the theater immersed in local strivings, our heads buzzing with sociopolitical trivia of who's in and who's out. Shakespeare seems willingly to begin his play in the same environment of Fortune's City. But he drives us away from fortune into nature, from relativities of rank and luck toward happy glimpses of teleological harmonies. Busy plotting and intellectual machinations aimed at atomistic gains give way to quieter resolutions of fellowship and song. Thus it is not surprising that the same critic who notes a "curious stillness at the heart of the play" also notes a "subordination of plot in the traditional sense to an intricate structure of meetings between characters, a concentration upon attitudes rather than action."[13] Characters, moreover, who are realistically English in type and manner, who are often victims of Fortune and butts of wit, seem at first unsuited to the nearly idyllic natural setting to which they come, but Shakespeare "softens" the humor, shades the bright light of wit, favoring gentler emotions of contentment rather than the "ebullition of outward merriment."[14] In *As You Like It*, despite the range of characters, action, and language, we achieve a serene vision of continuing blessings; we reach a source and end, a reason for going on. There is in Arden "a timeless world beset by time" where "voices of maturity" counsel just perspectives on human folly and promote a willingness to proceed with the major businesses of life.[15]

It has been suggested that, though "Shakespeare had no comic theory," a kind of teaching, a comic morality, is to be found embedded "in the whole substance of his comedies."[16] A combined questioning and acceptance throughout Shakespeare of overarching purposes in life accords well with the ethos of his comedy. In his Preface of 1765, Samuel Johnson defends Shakespeare's powers of "exhibiting the real state of sublunary nature" in which "many mischiefs and many benefits are done and hindered *without design*." A few lines later however, Johnson refers to "the successive evolutions *of the design*."[17] Therein lies, surely, one key to the secret of Shakespeare's comedy. He makes us muse: How can the seemingly undesigned fit a design? How can mistake and folly seem so embraceably happy? How can chance be so choice? And how is it that we may achieve "a point of view in which love is known for its absurdity, and yet retained with laughing certainty at the centre of human experience"?[18]

Because, lastly, love and its discontents are at the center of Shakespearean and probably most other comedy, comic theory involves, inevitably, social theory. The questions are often these: Who deserves to propagate and thrive? And in what style? It has been argued that English Renaissance theorists applied a class concept of decorum in assigning comedy to the common errors of the meaner sorts of men.[19] Such comedy, one might conclude, will celebrate, even as it attempts to purify, the great coming on of the middle class. In part, it does. But Shakespeare, in *As You Like It* and elsewhere, elevates his comedy, dramatizing romance and the fortunes of its nobility. He favors, in his late comedies particularly, plots in which generational succession is threatened: a prince or duke appears unlikely or disinclined to marry (*Twelfth Night, All's Well, Measure for Measure*), or the king or duke has or appears to have only female issue (*As You Like It, Pericles, Cymbeline, Winter's Tale, Tempest*), so that appropriate succession depends on breaking barriers to a *new* marriage. The central marriage, moreover, often requires nobility to marry beneath itself or to entertain that offered fallacy. Each "crisis of degree" is solved in its own way, but always the result is to remind audiences that, in and through marriage, the varied powers of class and sex may be made more even and, in the phrase of Hymen in *As You Like It*, may "atone together."[20] Through such means as these, Shakespeare makes his comedy of reconciliation remarkably complete.

INTERPRETING *THE WINTER'S TALE*

How does an interpreter begin to move beyond New Critical or objectivist or formalist styles of Shakespearean interpretation? "Eventually the resurrection of Hermione must be considered the most strikingly conceived, and profoundly penetrating, moment in English literature."[1] This is a large claim, and one that can never be validated. "Eventually," if its current ascent in critical valuation forecasts truly, *The Winter's Tale* may indeed challenge Shakespeare's more widely respected tragedies for power to be both striking and profound. Then the bravura statement of the interpreter may come closer to realization. But, at least onstage, the resurrection of Hermione has hardly been waiting for recognition and reverence: "as I descended from the pedestal and advanced towards Leontes, the audience simultaneously rose from their seats as if drawn out of them by surprise and reverential awe."[2]

This happened in the past century, and the entire drama of *The Winter's Tale*, no matter how much neglected by critics, has from the first been one of Shakespeare's most successful in the theater. Yet the interpreter first quoted is thinking of the play not as staged drama but as "literature," a poetry of themes and symbols whose significance we grasp only after deep study and visionary interpretation away from the stage. He deplores among interpreters any "tendency to neglect the deeper significances of the plays for an insistence on the dramatic nature of the composition,"[3] and he insists that interpretation, rightly considered, has to do not with the staged, temporal progress of the action but with a central and spatially conceived "vision," "theme," "idea," or "atmosphere."[4] The much vexed question of exactly what it is that interpreters of poetic drama interpret is answered obliquely:

literary analysis of great drama in terms of theatrical technique accomplishes singularly little. Such technicalities should be confined to the theatre from which their terms are drawn. The proper thing to do about a play's dramatic quality is to produce it, to act in it, to attend performances; but the penetration of its deeper meanings is a different matter, and such a study, though the commentator should certainly be dramatically aware, and even wary, will not itself speak in theatrical terms.[5]

Interpretation, then, aims at "deeper meanings," residual products of post-performance rumination. It follows that such deeper meanings in *The Winter's Tale* can never be interpreted through consideration of its dramatic technique or in theatrical terms.

An opposing chorus of interpreters would have us believe that the resurrection of Hermione reveals its deepest meanings not after but during the play, not in the study but in the theater:

we are forced through the process of ourselves coming to recognize that Hermione is alive. It is not something we knew all the time; it is not even a miracle which is reported to us or staged for us: it is a miracle in the full effect of which we participate.[6]

. . . we finally partake, in some way, of the "miracle" itself.[7]

Hermione's image is a symbol of *The Winter's Tale* itself, but whether or not the play succeeds in mirroring a reality beyond its fictive appearance depends finally upon its audience. Unlike Autolycus, Shakespeare does not advertise that his art is "Very true" or that it has practical results. No pack of witnesses can guarantee its truth. He must leave to his audience the question of whether, their imaginations seized by the surprise "resurrection," they stand in "lethargy," like Autolycus' trusting victims, or in the wonder of renewal, like Leontes.[8]

Amazingly enough, even the interpreter first quoted, who drew a sharp distinction between a play's dramatic and deeper meanings, has declared of Hermione's seeming resurrection: "the watcher's 'I' is, by most careful technique, forced into a close subjective identity, so that the immortality revealed is *less concept than experience*."[9]

We might dismiss this ill-sustained division between interpretation of Hermione's awakening with its deeper meanings, on the one hand, and direct apprehension of the awakening with its deeper meanings, on the other hand, as no more than a consequence of attempting to divide, artificially, concept from experience, play from performance, an unchanging object of interpretive focus from its ever changing manifestations on the stage. The division between interpretation and immediate apprehension, like the division between play and performance, refuses, however, to be so easily dismissed. We do recognize a distinction between thinking *about* a play and thinking the play directly. Both interpretation and criticism generally constitute post-play activity:

As long as we are reading a novel or listening to a play on the stage, we are following a movement in time, and our mental attitude is a participating one. It is uncritical, too, or more accurately precritical: we can make no genuine critical judgment until the work is all over. When it is all over, it assumes a quite different appearance. Now we see it as a simultaneous unity, something that has not so much a beginning, a middle and end as a center and a periphery. Criticism deals entirely with literature in this frozen or spatial way, and a distinction between criticism proper and the direct experience of literature which precedes it is fundamental to any coherent act of criticism.[10]

The trouble is that interpreters continually suffer misgivings as to whether meanings they discuss are truly separate from meanings apprehended in direct experience and, even if separate, sufficiently important to warrant an appellation such as "deeper."

Particularly in the case of *The Winter's Tale*, and perhaps more so than for any other Shakespearean play, do interpreters bow to the superior revelations of performance; the deepest meanings of the last scene and indeed of the entire play are performed meanings, meanings that can only be experienced at the time and place of direct dramatic encounter. Even the critic last quoted, who insisted that criticism deal entirely with meanings of the work when it is over, concedes later in the same volume that criticism cannot so deal with *The Winter's Tale*: "the meaning of the play is the play, there being nothing to be abstracted from the total experience of the play. Progress in grasping the meaning is a progress not in seeing more in the play, but in seeing more of it."[11] Again, the chorus of agreement is striking:

The Winter's Tale, like many other stories, deals with sin and forgiveness, and with the triumph of time—also a Christian theme. But we value it not for some hidden truth, but for its power to realize experience, to show something of life that could only be shown by the intense activity of intellect and imagination in the medium of a theatrical form. It is not a great allegory or a great argument, but a great play.[12]

[*The Winter's Tale*] is a supreme instance of Shakespeare's poetic complexity—of the impossibility, if one is to speak with any relevance to the play, of considering character, episode, theme, and plot in abstraction from the local effects, so inexhaustibly subtle in their interplay, of poetry and from the larger symbolic effects to which these give life.[13]

There is such a total blending of mood and subject matter that the bare description of themes, inadequate as it appears at any time in the discussion of Shakespeare, has a special sort of unsatisfactoriness here.[14]

Such commentators appear to have recognized that *The Winter's Tale* is precisely the opposite of a philosophic play, that is, one whose "deeper meanings" must be penetrated to. Instead, the whole tenor of their comments is that the play's meanings are inextricably bound up in its surface, its moment-by-moment existence on stage or in the reading. Yet their apparent deference to the unique shape of the experience fails to bring forth a means for dealing boldly and consistently with the play's affective and temporal dimensions. Interpreters inform readers at great length about rhetorical patterns, similarities and oppositions of characterization, and concepts of affection, art, and nature in *The Winter's Tale*, but they offer little understanding of the play's development from a cold beginning to a warm ending, or of how spectators begin by suspecting the suspicious Leontes and end by sharing in the general dance of awakened faith. They tend, therefore, in spite of all their protests, to veil the experience even as they reveal its meanings. Why?

Interpretation as yet has developed only rudimentary means for getting the affective aspects of a work into the interpretive account of it, adding what it does to what it is, or showing the true inseparability of does and is. Increasingly, nevertheless, interpreters are seeing a need to assimilate the concepts they discuss to both the "local effects" and the "total experience" mentioned above.[15] During the New Critical ascendancy, a critic expatiating on the "Fallacy of the First Night" described how Shakespeare's art "provides a stage action pleasurable to the immediate audience and at the same time dramatic literature suitable for prolonged contemplation, indeed yielding its secrets, if it yields them, only after long study and thought by the reader."[16] A decade later, the same critic is more eager to subordinate studied "secrets" to the theatrical encounter, where now "we are neither taking in propositions nor being taken in by emotional whirlwinds, but are taking part in an experience marked by complexity, not by confusion. . . . The spectator undergoes a two-sided but unitary experience which it is very difficult, if not indeed impossible, to replace by any one-dimensional substitute, such as being calmly lessoned, being wholly swept away, or being hung limply on an epistemological crux."[17] The search, in other words, is for a "very difficult," multidimensional interpretation, one that does justice to both thought and feeling, an interpretation that neither deals with the play in a "frozen or spatial way" nor kneels in speechless admiration before its inexpressible "wonder," "the shocked limit of feeling."[18]

How, then, can interpretation be more than a post-dramatic exercise, a kind of delicious regretful insight into what might have been found in the past? We want to put more meaning into our explorations of art as well as to pull more meaning from our explanations. How can interpretation fit into the endless antiphonal debate between our perception of art as the self-contained expression of precedent meanings and our perception of art as that which is first to be wondered at, then understood?

One way to counter the epistemological emphasis that tends to prevail in literary interpretation is to concentrate openly on the immediacy and passion of Shakespearean drama. Resisting the approach to drama as vehicle of certain "truths," some interpreters stress the "momentous and energizing experience" that drama offers, a "comprehensive excitement of the whole gamut of emotion, a general sharpening and broadening of all our powers of perception, and a joyous re-vitalization which operates at a profound level on the whole personality. To try to express all these things in a vocabulary of expressing moral insights 'concretely' is at bottom to deprive words of their meanings."[19] As in the remarks of interpreters quoted earlier, "experience" here tends to be opposed to concepts, ideas, truths. Though one can experience ideas, the term "experience" in this kind of interpretation associates itself with the de-intellectualization of the theatrical encounter. A specially charged terminology of feeling and action tends to accompany appeals to "experience": "excitement," "gamut of emotion," "joyous re-vitalization." Those who turn away from an issue-oriented interpretation of deeper meanings often gravitate toward an act-oriented interpretation of self-fulfillment and ritual release. "Experience" begins to point toward synthetic temperaments as opposed to analytic ones, toward self-sufficient subjectivity of feeling as opposed to endless translations of thought.

Unhappily, interpretation in terms of feeling has tended to be singularly uninformative:

The thrill that passed through the audience on the first raising of the curtain from the seeming statue, told how intensely the spiritual beauty of Miss Faucit's attitude and expression was felt. . . . It was the realizing of a sculptor's hopeless dream. . . . The spectator became an actor in the scene, and all "Held their breath for a time." The turning of the head, and the earnest gaze of the full eyes by which Miss Faucit, with the skill of a great artist, breaks the transition from repose to motion, was magical in effect, and made the suspended blood to throb.[20]

One is not likely to be convinced by an observer who merely records such impressions: "It enchanted my eyes. It made me weep. It enlivened my spirits."[21] Comments in this vein may testify to the emotive impact of the play on the writer but do little to help readers and spectators realize their own momentous and energizing experiences. A dubious insistence on conceptual meanings hidden within the play or found only after elaborate study surely fails to justify an equally dubious insistence on subjective impressionism. The text and its performance as they work on spectators or readers in a cumulative development through time must remain the focus of any interpretive study that would avoid the charge of solipsism.

An interpreter may try to reconcile polarities of feeling and thought by simply stating that experience, properly conceived, contains each in equal measure: experience "is only momentous when it has meaning."[22] Such meaning may be associated, we have been told, with "wisdom," "not a part of the play but a precipitate of the play as a whole." But wisdom, too, "proves misleading"; "vision," we are assured, is a "better" word: "To share this vision and this wisdom . . . is not to receive information or counsel but rather to have a 'momentous experience.' The momentousness is to be defined partly in emotional terms: according to the play in question there accrues joy, elation, exaltation, ecstasy, or whatever. But an essential part of our conviction that such an experience is momentous derives from what we take to be the import of the play." Here, just as "momentousness" ends up as the sum of

"emotions" and "import," so the phrase to which the interpreter subsequently turns, "the dignity of significance,"
again neatly matches a term of emotion with a term of import.
The result is unsatisfactory because thought, import, wisdom,
and significance still tend to remain "precipitates." The interpreter finds no way to make thought and feeling intermesh
verbally, to show that experience does not have meaning
attached or accruing to it, does not produce meaning as a precipitate, but is at once both meaning and emotion, both
thought and feeling, without separable identification.

Such cautious mediation, as that above, between old
approaches promises less progress in understanding how
plays work than the bold assay of a new approach can promise. "One of the dullest positions into which a critic can
maneuver himself is that of mediating between opposites.
The truth about a subject is usually a by-product of the clash
between extremists who feel and think strongly enough to
project their necks from their collars."[23] Extreme concentration on the momentous and energizing character of theatrical
experience can at least promote awareness of how deeply
action attacks theme, form absorbs content.[24] Those who
value art as experience are likely to recognize not only the self-
containment of aesthetic encounters but also their capacity for
ordering and sanctifying precious insights and states of
being. Theatrical experience in this sense uses up accumulated wisdom, celebrating it so thoroughly that the partici-
pants become elevated to the next stage in their growth, and
so sense a waking.

At worst, experience shows itself to be a dangerous refuge,
offering no real hospitality or warmth, only self-sufficiency,
the opaque tautology of "I am that I am." In the essays of con-
ceptualist interpreters, reference to "experience" tends to
appear, as shown, at the moment in which the concept or
deeper meaning being discussed manifests its remoteness
and detachment from the reader's or the watcher's encounter
with the play. There follows the reasonable and natural
attempt to absorb concept back into encounter. Deference to

the superior revelations of experience then becomes a kind of verbal throwing up of hands, the Frenchman's *je ne sais quoi*—a simple admission that, after all, the play's the thing, there the action lies. But just as experience becomes less useful as an interpretive term when pushed in the direction of pure, untranslatable feeling, so it becomes less useful when made to stand for "the irreducible individuality of the aesthetic fact."[25] Successive interpreters inevitably strive to penetrate past the play that they have learned about to the play that they do not know, to pure form or experience. As they find words for the experience, they seem to internalize it and freeze it, so that it can only relive again "out there" as something "other." "Indeed, the very obscurity of art is in a sense its more generic meaning. Prior to the neatly formulated questions of systematizing intelligence, there is the deep-set wonder in which all questions have their source and ground."[26] Recognizing the dangers of over-conceptualization, an interpreter who opposes that tendency may even go so far as to question the very relevance of interpretation to the thing in itself, saying: "Our task is not to find the maximum amount of content in a work of art, much less to squeeze more content out of the work than is already there. Our task is to cut back content so that we can see the thing at all."[27]

But the "thing," the play itself, is not, of course, contentless wonder; to apprehend the play involves an activity of mind partly interpretive in nature. The appearance, language, and action of each character, for example, must be assessed cumulatively in relation to those features in every other character. The sequence of events must be held in mind. As he relates the parts of the play to each other, the spectator also considers their mimetic relevance to the "outside" world. Are the play's concerns remote from the spectator's? Are the characters recognizable? Does the action build toward a relevant tension and a convincing resolution? The answers given to such questions necessarily register in degrees of interest or boredom manifested by audiences.

Theatrical experience, in other words, consists in part of analyzing, comparing, and generalizing. A problem for play-goers and interpreters alike is to make the analysis support the temporal encounter itself, so that not all the reactive detail, the mix of sharp thoughts and keen feelings, seeps away through a sieve of generalization. Those who would in partic-ular work beneath the supposed Christian allegory, pastoral romance genre, mythic symbolism, or Jacobean social com-mentary of *The Winter's Tale* should try, therefore, to account for the experience of it, not solely in terms of the feelings it engenders or of its irreducibility, but more nearly in the terms in which it probably appears to a sensitive and knowledgeable audience, as an emotion-charged activity of mind, a temporal tracking of the play as it unfolds scene by scene toward earned apprehensions of jollity.

One who would trace the elusive yet critically important temporal dimension of *The Winter's Tale* but who rejects as incomplete mere description of subjective experience, may turn for guidance to the growing study of drama in perform-ance. The furthest one could go to study the staging of the play "would be to try to produce it."[28] Undoubtedly, a good deal may in this way be learned about how the play is constructed and can be performed effectively. But there is a difference between craftsmanship and interpretation; to know how to offer a play to an audience is not necessarily to know what the audience may find there. As is more clearly the case with per-formers of musical works, directors and actors concern them-selves as much with matters of technique—serially arising questions of rhythm, tempi, and dynamics—as with the received force of the accumulating whole. Guides to play pro-duction and direction, while employing a vocabulary that helps to describe the intensity, impact, and emotive funding of a drama, a vocabulary that interpreters might more fre-quently draw on, still concentrate on questions of casting, characterization, sight lines, pictorial composition, lighting, special effects, cues, pace, shifts in tone, building of climaxes, improvisation, stage business, and the like.[29] True, a director's sense of the spirit of the play must inform the whole, but his sense of spirit is more like an actor's intimate feeling for prevailing moods and patterns of action sought onstage than like a spectator's interest in entering the theatrical format to be surprised, informed, and stirred, and to weigh the play against his own knowledge of life.

No slur is hereby cast on the study of drama in performance per se. The very inability of conventional interpretation to get beyond atemporal concepts, to account for the dramatic progress toward participation often realized by readers and watchers, suggests a need for such study. A selective history of the play's staging should sensitize one to its temporal dimension and, if only by examples of failed productions, to its potential growth within an auditor's consciousness. Theatrical study, moreover, should help to center us on potential enticement of the psyche toward heightened states of awareness that can be called neither thought nor feeling because they are both, each informing the other. That much is true. But such study is of little use to interpretation until integrated with other interpretive modes. Standing alone, it almost invariably overemphasizes action, emotion, and audience engagement, so much so that it rarely meets the full intellectual challenge of the play.

That students of drama in performance tend to slight the full challenge of *The Winter's Tale* is shown by the example of a theatrical scholar who advances what at first seems a persuasive theme: "The total solemnity of much criticism of the last plays that is current today would strike Elizabethans and Jacobeans as pompous and restrictive. Romance, for them, spelt wonder, delight, *and* mirth."[30] The conclusion to which this approach leads, however, is that the statue scene must be taken as a dreamlike fantasy that the audience only "accepts" because put in a "relaxed and uncritical condition" by the preceding antics of Autolycus. The "irresponsible enjoyment" of the feast and of its satyrs' dance, "another divertissement," it is argued, becomes acceptable to the audience as a contrast

with the more serious love of Perdita and Florizel, because
Autolycus's clowning establishes a general mood of laughter
and enjoyment. Such description overstresses the emotional
atmosphere of the scenes at the expense of their thematic content. Appreciation of the statue scene hardly requires a
"relaxed" condition; rather the opposite. "No foot shall stir,"
commands Leontes.[31] When Autolycus, moreover, works to
"gain the connivance of the audience" and makes his clowning dominate the feast, then the audience is in danger of
becoming overwhelmed by a scene that threatens to disrupt
the drive and continuity of the play. Performers, we are told,
often mar the shearing festival with "Mummersetshire buf-
foonery," "rowdy" realism, or a "fussy and feverish rustic
party."[32] Far better to mount a "graceful, measured production" where "gaily as the pastoral interlude is rendered the
jealous errors from which it stems are not quite forgotten."[33]
In such a production, the audience does not relax to accept a
statue scene of uncritical fantasy. The scene "grips their attention"[34] and proves itself the climax to a series of ascending
wakings—trial, betrothal, and this unveiling—in each of
which an elaborate and initially dreamlike artifice breaks
down under a call to faith, the faith that Leontes must achieve
in the Oracle and in Hermione, the faith that Florizel and Perdita must win out of tested love, the faith that those who view
the statue must find in forgiveness and renewal. Within this
process, Autolycus must play his vital but thoroughly subordinated and thematically relevant part.

The scholar who overstates the "connivance," the "irresponsible enjoyment," and the "relaxed and uncritical condition" clowned forth by Autolycus is one whose "whole book,"
in his own words, "advocates a decisive movement away from
literary criticism toward theatrical study."[35] But this does
inadequate justice, and pays insufficient attention, to the curious blend of engagement and disengagement, of psychic intimacy and homiletic detachment, that thought-threaded
closeness, which marks our encounter with Shakespearean
drama.[36] Spectator follows actor absorbedly, in the words of

Thomas Heywood, "pursuing him in his enterprise . . . wrapt in contemplation . . . as if the personator were the [actual] man personated."[37] At the same time, the spectator stands aloof, "admiring the subtile Tracks of [his] engagement."[38] Not only is it "possible for him to be aware quasi-objectively of his own mental state and to feel wonder on account of it,"[39] it is also imperative that he think intensely about the patterned meanings of the "subtile Tracks," those carefully placed prints of relatedness. While it may not promote the same kind of enjoyment and engagement that is promoted by theatrical study, literary interpretation has something of value to say about the meaning of each temporal encounter with Shakespearean drama. That much is suggested by the mere fact that the plays are not only worth seeing, they are also worth hearing and reading.[40] And while the interest of hearing and reading often intensifies with, it does not depend on, minutely imagined theatricality. The plays offer a venture, a journey of mind, so singular, intricate, and absorbing as to have a life of its own that can exist apart from the audience-companioned ritual, the more collective catharsis and renascence of theatrical experience. Still, undoubtedly, "it is to the theatre that all interpretation must consistently be referred if we are not to risk dealing in unrealities."[41]

No one approach to Shakespearean drama can serve much more than a limited purpose. The problem of how to approach *The Winter's Tale* is especially vexing because the play offers in close juxtaposition a wide variety of seeming incommensurables: philosophy and dance, satire and miracle, realism and romance, sheer poetry and sheer spectacle, dislocations of space and time. Yet to adopt an ad hoc approach and to apply whatever critical method seems to cast light on each local section would be to ignore the central need for a cohesive view of the play.[42] As everyone knows, however, a cohesiveness gained through a single interpretive approach often proves disappointingly limited and resists assimilation into the living encounter of reader or spectator with the play. Several modern studies, for example, approach *The Winter's Tale* as "romance," "pastoral," "pastoral comedy," "melodrama," and "tragicomedy."[43] From these studies much may be learned about meanings gleaned from the play when its elements are gathered into varying generic collectivities or types. But if we think of the Polonian scramble of genres ridiculed in *Hamlet* or of Touchstone's laughable list of rebukes in *As You Like It*, we may doubt whether any typological scheme will fully reflect or be adequate to Shakespeare's authorial purposes or to the spectator's perceptions. For the unity, rhythm, and progress of *The Winter's Tale* appear at once more accessible to common understanding and yet more mysterious and complex than generic stylization will allow.

Because the focus of "genre" is flexible and can be turned in the direction of formal or stylistic requirements or in the direction of content in action or idea, the approach through genre may seem, as varieties of recent studies suggest, specially appealing. But generic studies are essentially comparative, rarely designed to get at, except by negative definition, the uniqueness of a work. What is more, they tend to concentrate on areas of literary discourse between the linguistic intricacies and immediacies of the text, on the one hand, and the experiential impact of the work, on the other. Studies of language in *The Winter's Tale* as well as studies of its psychosocial dimensions may be highly illuminating; genre study, however, displays little capacity to respond to them.[44]

All knowledge of the play, of course, must be contextual. Locus follows focus, that is, what one makes of the play depends on the purposive environment of one's study. There is no way to apprehend "the play itself" freed from burdens of generic classification, historical origins, linguistic ambiguities, meanings as myth and ritual, psychoanalytic implications, vagaries of affective response, and the like. Strategies for attaining a single cohesive view range from reductive concentration on "the text per se," or on "what the author meant," or on themes or structure or spatial design or archetypal meanings, to complete histories of staging and criticism, studies of sources, analogues, and influences, accounts of the drama's probable effect on an Elizabethan or modern audience, and various combinations of "approaches." What we need today in the case of *The Winter's Tale*, I suggest, is not only a renewed attention to its full stage history and critical history and not only a much better understanding of the play in relation to its source and to Shakespeare's artistic development but also several interpretive "performances" of the play. We require a variety of sensitive and sustained attempts to posit the impact of successive speeches and scenes on readers and spectators. Such interpretation, which might be termed "temporal-affective," would treat the living play as it comes to us, not a bundle of abstracted concepts. It would deny the primacy of "meaning" conceived as external to or self-sufficient apart from performance and reception. It would help us test what the play does in staged or in readers' mental performances against what it allegedly *means* symbolically, allegorically, or otherwise. By making us pay attention to the order of speeches and actions, it should help us see the central dramatic progress and so permit a shift of focus from the statically conceived "world" of the play to its temporally conceived metabolism or orchestration, the developing progress of verbal and visual effects determined by the sequential cross-commentary of speeches and by dramatic alterations in mood, tone, diction, volume, pace, numbers of actors, their placement, and their action.[45]

What is needed is not scene-by-scene commentary, the conventional private "reading," but rather analysis and synthesis of the central constructive patterns through which the parts accumulate toward a whole. By "central constructive patterns" I mean features such as thematic contrasts and parallels among scenes, patterns of dramatic preparation, systematic disengagement and re-engagement of audience empathy, consistent association of characters and themes with repeated devices of style such as images that are both staged and spoken, all features that may contribute significantly to the developing dramatic design. We need to understand much more clearly, for example, to what effect Shakespeare alternates with such impressive regularity the loud and crowded scenes of Leontes' divisive jealousy with brief, interstitial scenes in which lesser characters come together and dare to hope. We need to grasp how the sequence of scenes in each of which a single, still woman faces curious but uncomprehending onlookers prepares us for the statue scene or how the carefully spaced appearances of Autolycus work to inflict and dispel ironic contemplation on preceding and following scenes. We need to follow out the battle of styles—ornate, Latinate, ratiocinative versus plain, native, emotive—within Leontes and between Leontes and others. We need to understand why and to what effect Shakespeare turns about the center of his play the three soliloquies of Antigonus, Time, and the Shepherd, all of whom meditate on relations of age and youth. How should these matters affect audiences? What should be their playhouse life? How may readers best perceive and perform the play in theaters of thoughtful feeling?

In these paragraphs I hover, obviously, between indicative and optative moods as between descriptive and normative views of interpretation. Each interpretive "performance" can, on the one hand, reveal an inner circle of truths about the play, truths that will win, because they deserve to win, the continuing assent of most readers. The outer circles of interpretation remain, on the other hand, more suggestive than certain. Working from the inner circle, directors, actors, and audiences should note, for example, that spectators in the play at the statue scene are themselves described as art works. Leontes is "more stone" than the statue; Perdita stands "like stone" watching it. Camillo describes Leontes' sorrow as "too sore laid on"; Polixenes would "piece up in himself" Leontes' grief. Leontes becomes "wrought" by the sight of the image, and Perdita could for "twenty years" "stand by, a looker on." Shakespeare takes pains to suggest that the statue is in some sense more alive than its beholders. In the strange analogy of Paulina, it imitates life as sleep imitates death. Beyond the stone veil of the statue lies a superior life. There is magic in its majesty, conjuring evils to remembrance and taking "the spirits" from onlookers. We are invited to think not only of the central Shakespearean play metaphor, which interfuses art and life, but also of the promised end, the judgment day when evils will be conjured in remembrance, spirits breathed back into those of "awakened faith," the grave filled up, and "numbness," through holy action, bequeathed to death by redemptive life.

Like the circle of bystanders about the statue, the playhouse audience accepts an artificial stillness for a time in order that art may renew its moving life. Such a notion may be readily grasped and widely held, but the notion will grow toward fullness and light only as presenters of the scene coordinate it with analogous artifice at the trial and festival scenes and as spectators gather in cumulative memory the sheaves of the play metaphor from throughout *The Winter's Tale*. An "interpretive performance," therefore, aims not at describing the necessary response of any spectator to any production of the play but rather at desired responses to productions and reading deemed desirable.[46] For the purpose of such interpretation is to enrich not only post-play rumination but also, more importantly, future engagement with the play.

The focus on productive and receptive "response" (as opposed to "meaning" embedded in a text) keeps before us the transactional nature of dramatic performance. It brings forward the problem of subjectivity in establishing meaning. Attempts to describe collective responses promoted by the text and perhaps attainable under ideal or at least favorable conditions should not re-obscure the problem of subjectivity. There are, certainly, both silly quirks and brilliant imaginings limited to individual experience, but drama is a supremely social art, and a play such as *The Winter's Tale* drives toward the conclusion that each person may "Demand, and answer to his part / Perform'd" in a pattern that assumes a collective undertaking and the rightness of collective intercourse. To ask what the play intends of its audience or how that audience may find and become what the play seems to expect is not to ask in a

disguised form what the individual interpreter gets out of it.[47]
Nor is it to ask what the lowest common denominator of an
audience, call it inattentive ignorance, would derive. Successive interpreters may work toward the play's probable
impact on reasonably sensitive and informed audiences and
hope to reach an inter-subjective overlap or unity of some
significance.[48]

Individual interpretive performance, then, should contribute to a coherent, developing conversation. Thus:

> in recognizing from the beginning that the immediate and fluctuat-
> ing response to the play during performance is not to be our last
> word, we can come a little nearer to the position of the true critic. . . .
> If we are resolute and searching enough, we can in retrospect
> bestow on a work of the theatre something of that very stability
> which during the time of performance, it necessarily lacks. This
> means that the theatre can escape from its purely ephemeral condi-
> tion: memory, consideration, comparison have made it truly public,
> a proper subject of discourse.[49]

We want *The Winter's Tale* to be, ultimately, a subject of discourse as well as dramatic experience, because, if we believe
in criticism, we believe that the discourse and the experience
can become mutually enlightening. Yet, as the critics attest
who were cited earlier for the denials that interpretation can
advance or finally explain the impact of *The Winter's Tale*,
Shakespeare, of all writers perhaps, most fully resists the
inevitable translation of critical discourse. It may be the case,
indeed, that "Shakespeare is responsible for the openly
empirical bent of English criticism," so that, given "a mark-
edly 'English' prejudice against mixing art with anything,
especially with philosophy," the task for Anglo-American
critics of finding a proper subject of discourse among interpretations of *The Winter's Tale* remains especially challenging.[50] Various attempts, so far, to read the play in terms of
social, political, and intellectual history have proved only
marginally relevant and useful.[51] It seems best, for the present, to concentrate on the play's more immediate significance
in terms of its playhouse life or temporal impact on readers

and in terms of basic, close-in ruminations on language, psychology, and meanings as family romance.

Having said this much, one recoils from any sense of confidence in assisting oneself or others to approach such a bravely intricate play. We interpreters may all resemble the confused Leontes who sadly mistook Hermione. She admonished:

> How this will grieve you,
> When you shall come to clearer knowledge, that
> You thus have publish'd me!
>
> (2.1.96–98)

Perhaps we, too, will come to clearer knowledge beyond our publications, grieve as necessary, and then gather at last, as do the Sicilians and Bohemians of the play, in just celebrations of our joys. For does not *The Winter's Tale* demand and promise that in such a spirit we can recover a nearly miraculous communion? Interpreters of the play, one hopes, may yet work and thrive in the spirit of Paulina's charge:

> Go together,
> You precious winners all; your exultation
> Partake to everyone.
>
> (5.3.130–32)

IV

THE TEMPEST AND THE NEW WORLD

Shakespeare sets the action of *The Tempest* on an island in the Mediterranean, an island somewhere between Naples and Tunis. Yet there appear to be, at the very least, several glances in the play toward the New World. Ariel speaks of fetching magic dew from the "still-vex'd Bermoothes" (1.2.229). Caliban says that Prospero's Art is powerful enough to control the god worshiped by Caliban's mother and, apparently, by Caliban, a god named "Setebos" (1.2.375; 5.1.261), who was in fact worshiped by South American natives. Trinculo mentions the English willingness to pay a fee "to see a dead Indian" (2.2.33). And Miranda exclaims on seeing the courtiers resplendent in their finery: "O brave new world / That has such people in 't!" (5.1.182–83).[1]

In the eighteenth century, scholars traced Shakespeare's use of Setebos to Richard Eden's sixteenth-century accounts of Magellan's experience with Patagonian natives who "cryed upon their great devil Setebos to help them." In 1808, Edmond Malone argued that Shakespeare derived the title and some of the play's incidents from accounts of a storm and shipwreck experienced by Sir Thomas Gates and other Jamestown colonists on the Bermuda islands in 1609.[2] Ever since these discoveries or, more precisely, these allegations of source and influence, Shakespeareans have been asking, "What has *The Tempest* to do, if anything, with the New World?"

Commentators in the nineteenth century were, for the most part, unwilling to advance beyond recognition of such casual and fragmentary borrowings from Eden and the Bermuda pamphlets as have been mentioned. But at the turn of the century and thereafter, Sidney Lee, Morton Luce, Charles Mills Gayley, and others began to assert much more detailed and sweeping connections between Shakespeare and the entire colonial enterprise of the Virginia Company.[3] Luce, in the introduction and appendix to his Arden edition of *The Tempest*, worked mainly in terms of parallel passages. But Gayley tried to go further. According to Gayley, Shakespeare knew many of the men who were active in the Jamestown venture and, as an "aristo-democratic" meliorist, supported such vaguely defined colonial ideals as independence, freedom, and a sense of obligation to society.[4] Shakespeare, thought Gayley, was "above" the average beliefs of his day, and in his wise and conscientious patriotism he should provide inspiration to an England engaged in righteous battle against the tyrannous Hun. Gayley's thesis that Shakespeare acquired liberal views from men of the Virginia Company was swiftly countered and partially refuted by A. W. Ward. But enthusiasts such as Sidney Lee and Robert Cawley insisted that in *The Tempest* problematic relations between Caliban and the rest were meant to reflect problematic relations between the American natives and the Virginia settlers.[5]

At this point entered the genial skeptic E. E. Stoll. Taking his cue from Juvenal's remark that it is difficult not to write satire, Stoll excoriated Gayley and his followers for taking such "great pains to endeavor to prove acquaintance on Shakespeare's part with the promoters of colonizing in Virginia, and sympathy with their motives and aspiration . . . Shakespeare himself says not a word to that effect. Spenser, Daniel, Drayton, and the rest sing of the New World and Virginia, but not Shakespeare." Determined to cancel out the image of "Shakespeare with his prophetic eyes upon us!" Stoll argued, "There is not a word in the *The Tempest* about America or Virginia, colonies or colonizing, Indians or tomahawks, maize, mocking-birds, or tobacco. Nothing but the Bermudas, once barely mentioned as a faraway place, like

Tokio or Mandalay. His interest and sympathy Shakespeare keeps to himself."[6]

Despite Stoll's protestations, however, the Virginia or New World claimants, if we may call them that, have continued, undeterred to maintain and in some respects to strengthen their position. Most persuasive to contemporary Shakespeareans, perhaps, are essays by scholars such as Frank Kermode, Geoffrey Bullough, and Hallett Smith discussing New World materials as they may have influenced *The Tempest*. Speaking of certain Bermuda pamphlets, Professor Kermode concludes that in writing *The Tempest* "Shakespeare has these documents in mind." Professor Bullough lists a host of notions found in travel literature on the New World and says, "All these ideas came into Shakespeare's mind and affected the characterization and texture of his play. He was not writing a didactic work; nevertheless, approval of the Virginia Company's aims, and recognition of its difficulties seem to be implied in his depiction of Prospero, Caliban, and the intruders into the island."[7] Professor Smith notes that Richard Eden's accounts of explorations by Magellan and others tell of St. Elmo's fires in ship's rigging, Indians who die before their captors can exhibit them in Europe, Caliban-like natives who seek for grace, Utopian, golden world innocence, strange roaring sounds heard in woods, dogs used to pursue natives, natives interested in music, mutinies suppressed, and so on. Smith concludes, "Shakespeare's imagination, at the time he wrote *The Tempest*, would appear to have been stimulated by the accounts of travel and exploration in the new world."[8]

Kermode, Bullough, and Smith typify those scholars concerned to show what accounts of the New World Shakespeare probably had in mind when he constructed *The Tempest*. Other scholars form a second group of New World advocates more concerned to show how prophetic the play seems today, particularly in its depiction of sociopolitical problems within colonial and developing nations. As Leslie Fiedler, one of the more extreme proponents, would have it, by the time Prospero has put down the plot of Caliban, Stephano, and Trinculo,

the whole history of imperialist America has been prophetically revealed to us in brief parable: from the initial act of expropriation through the Indian wars to the setting up of reservations, and from the beginnings of black slavery to the first revolts and evasions. With even more astonishing prescience, *The Tempest* foreshadows as well the emergence of that democracy of fugitive white slaves, deprived and cultureless refugees from a Europe they never owned, which D. H. Lawrence was so bitterly to describe. And it prophesies, finally, like some inspired piece of science fiction before its time, the revolt against the printed page, the anti-Gutenberg rebellion for which Marshall McLuhan is currently a chief spokesman.[9]

Writers in this mode tend to weave elaborate themes of colonialism, race relations, and cultural history out of *The Tempest*.[10] But they sometimes work out themes of even broader design, as when Leo Marx, with convincing particularity, suggests ways in which "the topography of *The Tempest* anticipates the moral geography of the American imagination."[11] If Kermode, Bullough, and Smith tend, in the fashion of traditional source study, to connect *The Tempest* to the history that predates it, the visionary group that includes Fiedler and Marx connects the play more to the history that postdates it. Both groups are willing, however, to go beyond the local, immediate, sensuous life of the text. And it is in this respect, primarily, that they challenge Stoll's assertion that there is nothing in *The Tempest* about America.

Professor Stoll would have us view *The Tempest* solely as drama, distrusting any source-hunting that might turn us away from the local artistic context. It is always tempting to see art as self-contained and autonomous, as having no need for any cumbersome historical "interpretation." Thus Northrop Frye writes:

It is a little puzzling why New World imagery should be so prominent in *The Tempest*, which really has nothing to do with the New

World, beyond Ariel's reference to the "still-vexed Bermoothes" and a general, if vague, resemblance between the relation of Caliban to the other characters and that of the American Indians to the colonizers and drunken sailors who came to exterminate or enslave them.[12]

Frye concedes a degree of New World presence in the very text of the play, of course, primarily in the imagery (though just what *images* are truly indigenous to the New World, in the seventeenth *and* twentieth centuries, remains problematic). But he resembles Stoll in asserting that the historical context of the New World bears little relevance to the inner, self-enclosed, self-referential working of the play. The real argument here is over the functions of drama—over, in Hamlet's terms, the purpose of playing. Professors Stoll and Frye, in arguing that *The Tempest* has nothing to do with the New World, associate themselves with a kind of formalism or aestheticism that is too little concerned with historically conditioned meanings of language. They commit, as Robert Weimann puts it in his essay on "Shakespeare and the Study of Metaphor," the "autonomous fallacy."[13]

When works of art are asked to generate their own meanings, they and culture generally suffer. For language is never autonomous. Considered in its most elemental form, as the paper and ink of a text, *The Tempest* has no content at all. It is only when we assign to the print information in our minds that it takes on meaning. The issue is always, What information shall we assign? What are the best standards of relevant information?

For centuries, men and women have read or heard Caliban promise Stephano:

> I prithee, let me bring thee where crabs grow;
> And I with my long nails will dig thee pig-nuts;
> Show thee a jay's nest, and instruct thee how
> To snare the nimble marmoset; I'll bring thee
> To clustering filberts, and sometimes I'll get thee
> Young scamels from the rock.
>
> (2.2.167–72)

Any reader or hearer's imagination may supply a general context, no matter how vague, for pig-nuts and the nimble marmoset. But "scamels" is another matter. What happens in the brain when the word is first perceived? One may be totally at a loss. Or one may assume that a variety of bird or shellfish or other edible, unknown to one because of limited experience, is referred to. A reader who consults notes or reference works will find that "scamel" appears, without much authority, in a dialect dictionary as the name for a kind of bird. But the majority of editors favor emending "scamel" in *The Tempest* to "seamell," another variety of bird. My point is that we must go "outside" the play to apprehend and create meanings for words and passages within it.

Useful evidence for many such meanings in *The Tempest* is provided by outside reading in travel literature of the New World. There is good reason to believe that Shakespeare had read or heard of Magellan's encounter with the Patagonians who worshiped Setebos. French and Italian accounts of Magellan's or, more properly, El Cano's circumnavigation of 1519–1522 were widely circulated and discussed in Shakespeare's day; they relate that the men, off Patagonia, ate small fish described as "*fort scameux*" and "*squame.*"[14] The possibility that Shakespeare, in referring to "scamels," is adapting a foreign word like "*squamelle*" (that is, furnished with little scales) would seem worth investigating.[15] But, whether or not a new source and image for "scamels" became thus established, the larger question would remain: not so much what Shakespeare's actual sources were but what linguistic and narrative force-field we should bring to the play to disclose its meanings.

Shakespeareans interested in accounts of the New World voyagers have tended to restrict their focus to those accounts that Shakespeare is traditionally assumed to have read, as if only his reading could make the accounts inform *The Tempest* and, further, as if his reading necessarily *would* make a given account inform the play. I believe that we should question whether such source study is in fact the most productive and rewarding approach to a play such as *The Tempest*. Whether or not Shakespeare had read Eden's narrative of Magellan's voyage, such accounts can inform or illuminate *The Tempest* because they provide models of Renaissance experience in the New World.

The French and Italian accounts cited above were well-known in Shakespeare's time, and they mention that two of the mutineers against Magellan were named Antonio and Sebastian. With the help of one Gonzalo Gomez de Espinosa, Magellan put the mutiny down.[16] We are told, in addition, that one of the ships in Magellan's fleet was wrecked but that "all the men were saved by a miracle, for they were not even wetted."[17] One recalls the assertion by Shakespeare's Gonzalo that "almost beyond credit" the garments of the court party hold their freshness and are "rather new-dyed than stained with salt water" (2.1.61–62). It would begin to appear that a New World venture in addition to the Jamestown one provides a model for the play. Whether or not Shakespeare read this or any other account of Magellan's voyage, these were the sorts of terms, names, and incidents that were being bruited about. Magellan's voyage was discussed as polar or lunar expeditions have been in modern times. We need to read the voyage literature, therefore, not necessarily to find out what Shakespeare read but to ascertain what Shakespeare and his audience together would have been likely to know—what they would have gathered from a variety of sources. We need to determine what information and what special responsiveness we as readers and spectators of *The Tempest* should bring to the play.

To gain a command of notions about the New World that an Elizabethan would have found embodied in *The Tempest*, modern students of the play's backgrounds must read not only Eden's sketch but also the other accounts of Magellan and, beyond those, the various accounts of other voyages and voyagers. To do so is to find that there are telling patterns of entry into the New World.

To some extent, the voyagers carried their perceptions with them ready-made. It is a truism that from Columbus onward

Old World names for flora and fauna, Old World beliefs about golden-age primitives, and so on were imposed on the life of the New World.[18] But, in journeys involving thousands of miles and thousands of days, the old order was left behind, too. Voyagers attempting circumnavigation from Europe around the tip of South America usually sailed down the west coast of Africa, arced across to Brazil, and then worked their way south into the colder and stormier latitudes of Argentina's coast. It was at about this point, on entering the vicinity of Port San Julian (somewhat north of Tierra del Fuego) and on encountering the strange, big, naked Patagonian natives, that voyagers began to lose their confidence and their imported "understanding." Here we find repeated accounts of mutiny and miracle.

When Drake circumnavigated the globe between 1577 and 1580, he partially followed Magellan's route. His party knew in some detail of Magellan's experiences. And Drake, like Magellan, suffered a mutiny at Port San Julian, a mutiny that he, too, suppressed. At about the same time, his men were encountering the Patagonian natives and hearing, once more, of their god—this time heard pronounced as "Settaboth." Drake's chaplain, one Francis Fletcher, kept a journal in which he recorded details of the encounters with the Patagonians. Again, some of the resemblances to happenings in *The Tempest* are striking. It will be recalled that when Alonso and his party come upon the banquet presented by the "several strange Shapes" Prospero and Ariel have summoned, the response of Gonzalo is one of amazement and gratitude:

> If in Naples
> I should report this now, would they believe me?
> If I should say, I saw such islanders,—
> For, certes, these are people of the island,—
> Who, though they are of monstrous shape, yet, note,
> Their manners are more gentle, kind, than of
> Our human generation you shall find
> Many, nay, almost any.
>   (3.3.27–34)

Compare Francis Fletcher's account of the first meeting between Drake's men and the Patagonians. Fletcher speaks of "making a stay to look for the coming of the ships which were not yet come after a most deadly tempest":

Herewith the General with some of his company went on shore where the Giant men and women with their children repaired to them showing themselves not only harmless, but also most ready to do us any good and pleasure. Yea they showed us more kindness than many Christians would have done, nay more than I have for my own part found among many of my Brethren of the Ministry in the church of God.[19]

Fletcher goes on to say that the natives brought them such food "as their country yielded in most kind and familiar sort." A little later, the party lands on a small island. Thinking to gather eggs there, they are overwhelmed with birds, in Fletcher's words, "more and more overcharged with feathered enemies whose cries were terrible, and their powder and shot poisoned us unto even death if the sooner we had not retired." In *The Tempest*, of course, Ariel, in guise of a harpy (reminiscent of the one encountered in the *Aeneid*), claps his wings on the banquet table and drives back the court party who, like Fletcher's party, have drawn their swords.

The next incident Fletcher describes is that of seeing the natives "in divers companies upon several hills not far from us with leaping, dancing, and great noise and cries with voices like the bulls of Basan." One recalls Gonzalo's mention at the banquet scene of "mountaineers / Dew-lapp'd like bulls" (3.3.44–45).

Fletcher also tells of a native being introduced to wine:

Another of the Giants standing with our men taking their morning's draughts showed himself so familiar with us that he also would do as they did who taking the glass in his hand (being strong with canary wine) it came not to his lips when it tooke him by the nose and so suddenly entered into his head that he was so drunk or at the least so overcome with the spirit of the wine that he fell flat.

Fletcher says that the giant then sat up and tasted the wine and conceived an insistent liking for it—all reminiscent of Caliban's inebriating encounter with Stephano and Trinculo. Finally, Fletcher recounts an incident that could well stand behind Caliban's famous speech to his companions on hearing Ariel's tabor and pipe. Caliban says:

> Be not afeard; the isle is full of noises,
> Sounds and sweet airs, that give delight, and hurt not.
> Sometimes a thousand twangling instruments
> Will hum about mine ears; and sometime voices,
> That, if I then had wak'd after long sleep,
> Will make me sleep again: and then, in dreaming,
> The clouds methought would open, and show riches
> Ready to drop upon me; that, when I wak'd
> I cried to dream again.

$$(3.2.133-41)$$

Fletcher writes of the Patagonians:

They begin to dance and the more they stir their stumps the greater noise or sound they give and the more their spirits are ravished with melody in so much that they dance like madmen and cannot stay themselves unto death if some friend pluck not away the baubles, which being taken away they stand as not knowing what is become of themselves for a long time. In the great storms whereof we have spoken before, myself having some loss of good things spoiled in my trunk . . . , among other things glass vials, bottles, went to wreck among the which, some being covered with wicker rods, the broken glass remained within the cases, whereof one being in my hand and making noise, one of the Giants supposing it to be an instrument of music must of necessity have it, which, when he had received, he and his companies were so overcome with the sweetness of the music that, he shaking the glass and dancing, they all followed and danced after his pipe over mountains and valleys, hills and dales, day and night, till all the strings were consumed. For, the glass being continually laboured, did become small powder and wasted by little and little quite away, and the music ended. The next day they came again but all a morte that their sweet instrument had lost its sound and made great means to have another.

In *The Tempest,* Caliban leads his companions after Ariel's music, and Ariel later says that he "charm'd their ears," led them long ways, and left them "dancing." And, somewhat in the fashion of Fletcher's natives, they, too, lament the loss of their bottles.

We thus find combined in Fletcher's narrative the tempest; the mutiny; the natives with their god Settaboth; the natives' kindness, thought to exceed that of many Christians (with the telling repetition of Fletcher's "more kindness than many . . . nay more than I have . . . found among many" in Shakespeare's "more . . . kind, than . . . you shall find / Many, nay, almost any"); the incident of swords drawn against birds who prevent food-getting; the description of a giant becoming drunk; and the incident of the giants ravished with sweet music and dancing after it. Fletcher may have made part or all of it up, or he may have put together an amalgam of travelers' tales. But the similarities between his narrative and Shakespeare's play help us define what Elizabethans wanted to crystallize out of a strange and brave new world. Reading contemporary accounts of the voyagers illuminates *The Tempest,* in part, by widening our notions of New World concerns beyond colonial politics and race relations to the very stuff of romance. Shakespeare shared with Fletcher, the Bermuda pamphleteers, and others an interest in tempests, shipwrecks, and mutinies, an interest in exotic fish and fowl, an interest in natives and their offerings, an interest in native manners and native music—in short, an interest in the same matters that absorbed all the travelers of his day. We will never settle how much of this material was indigenous to the Western Hemisphere and how much was imported in the minds of men who came from Europe. But that Magellan, Drake, Cavendish, and, no doubt, others should have met with tempests, mutinies, and cross-kind natives all in a particular part of the New World seems less important than the way their overlapping experiences helped define what a new world might be.[20] By reading the voyagers, in other words, we can read Shakespeare with a keener appreciation of how aspirations and events having to do with the New World become universalized in *The Tempest*.

Just as reading about the southern voyages can help to enlarge and vivify our perception of New World concerns, so reconsideration of connections between *The Tempest* and Jamestown can help to refocus the issues, particularly with relation to the balance of interest between history and romance.

Among the Virginia backgrounds, for example, is a pamphlet of 1610 by one of the Bermuda survivors, Richard Rich. Though Rich's *Newes from Virginia* has been noted by Luce and others for its spelling "Bermoothawes" (closer to Shakespeare's than the spellings elsewhere), the full suggestiveness of the pamphlet has never been brought out. Writing in eight-line tetrameter stanzas, Rich describes the miraculous survival of the group shipwrecked in the Bermudas in 1609. He then goes on to proselytize on behalf of Jamestown. He mentions that two members of the company were lost. And though a son and daughter were born during the Bermuda stay (as if in compensation), the colonists were, in Rich's words,

> . . . opprest with grief
> and discontent in mind.
> They seem'd distracted and forlorn,
> for these two worthies' loss,
> Yet at their home return they joyed,
> among'st them some were cross.[21]

Into the midst of these Alonsos, Gonzalos, and Antonios— the distracted, the joyful, and the cross—comes the "noble Delaware" who, in Prospero's manner, "comforts them and cheers their hearts." Rich mentions a worthy knight named Ferdinando among the men who assist Delaware and, like Shakespeare's log-bearing Ferdinand, "unto their labor fall, / as men that mean to thrive." As for the Virginia commonwealth, Rich speaks of "this plantation" and says, "We hope to plant a nation, / where none before hath stood." Gonzalo in

The Tempest, imagining the "plantation" of the isle, insists that there "all things in common nature should produce." Rich, too, writes of nature's plenty—fish, fowl, grapes, strawberries—and of a land like Gonzalo's "commonwealth" where "There is indeed no want at all," where "every man shall have his share," "every man shall have a part." And in an address to the reader, Rich concludes, á la Prospero, with an epilogue:

> As I came hither to see my native land,
> To waft me back lend me thy gentle hand.

My point is not that Shakespeare must have read Rich, though it seems likely he did. My point is that we tend not to appreciate the extent to which some themes, situations, incidents, and even phrases in *The Tempest* were part of the common coin of Shakespeare's day. To examine this coin, to read such accounts of the voyagers and adventurers, is to enrich one's understanding of the play. Shakespeare shows how what happened and what was hoped for tended to mingle in the minds of far travelers who said they found what they sought, their woes all changed to wonder, and their losses yielding to greater gain.

A final example must suffice. At the heart of *The Tempest* lies the scene in which Ferdinand labors for love. He asks Miranda, "What is your name?" She replies,

> Miranda.—O my father,
> I have broke your hest to say so!
>   Fer.   Admir'd Miranda!
> Indeed the top of admiration! worth
> What's dearest to the world! (3.1.36–39)

One has but to turn to the title page of Thomas Harriot's *Brief and True Report on Virginia* (in de Bry's widely circulated Latin translation of 1590) to find the striking head-phrase describing what is to follow in the report: ADMIRANDA NARRATIO, it says.[22]

We now come to the dynamic crossing of history and romance. What Harriot, the sober scientist and historian, would describe as a brief and true report, de Bry, the publisher, sees as a narration to be admired. What grime and agony Richard Rich experienced in the Bermudas and at Jamestown become transmuted into the glitter of the balladeer. What tempests and shipwreck, mutinies and discontent were suffered by travelers often become, in the eventual success of the journey, metamorphosed into fortunate falls. In melding history and romance, therefore, Shakespeare merely dramatized what his contemporaries enacted.[23] Richard Rich promises that each of his fellows who comes to Virginia will have a house and a "garden plot." In Prospero's masque for Miranda and Ferdinand, Ceres is summoned from the "seamarge, sterile and rocky-hard," to "this grass plot," "this short-grass'd green." And Ferdinand finds that this "most majestic vision" makes him want to "live here ever" with Miranda and the "wonder'd" Prospero who "makes this place Paradise" (4.1). As Shakespeare saw, our imaginations project in every world, old and new, the same surpassing story of a will to make a garden in a wilderness, to find the human fellowship that lies beyond all storm.[24]

Shakespeare's *Tempest* ends with a grand gathering. Prospero in his ducal attire confronts his one-time enemy Alonso, forgives him, embraces the good counselor Gonzalo, and offers forgiveness to Antonio, whom many have found not only unworthy of such forgiveness but also unwilling to respond in kind. Then Miranda and Ferdinand are discovered. The sailors return, amazed at their own survival. And, lastly, Stephano, Trinculo, and Caliban enter to stand in wonder before the gathering. Says Caliban, all breathless, "O Setebos, these be brave spirits indeed!" (5.1.261). We are invited, for a moment, to look at representatives of the Old World through New World eyes. As it turns out, Setebos could not ward off, was no match for, such Europeans. To read about the New World voyagers is to see why. In their combination of apparent magic and mastery over the elements, in their greed and missionary zeal, in their hope for gain and for grace, the voyagers, like the visitors to Prospero's isle (or is it

Caliban's?), earned for themselves that peculiar mix of mockery and admiration that an audience finds in Caliban's term "brave spirits."

The question, finally, of what *The Tempest* has to do with the New World becomes wonderfully rich and strange. I should not wish to impel the play totally out of history into an autonomous imaginative construct, nor would I impel it too far in the other direction, reducing it to an historical document.[25] With many new worlds, including ours, *The Tempest* does, in truth, have much to do. And as I have tried to suggest, in order to explore the meanings implicit in the play's peculiar merger of history and romance, interpreters must travel and labor still onward.

"O SACRED, SHADOWY, COLD, AND CONSTANT QUEEN"
Shakespeare's Imperiled and Chastening Daughters of Romance

Shakespeare's plays often open with generational conflicts that point up distressing consequences of patriarchy. We find fathers and husbands treating children and wives as mere property or appurtenances of themselves (for example, the Duke of Milan in *The Two Gentleman of Verona*; Egeus in *A Midsummer Night's Dream*; several men in *The Taming of the Shrew* and *The Merry Wives of Windsor*; the Capulets; Lear; Brabantio). We see children greedy for patrimony (Oliver in *As You Like it*; various characters in the Histories; Edmund, Goneril, and Regan in *Lear*). The elder generation often adheres, moreover, to a code of revenge or war in which it seeks to overinvolve the younger generation (*Titus Andronicus, Romeo and Juliet, I Henry IV, Hamlet, Lear*), so that the procreative process becomes interrupted by misdefinitions of roles or unfortunate expectations of family loyalty and "inheritance." Sons, in particular, become tragic losers in this patriarchal overdetermination of loyalties, because they are, typically, used up in fighting feuds of their fathers; the desire for primogenitural progeny becomes thwarted when the male line is forfeited in parental wars. The particular conflict between values of war (or protection of family) and love (or extension of family) shows up most clearly in tragedies such as *Romeo and Juliet* and *Hamlet*. In *Lear, Othello*, and *Macbeth*, plays shot through with sexual and familial confusion and unwholesomeness, we see the inability of an authoritarian, aggressive male to enter reciprocal, fruitful relations with women or to foster life or line.

Given such often-disastrous results generated by the system of near-absolute male authority, a major issue in Shakespeare's plays is, What part may women play simply to survive, and then, beyond that, what part may women play to right at least some of the wrongs of patriarchy? In what follows, I shall examine Shakespeare's evolving depictions of daughters' responses to the familial pressures outlined here. I shall consider particularly the plights and flights of daughters in Shakespeare's later plays, daughters who respond to expectations of love and matrimony in surprisingly contradictory, and modern, or perhaps timeless, ways.

To say, initially, that Shakespeare's women are to some degree victims of patriarchy is not to say that, among the range of Shakespeare's characters, one finds a dearth of spirited, knowing women; one has but to think of Rosalind or Beatrice or Viola or Helena, or of Cordelia, Cleopatra, and Imogen. Such women manage to assert themselves, however, in spite of the odds against them, as heroic exceptions to the more general rule of depressing male domination. To take a very significant theme, think of how often and how keenly Shakespeare concentrates on the perversity of fathers' claims to direct their daughters' destinies in marriage. We hear throughout the plays of proprietary acts and attitudes taken by fathers in regard to or rather disregard of their daughters:

> I beg the ancient privilege of Athens;
> As she is mine, I may dispose of her;
> Which shall be either to this gentleman,
> Or to her death. . . .
>
> (*MND*, 1.1.41–44)

> A' Thursday let it be—a' Thursday, tell her,
> She shall be married to this noble earl.
> Will you be ready? do you like this haste?
> (*Rom.*, 3.4.20–21)

> This is for all:
> I would not, in plain terms, from this time forth
> Have you so slander any moment leisure
> As to give words or talk with the Lord Hamlet.
> Look to't, I charge you. Come your ways.
>
> (*Ham.*, 1.3.131–35)

> Thou must go to thy father, and be gone from Troilus.
>
> (*Tro.*, 4.2.91)[1]

To the father's combined claims of legal and emotional interest in the daughter's marriage choice, the Elizabethans were, obviously, well attuned. So intense, moreover, is the emotional investment of Shakespeare's fathers in their daughters' love that the thwarting of the fathers' expectations often brings forth imprecations and diatribes of surpassing bitterness:

I would my daughter were dead at my foot, and the jewels in her ear! (*MV*, 3.1.87–89)

> Do not live, Hero, do not ope thine eyes;
> For did I think thou wouldst not quickly die,
> Thought I thy spirits were stronger than thy shames,
> Myself would, on the rearward of reproaches;
> Strike at thy life.
>
> (*Adc*, 4.1.123–27)

> Look to't, think on't, I do not use to jest.
> Thursday is near, lay hand on heart, advise.
> And you be mine, I'll give you to my friend;
> And you be not, hang, beg, starve, die in the streets,
> For, by my soul, I'll ne'er acknowledge thee,
> Nor what is mine shall never do thee good.
>
> (*Rom.*, 3.5.189–94)

> The barbarous Scythian,
> Or he that makes his generation messes
> To gorge his appetite, shall to my bosom
> Be as well neighbor'd, pitied, and reliev'd
> As thou my sometime daughter.
>
> (*Lr.*, 1.1.116–20)

Examples of such bitterness could be multiplied from other plays, and such multiplication would merely serve to support one's natural response and question: Why? Why do Shakespeare's fathers often hate their daughters so ambitiously, with a hate that borders on disintegration and madness? Part of the answer lies, no doubt, in the special relations between father and only or best-loved daughter. More important is the concomitant absence, at least in the plays quoted above, of any sons.

Some of the fathers mention their reliance on their daughters for comfort and security in old age. Thus the Duke in *The Two Gentlemen of Verona* says, "I thought the remnant of mine age / Should have been cherish'd by her child-like duty" (3.1.74), and Lear says, "I lov'd her most, and thought to set my rest / On her kind nursery" (1.1.123). Such considerations—of emotional and economic security and of political control and generational extension of line—help to dictate the father's interest in the choice of his daughter's marriage partner. Lack of sons not only may make plain the father's need for the daughter's support and thus for a congenial son-in-law, but it also may turn the son-in-law into substitute son, the inheritor of family power and values. When the daughter chooses radically against the father's will, she effectively shuts him off from patriarchal domination of the son-in-law and consequent sonlike extension of his power and values. In the earlier comedies, the daughter's choice does not really extend beyond the father's range. Who can tell a Lysander from a Demetrius? When the choice does extend vastly beyond the father's range, as in the case of Jessica and Shylock, the results, for the father at least, are tragic.

In the earlier comedies, the society with which we are presented at the opening does not need fundamental revision, and the daughter's choice of a partner, even if against her father's will, serves eventually to confirm existing values. In tragedies such as *Romeo and Juliet*, *Othello*, and *Lear*, where the order existing at the outset is often superficial, narrow, or archaic, the daughter marries someone far beyond her father's range who challenges his sociopolitical security. Romeo's family is the age-old enemy of Juliet's family; Brabantio finds Othello repugnant as a son-in-law; France is inevitably under suspicion as rival or enemy of Lear's England, which he indeed invades later in the play. Given these special circumstances, fathers such as Capulet (though he may be on the brink of giving up the feud), Brabantio, and Lear cannot or will not think to extend their line through their rebellious daughters. Yet they have little alternative. Dreams they might have of patrilineal extension are shattered by their daughters' choices of marriage partners. Their resultant rage may be better understood in this light, as may the terrible consequences of the rage.

Terrible as the consequences are in terms of individual deaths, the revolts in the tragedies of daughters against their fathers' wills become essential elements in the whole process of loss and at least partial redemption that marks the tragic catharsis.[2] In Shakespeare's tragedies, as in his comedies, a daughter who defines herself against her father, who takes a husband, as it were, in spite of him, usually becomes associated with regenerative forces and outcomes. Where the problem, or part of it, is to break the death-dealing feud or prejudice of the father, the daughter manages to help, but in the tragedies she helps in a way that costs very dearly. Viewed in the most basic terms of patriarchal expectations, tragedies such as *Romeo and Juliet* and *Hamlet* portray fathers who employ sons to carry on their concerns, to enforce their continuing images in patrilineal succession but also to fight in the fathers' feuds. Where sons are denied to such patriarchal fathers, they may become resentful or seek substitutes. Macbeth, whose ambition to be king is threatened by Duncan's election of his son as successor, does manage to become king, but he himself has no son and remains threatened not only by Malcolm but also by Banquo's line, prophesied to succeed to the throne. Macbeth becomes cast in the role of one who kills the sons of others. Unable to reach Malcolm, he attempts through hired killers to murder Banquo's son (as well as Banquo) and almost succeeds. His killers do kill Macduff's son, onstage, and finally, near the end of the play, we see Macbeth himself hack down Siward's son, "Young Siward." The most significant fact about Macduff, who at last kills Macbeth, is that Macduff is "not of woman born," as if only such a person could get around Macbeth's malevolence against issue. Lear, too, has no son, but our first glimpse of him is in the act of arranging to acquire appropriate sons-in-law. He thinks to extend his line through daughters. Two of them, however, turn out to be his enemies, and the third marries France, who becomes Britain's enemy, albeit in a war of "liberation." Still, as in *Romeo and Juliet*, the daughter's choice of a husband who is independent of her father's influence proves a catalyst, though a bitter one, for the changes necessary to a revitalization of the home society. Thus the tragedies rather insistently criticize the patriarch's own attempts to manipulate sons or sons-in-law for his own interest.

In the romances, these themes intensify. Here problems of sons as tragic victims of their fathers' feuds are largely eliminated (save, possibly, for the example of Mamillius in *The Winter's Tale*). In *Pericles, Cymbeline, Winter's Tale,* and *Tempest,* such sons are nonexistent, lost, or killed, and only daughters are looked to for continuation of the central family. Pericles, Cymbeline, Leontes, and Prospero all have enmities in which they could tragically involve any sons of theirs, but when each such son appears to be eliminated (together with the wives of the fathers), the relation between each father and his sole daughter becomes central. The function of each daughter is not to represent, as a son might, the father in the father's battles but rather to leave home, travel widely, perhaps marry the son of her father's chief enemy (as in *Winter's Tale* and *Tempest*), and return home to instill virtues of forgiveness and the lesson of pardon in the father. The solution for patriarchal overcontrol and quasi-incestuous inwardness thus seems to be a dramatic destruction of the progenitive center and an explosion outward through time and space that leads to regroupings at the end and visions of a wide incorporative harmony.

It seems apparent that Shakespeare in these four romances celebrates a view of women as protectors and givers of life in a very special sense. Daughters such as Imogen, Perdita, and Miranda not only marry in ways that heal enmities but also prove their love viable in settings that harbor lustful or permissive appetites, that is, they encounter in "nature" a rapacious Cloten or Caliban or a bawdy Autolycus but remain chaste and eventually chasten the appetites of their true lovers. Marina, of course, chastens even the brothel. Often we see these daughters, moreover, rising from sleep and seeming death, as if to prove their miraculous power to awaken fresh life.

In all the romances (as in other Shakespearean plays), lesser characters may be seen as representing in part components within the psyche of a central character. Each father—Pericles, Cymbeline, Leontes, Prospero—works out his emotional maturation, partly through recognition of his daughter as she embodies nature's powers to renew itself rhythmically and human powers to delay acting on desires that else might become confused and blighted. Recognition of this sort is not easily won, however, and the romances are notable for their repeated images of fathers trying to dominate their daughters as well as to learn from them. In *Pericles*, Antiochus commits incest with his daughter. Cymbeline berates Imogen and orders her locked in her chamber. Prospero admonishes Miranda to listen and to obey. In the instant before recognizing his daughter, Pericles pushes her back. Leontes, too, makes menacing gestures at the infant Perdita whom he denies is his, and later, still not knowing her, he makes a kind of romantic overture in her direction (5.1.223). The passionate interaction of all the romance fathers and daughters perhaps thus necessitates in psychic terms the far journey of each daughter away from home and the taking a husband in each case so clearly set apart from the father.

Despite these apparently happy solutions to problems of patriarchal domination, and though the romances have witnessed in our supposedly liberated age a mounting tide of enthusiasm, they may be more patriarchal and patrilineal in perspective than Shakespearean interpreters have yet cared or dared to recognize. To ask the following question is to ask, in some respects, how many children had Lady Macbeth? Still, is not the engendering of a daughter in each romance taken implicitly as a guilty act that signals the impotence of the father or his receipt of divine displeasure? Else why should he have lost or in the course of the play lose wife and any sons he may have had? Kings need sons.

When they produce daughters, in a patrilineal society, they do less than the optimum to further a secure succession. When their sons die or they produce a daughter or daughters alone, they become as vulnerable as Henry the Eighth, who says, according to Shakespeare:

> First, methought
> I stood not in the smile of heaven, who had
> Commanded nature, that my lady's womb,
> If it conceiv'd a male-child by me, should
> Do no more offices of life to't than
> The grave does to th' dead; for her male issue
> Or died where they were made, or shortly after
> This world had air'd them. Hence I took a thought
> This was a judgment on me, that my kingdom
> (Well worthy the best heir o' th' world) should not
> Be gladded in't by me. Then follows, that
> I weighed the danger which my realms stood in
> By this my issue's fail, and that gave to me
> Many a groaning throe.
>
> (H8, 2.4.187–200)

In Pericles, Cymbeline, Winter's Tale, and Tempest, each leader of the state is threatened with similar "issue's fail." The plays might seem to strike at patriarchal chains when they take up the device of extending a family not through sons but through a daughter's adventure in finding a son-in-law. Through this infusion of fresh male blood, the plays seem to say, a king can more truly revitalize his kingdom. And, given the English experience with Henry the Eighth and his children, the pattern of the saving daughter might well be regarded as much more than an anomalous and irrelevant residue of folktale origins of the romances. Shakespeare could be saying, in the style of Lear's Edmund, "Now, gods, stand up for daughters!" Still, assuming that Shakespeare (who himself lost a son and, judging from the terms of his will, looked wistfully to his daughters for continuance of his line) has raised in the romances a kind of argument for daughters otherwise demeaned by patriarchalism, are not the daughters exalted more as potential wives and father-comforters than as persons in their own right? Marina, Imogen, Perdita, and Miranda are, to be sure, spirited and, at times, independent. Consider Marina speaking to Boult in the bawdy house:

> Thou art the damned door-keeper to every
> Custrel that comes inquiring for his Tib.
> To the choleric fisting of every rogue
> Thy ear is liable, thy food is such
> As hath been belch'd on by infected lungs.
> (*Per.*, 4.4.165–69)

or Imogen speaking of Posthumus and Cloten:

> I would they were in Afric both together,
> Myself by with a needle, that I might prick
> The goer-back.
> (*Cym.*, 1.1.167–69)

or Perdita:

> I was about to speak, and tell him plainly
> The self-same sun that shines upon his court
> Hides not his visage from our cottage, but
> Looks on alike. Will't please you, sir, be gone?
> I told you what would come of this.
> (*WT*, 4.4.443–47)

Or consider Miranda, calling Caliban "abhorred slave" to his face, breaking her father's command that she not tell her name to Ferdinand, and accusing Ferdinand of false play at chess. Despite such displays, however, the chief function of the daughter in each romance is to bring home a husband and to teach or permit her father a newfound love and forgiveness made possible and believable amid the restored patriarchal security. At the end of each romance, the daughter's father explicitly rejoices over the presence of his son-in-law. Pericles says to his wife, "Thaisa, / This prince, the fair-betrothed of your daughter, / Shall marry her at Pentapolis" (5.3.70–72). Cymbeline says, "We'll learn our freeness of a son-in-law: / Pardon's the word to all" (5.5.421–22). Leontes' last act is to introduce Florizel to Hermione: "This your son-in-law, / And son unto the King, whom heavens directing / Is troth-plight to your daughter" (5.3.149). Prospero tells Alonso of his "hope to see the nuptial / Of these our dear-belov'd solemnized" (5.1.309–10).

In terms of what their worlds and plays obviously expect of them, Shakespeare's daughters of romance have done well, and Shakespeare has, in a sense, "solved" problems of over-controlling fathers and overrebellious daughters that appeared in tragedies such as *Romeo and Juliet*, *Othello*, and *Lear*. In place of patrilineal succession, we have a new pro-creative process in which direct male issue are bypassed— perhaps as too competitive, aggressive, promiscuous, or death-dealing—in favor of virginal daughters who promise to win reinvigoration of the family through outside stock that is now more readily accepted by the fathers than it was before. The daughters themselves, however, are hardly permitted the alternative of not choosing a mate. To do so would be unthinkable. They must take mates to save and extend the families of their fathers, who remain so much in evidence. After working out this "solution" in the romances, Shake-speare went on, nonetheless, to consider the matter further (as was his custom) and even to question the solution.

In *Henry VIII*, we find the familiar romance patterns of ostracized queen, restorative daughter, and great hopes for the younger generation, but now the daughter, Elizabeth, becomes exalted in virginal radiance:

> Good grows with her;
> In her days every man shall eat in safety
> Under his own vine what he plants, and sing
> The merry songs of peace to all his neighbors.
> God shall be truly known, and those about her
> From her shall read the perfect ways of honor
> And by those claim their greatness, not by blood.
> Nor shall this peace sleep with her; but as when
> The bird of wonder dies, the maiden phoenix,
> Her ashes new create another heir
> As great in admiration as herself,
> So shall she leave her blessedness to one
> (When heaven shall call her from this cloud of darkness)
> Who from the sacred ashes of her honor
> Shall star-like rise as great in fame as she was,
> And so stand fix'd.
>
> (5.4.32–47)

If we compare Elizabeth to the heroines of the preceding four romances, we find that the romance pattern is transcended. Though the father's search for male issue remains important, is never more important than here, the daughter need now elect no husband to fulfill her function. She becomes herself a "pattern to all princes," and this, it seems stressed, is "not by blood" but by "honor," meaning, among other things, her sexual purity. Cranmer continues:

> Would I had known no more! but she must die,
> She must, the saints must have her; yet a virgin,
> A most unspotted lily shall she pass
> To th' ground, and all the world shall mourn her.
> (5.4.59–62)

Praise of woman beyond or even in opposition to the supposed virtues of marriage and childbearing seems to be

Shakespeare's purpose not only in his depiction of Elizabeth but also in his treatment of Katherine in *Henry VIII*. Katherine, who "failed" to give Henry the male issue he so desperately wanted, follows the lead of Buckingham and Wolsey by converting her secular fall into spiritual ascent. On her sickbed (4.2), she learns to forgive Wolsey; meditating on "celestial harmony," she falls asleep and sees a heavenly vision that promises "eternal happiness." She asks that, when she is dead, she be "us'd with honor" and strewn with "maiden flowers." All this fits the general tenor of the play as it suggests the vanity of earthly pageantries, the paltriness of bodily appetites, and the insufficiency of love's whole enterprise. Reminiscent of *The Tempest*, and reaching perhaps beyond, is the strange power of *Henry VIII* to present bodily and earthly life, especially in the getting of children, as somehow inconsequential, even petty. In its revelation of brave but diaphanous masques, of vain attempts to solidify the stage and state of earthly shows, the play points heavenward. Miranda's admirable chastity evolves toward Elizabeth's sacred virginity.

In *The Two Noble Kinsman* (which for present purpose I treat as dominated by Shakespeare's conception and handling),[3] Shakespeare, from the outset, makes his heroine one of Diana's great devotees. Emilia describes her affection for a childhood companion in these terms:

> The flow'r that I would pluck
> And put between my breasts (O then but beginning
> To swell about the blossom), she would long
> Till she had such another, and commit it
> To the innocent cradle, where phoenix-like
> They died in perfume. On my head no toy
> But was her pattern, her affection (pretty,
> Though happily her careless wear) I followed
> For my most serious decking. Had mine ear
> Stol'n some new air, or at adventure humm'd one
> From musical coinage, why it was a note
> Whereon her spirits would sojourn (rather dwell on)
> And sing it in her slumbers. This rehearsal
> (Which, ev'ry innocent wots well, comes in

Like old importment's bastard) has this end,
That the true love 'tween maid and maid may be
More than in sex dividual.

(1.3.66–82)

Asked later to choose as husband either Arcite or Palamon, Emilia decides, momentarily, that her "virgin's faith has fled" (4.2.46) and she loves them both, but, still later, when the two kinsmen are about to fight for her hand, she prays at the altar of Diana:

O sacred, shadowy, cold, and constant queen,
Abandoner of revels, mute, contemplative,
Sweet, solitary, white as chaste, and pure
As wind-fann'd snow, who to thy female knights
Allow'st no more blood than will make a blush,
Which is their order's robe: I here, thy priest,
Am humbled 'fore thine altar. O, vouchsafe,
With that rare green eye—which never yet
Beheld thing maculate—look on thy virgin,
And, sacred silver mistress, lend thine ear
(Which nev'r heard scurril term, into whose port
Ne'er ent'red wanton sound) to my petition,
Season'd with holy fear. This is my last
Of vestal office; I am bride-habited,
But maiden-hearted.

(5.1.137–51)

We could say that Shakespeare simply took his plays and themes in no special order, as they came to him. The evolution of his heroines toward virgin faith would remain, nonetheless, to be accounted for. The entire action and atmosphere of *The Two Noble Kinsmen* help account for Emilia's lack of love. Arcite and Palamon are made to seem simpleminded, outer-directed followers of Mars and Venus, respectively, but the best exposure of the post-romance attitude occurs in two prayers that Arcite and Palamon give just before Emilia's. Arcite prays to a Mars of destruction and waste, the "decider / Of dusty and old titles," whose "prize / Must be dragg'd out of blood" (5.1.63–64, 42–43). Palamon prays to a Venus who commands the rage of love throughout man and woman unkind, whose "yoke . . . is heavier / Than lead itself, stings more than nettles," who incites gross geriatric lusts, and "whose chase is this world, / And we in herds thy game" (95–97). Through these debased, decadent visions of chivalric and courtly ideals, Arcite and Palamon develop further Shakespeare's critique of patriarchalism and the potential murderousness and sterility that often accompany its political, social, and sexual hierarchies. Small wonder that Emilia, faced with two such votaries, chooses to remain "maiden-hearted."

Shakespeare's post-romance has moved far beyond the paradigmatic plots of *Pericles, Cymbeline, Winter's Tale,* and *Tempest,* in which the needs of a society for restoration, needs embodied in its leader, are answered by the restorative instincts of the leader's daughter. For Emilia, as for Elizabeth the Queen, choice of a marriage partner is dictated neither by a father's will nor by resistance to it. Remote from the dynamics of patripotestal interests, left to her own devices, Emilia displays no sense of familial drive. Lacking a father, a brother, or other male to define herself against, the daughter tends perhaps to resist marriage or to see it as especially troublesome. In contrast to Emilia, moreover, we find in this play the Jailer's Daughter, whose father wants her to marry her Wooer but who loves her father's prisoner (Palamon) and even frees him from her father's prison. She thus represents a filial pattern seen in the comedies. Irony descends again, however, as the Jailer's Daughter loses Palamon and goes mad. In this late stage in his career, Shakespeare enters an especially problematic zone in his conception of our romantic instincts and their functioning.

In the tragedies, Shakespeare's lovers—Juliet, Desdemona, Cleopatra—exercise free and vivid imaginative powers and make real, in some sense, the vigorous wide-embracing males with whom they flee, fight, and die. In the romances, the daughters no longer display the tragic force of will that finds and loses itself in an all-consuming love. They become subordinated to the pattern of generational renewal prompted by needs of their inescapable fathers. Their husbands, too, are conceived in terms of function rather than given an independence of being. They lack, consequently, the splendid willfulness and freedom of self-definition possessed by Romeo, Othello, and Antony. Lysimachus, Posthumus Leonatus, Florizel, and Ferdinand become, like the societies they inhabit, chastened and subdued by redemptive responsibilities their betrotheds place on them. This is a typical pattern in such dramatic romances as *Alcestis, The Beggar's Opera, When We Dead Awaken, The Caucasian Chalk Circle,* and *The Cocktail Party.*[4] Women are made to undertake journeys that will redeem their families and societies from some version of sterility, but the redemptive journey and return renders both husband and society strangely quiet, meditative, less lusty, and more spiritual. For Antony and Cleopatra (and perhaps even for Romeo and Juliet or Othello and Desdemona) one could almost substitute Mars and Venus, their heterosexuality and the vigor of their interchange is so strong, but for Ferdinand and Miranda and other romance couples one would prefer, at best, Apollo and Diana.

In Shakespeare's post-romance, Diana appears to win. After the womanizing excesses of Henry the Eighth, the virgin faith and phoenix-project of Elizabeth sound persuasive, and given the unconvincing, fatuous romanticalities of Arcite and Palamon, Emilia's chaste reserve appears appropriate. But societies are not renewed by chaste reserve, and Shakespeare, whose great subject has always been the renewal of family and society, is unlikely to settle, finally, for so sterile a solution. Emilia is made, at the end, to accept Palamon, the devotee of Venus, and, though the ending is hardly celebratory in tone, what makes the union of Palamon and Emilia acceptable, I submit, is the preceding incident of the Jailer's Daughter. Her idealizing eagerness for Palamon in part subjects him to ironic scrutiny but also in part marks the preservation in the play of an essential, sincere, and effective romantic imagination. That is, in the Jailer's Daughter, and through her in Palamon, we see that a creative passion of this romantic or romance-ic sort must be heeded and welcomed. The Jailer, Doctor, and

Wooer give in to the Daughter, humor her passion, and try their best to shape her world to her liking. She responds well and takes the Wooer for Palamon. The Doctor promises, convincingly, that by these means the Daughter will in three or four days become "right again."

The Two Noble Kinsmen, then, simultaneously attacks and defends romantic imagination, attacks the moribund mythologizing of Arcite and Palamon as embodied in their prayer to Mars and Venus, and purges their conception of humanity as passive and powerless before secret forces of hate and love raging in the blood, even to senility. The play first substitutes, for Arcite and Palamon, Emilia set on contemplative purity and blamelessness, praying to her sacred mistress, Diana, the "constant queen, / Abandoner of revels" (5.1.137–38). Then the play celebrates more positively and warmly the laughable but vital madness of the Jailer's Daughter, who makes the world try to create her imagined love before her eyes. Love is thus purged and renewed. The perverse and uncreative passions must yield to shadowy cold "Diana." Emilia is never a shining vital heroine. She seems to represent a stage in the development of successively more chaste, virginal heroines away from, say, Cleopatra through the likes of Imogen, Perdita, and Miranda, to Queen Katherine Elizabeth (as imaged in *Henry VIII*), and beyond. But Emilia, unlike Elizabeth, does marry. And her marriage is made possible and believable, I suggest, because its aim and function are supported by the warmer eagerness of the Jailer's Daughter toward Palamon and love.

Further investigation into Shakespeare's treatment of these acts and themes might seem foreclosed at this point by the absence of any more plays to contemplate. There are, however, significant links or overlaps between *The Two Noble Kinsmen* and the Cardenio episode in *Don Quixote*, the episode on which is based, almost certainly, the lost play *Cardenio*, attributed to Shakespeare and Fletcher in a significant "blocking entry" of the Stationer's Register and acted by the King's Men in 1613.[5] Cardenio falls in love with Lucinda, but Cardenio's friend Ferdinand (who had betrothed himself to Dorothea and jilted her), by a series of strategems, contrives to marry Lucinda in Cardenio's supposed absence. Lucinda, at any rate, submits to a marriage ceremony with Ferdinand, and Cardenio, who returns just in time to spy on the ceremony, is so horror-struck that he flees to the wilds where he meets Don Quixote and relates his misfortunes. It turns out that Dorothea, Ferdinand's betrothed, also comes to the wilds. She meets the friends of Don Quixote, and they persuade her to help them humor his madness by pretending to be a damsel in distress whom Don Quixote can aid. After elaborately playing up to Don Quixote's chivalric whims, Dorothea, Cardenio, Sancho Panza, the Barber, and the Curate bring Don Quixote to an inn where, eventually, Ferdinand and Lucinda also arrive. After the inevitable recognition, Lucinda is restored to Cardenio and Dorothea to Ferdinand. In chart form, striking similarities between the plots of *The Two Noble Kinsmen* and the conjectural *Cardenio* may be observed:

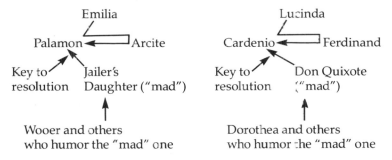

"I saw her first," says Palamon to Arcite (2.2.160) concerning Emilia. Cardenio saw Lucinda first. But both "first" lovers appear to lose out in dramatic fashion to their more active, scheming rivals. In each case the rival's intervention appears institutionally sanctioned, as when Arcite wins the battle at the pillar and is given Emilia by Theseus and, similarly, when Ferdinand marries Lucinda in a church ceremony. Then there is the eventual return of the heroine to her first love, but not before he is aided in each case by a mad romantic. The Jailer's

Daughter frees Palamon and brings him food in the forest;
Don Quixote, meeting Cardenio in the wilds, embraces him,
gives him food, and vows to serve him. In each case the mad
romantic's passionate desire to serve a disconsolate lover is
finally gratified by friends who, through impersonation,
humor the mad fancies and change the world so as to satisfy
their intentions.

When Palamon asserts his prior claim to Emilia, saying to
Arcite, "You must not love her" (2.2.161), Arcite replies:

> I will not, as you do—to worship her
> As she is heavenly and a blessed goddess;
> I love her as a woman, to enjoy her,
> So both may love.

In *The Two Noble Kinsmen* and the conjectural *Cardenio,* the first
lover is relatively passive, a worshiper of woman rather than
an enjoyer. The second lover, more lusty-active, "wins" the
woman but has less right and is presented with less sympathetic interiority of love. The mad romantics, the Jailer's
Daughter and Don Quixote, intervene and support with
intensity of conviction the worth and quest of the first lover.
Both Emilia and Lucinda, moreover, are represented as rather
passive and shrinking, tossed between extremes of ineffective
spiritual esteem from one man and primarily physical lust to
another. In each story the development of the main plot lies
secretly in the hands, or minds, of the subplot characters—the
Jailer's Daughter and Don Quixote—who must, as it were,
dream the main plot onward, substituting their creative faith,
their active idealizing eagerness, for the split love of the main
characters.

Both *The Two Noble Kinsmen* and the *Cardenio* story are, in
one sense, satires. The state of mind that overcomes the
impasse of love that is split into effete worship and Mars-like
rapacity is a state of mind represented as madness, an
unthinkable dedication of unified mind and heart, spirit and
flesh. But behind the satire, in each case there lies, I suggest,
the secret project of resuscitating the romance-ic spirit. Shake-

speare, like Cervantes, may have seen ahead in his very last works to an age of satire looming up on the horizon, but he also honored, as did Cervantes, the unquenchable desire of romantic will to purge and renew itself toward some version, no matter how strangely won, of ongoing and productive love. Ever since *All's Well* and *Measure for Measure*, if not before, Shakespeare had honored the beleaguered maiden's often-instinctive retreat to Diana, to the purer precincts of that shadowy queen, and never was this honor made more telling than in *The Two Noble Kinsmen*, but Shakespeare made Emilia—wrought even beyond Diana with impossible longings ("Were they metamorphis'd / Both into one," 5.3.84–85)— yield, finally, to her fated marriage. As Emilia exits hand in hand with Palamon, there linger still the singsong cracked remarks, the deepest hopes and fears of the Jailer's Daughter:

> *Daugh.* We shall have many children . . . .
> . . . .
> *Wooer.* Come, sweet, we'll go to dinner,
> And then we'll play at cards.
> *Daugh.*   And shall we kiss too?
> *Wooer.* A hundred times.
> *Daugh.*   And twenty?
> *Wooer.*   Ay, and twenty.
> *Daugh.* And then we'll sleep together?
> *Doct.*   Take her offer.
> *Wooer.* Yes, marry, will we.
> *Daugh.*   But you shall not hurt me.
> *Wooer.* I will not, sweet.
> *Daugh.*   If you do, love, I'll cry.
>   (5.2.95–112)

Shakespeare understood and made vivid, as have few artists before or since, the spirit of the maiden phoenix that flutters up periodically in women, if not in men as well, and he traced with surpassing skill the intricacies of that endless dance where daughters escape and follow, reject and recreate, their once and future fathers.

CORDELIA WEEPING

"With wash'd eyes / Cordelia leaves you." Saying farewell to her sisters toward the end of the first scene in *King Lear,* Cordelia confesses that she weeps. But why does she weep? And what does her weeping signify? Is she to be played as finally letting go after Lear's dismissal that precedes her own exit? "Wherefore be gone," Lear says, "Without our grace, our love, our benison" (1.1.264).[1] Or has she been quietly weeping during more or even much of the scene in pity for Lear, for herself, for "all"? "Wash'd eyes" in Shakespeare's plays often reveal true sight, clear conscience. "There are no faces truer than those that are so wash'd" (*Ado,* 1.1.27). Cordelia, in mentioning her tears, may be suggesting not so much her deeper sympathy for Lear as her own sincerity and her clear knowledge of her sisters' fault. It is after France asks Cordelia to bid farewell to her sisters that she addresses them directly: "The jewels of our father, with wash'd eyes / Cordelia leaves you. I know you what you are" (1.1.268). In a play so keenly focused on problems of blurred and clear physical and moral vision ("See better, Lear"; "I see it feelingly"), the reference to "wash'd eyes" must allude in part to Cordelia's clarified perception of her sisters.

Cordelia's tears were not summoned, however, as aids to perception. In his fashion, Shakespeare sets up a telling comparison between "the jewels of our father" and Cordelia's "wash'd eyes." Goneril and Regan have falsely established themselves as jewels in the view of Lear; they have also obtained his jewels, his wealth. "The jewels of our father . . . Cordelia leaves [to] you." Cordelia's eyes are, moreover, shining jewels themselves. Later, Edgar tells of meeting his "father with his bleeding rings, / Their precious stones new lost" (5.3.190). The washing of watery eyes makes them precious because it brightens them and because the tears, like Gloucester's blood, suggest a cleansing of inner sight as well as a freshening of whatever the tears touch. Sir Thomas More admonishes the mob: "Wash your foul minds with tears" (*STM*, 2.C.108), and Richard the Second's Queen asks her attendants to "wash him fresh again with true-love tears" (*R2*, 5.1.10). In *King Lear*, we next see Cordelia in the fourth scene of the fourth act, when again she not only weeps but also speaks of her weeping. In the scene preceding this one, Kent had learned the effect of his letters on Cordelia: "now and then an ample tear trill'd down / Her delicate cheek" (4.3.12):

> You have seen
> Sunshine and rain at once; her smiles and tears
> Were like a better way: those happy smilets
> That play'd on her ripe lip seem'd not to know
> What guests were in her eyes, which, parted thence,
> As pearls from diamonds dropp'd. . . .
> . . . There she shook
> The holy water from her heavenly eyes,
> And, clamor-moistened, then away she started
> To deal with grief alone.
>
> (4.3.17)

This mingling of tears, rain, ripeness, and holy water continues when Cordelia and the Doctor enter on the theme of Lear "mad as the vex'd sea" and crowned with "all the idle weeds that grow / In our sustaining corn" (4.4.2). Cordelia's tears are like a heavenly rain that fosters physical growth and moral birth. "All blest secrets," she says, "All you unpublish'd virtues of the earth, / Spring with my tears; be aidant and remediate / In the good man's distress!" (3.4.15).

In the same scene, Cordelia describes France as pitying her "mourning and importun'd tears" (4.4.26). She refers to herself as if weeping her way to England. Her weeping in the first scene, the description of her offstage weeping, her weeping when she next appears, and her allusions to her own weeping onstage and offstage build to a composite portrait of the weeping maid. When she enters to wake the sleeping Lear, she weeps once again. Lear responds, "Be your tears wet? Yes, faith. I pray weep not" (4.7.70). Cordelia next appears, according to stage directions, crossing over the stage with Lear. Should the actress portray her as weeping? In the succeeding scene, when she appears for the last time alive, now a prisoner of Edmund, Lear again alludes to her weeping: "Wipe thine eyes," he commands, or begs. Cordelia exits not to reappear save as a corpse in Lear's reverend arms. Then Lear will be seeking that moisture in her very breath that may "mist or stain" the looking-glass (5.3.262).

Thus, *every single speaking appearance* for Cordelia involves her weeping *and also* words about her weeping. I do not know that attention has been drawn before to the pervasiveness of Cordelia's weeping, but it has less significance in itself, perhaps, than in relation to Lear's own experience with tears. For Lear, in his battles with his daughters, echoes the sentiments of many a Shakespearean protagonist who thinks to take the man's dry way.

Some Shakespearean feminists, in the drive to free his female characters from degrading stereotypes, have denied that Shakespeare distinguishes between the natures of men and of women. We have been told that Shakespeare "did not divide human nature into the masculine and the feminine. . . . To talk about Shakespeare's women is to talk about his men, because he refused to separate their worlds physically, intellectually, or spiritually."[2] And we are told, "Shakespeare disavows the womanishness of weeping. Some of his noblest women do not weep."[3] The two examples then given of noble women who allegedly do not weep are Queen Katherine in *Henry VIII* and Hermione in *The Winter's Tale* at moments when each is refusing to ask for pity and is asserting instead the justice of her cause. Katherine in fact says that she *is* about to weep but will make sparks of fire out of her tears (*H8*, 2.4.70), and Hermione actually avows that weeping *is* womanish. She says, "I am not prone to weeping, as our sex / Commonly are" (2.1.108). Is she, moreover, saying something about herself that receives our unqualified admiration? Or has she the task of learning a maturity of tears? After Hermione swoons at the trial, Paulina castigates Leontes, telling him that even a devil "would have shed water out of fire" before committing Leontes' crimes. Leontes resolves to honor the memory of Hermione and Mamillius: "Once a day I'll visit / The chapel where they lie, and tears shed there / Shall be my recreation" (3.2.238). Hermione then appears, weeping, in a dream to Antigonus and tells him to convey Perdita to Bohemia: "There weep and leave it crying." Camillo later imagines Leontes "opening his free arms, and weeping / His welcomes forth" (4.4.548).

Womanish weeping is often mentioned and, it is true, sometimes denigrated by Shakespeare's characters. Some of the plays are quite flooded with such phrases as "tender womanish tears" (*Jn.*, 4.1.36); "tears do not become a man" (*AYL*, 3.4.3); "a woman's gift / To rain a shower of commanded tears" (*Shr.* Ind., 1.124); "I am a soldier and unapt to weep" (*1H6*, 5.3.133); "their gentle sex to weep are often willing" (*Luc.*, 1237). We cannot easily explain away such sentiments as illusions of misogynists, for they are mouthed by men and women, low and high, foolish and wise. Indeed the notion that women are more prone to weeping than are men stems in part from humoral psychology. In *Doctrine for the Lady of the Renaissance*, Ruth Kelso has noted how pervasive was the notion that the elements in woman "are badly mixed; humidity and cold prevail over heat and dryness with the result that she is timid, even cowardly, by disposition and shrinks from the great exploits that make the name of man glorious." In connection with this declared moistness of humor, women's weeping was made much of: "tears were of course scorned as a sign of great weakness in men, and women's tendency to let them fall on every occasion, big or little, was often used against them."[4] Yet there were defenders, too, and Kelso summarizes their response:

Woman's temperament, in which the humid and cold humors admittedly prevail, should not be made a reproach, for both men and women have all four humors in common, and only relatively can the humid and cold be said to dominate women, and the hot and dry men, and that not always in the same degree. Grant that the nature of heat, providing it is not excessive, is to be more quick and lively and better disposed toward every kind of activity. Yet nature has ordered each temperament for the special office assigned, and woman's is better for bearing and nurturing children because of its greater humidity even though it is more cold.[5]

Another example of this sort of backhanded praise comes from Thomas Puttenham, who, in his *Arte of English Poesie* (1589), defended women's weeping as a sign of good nature, meekness of mind, devotion, charity, and commiseration.[6] In a treatise concerning honor, Girolamo Camerata argued, "If we consider the more temperate complexion of women, who are thereby more stable, chaste, healthy, and long-lived, they surpass men in disposition to understand all the disciplines."[7] This discussion of woman's weeping kindness fits, it should be added, the context of Ruth Kelso's suggestion that ideals of self-glorification, lustihood, and nobility, set up for gentlemen in the Renaissance were essentially classical or "pagan" ideals whereas the ideals of chastity, patient suffering, and teary tenderness set up for women were essentially Christian. (Compare Cordelia echoing Christ's words [*Luke* 2.49]: "O dear father, / It is thy business that I go about" [4.4.23]). This rough division between the honor of the spending male and the honor of the saving female may open up another significance of the "double standard" for men and women.

Shakespeare's plays teem with references not only to women's frailty and cowardice but also with references to their pity and kindness. This may be precisely the portrait most galling to many feminists, and Shakespeare presents counterexamples enough to suggest how inaccurate the portrait can be. Certainly the plays yield a gallery of diversely strong, courageous women as well as those of "manly" cruelty and stony-heartedness. But there is little in the plays to suggest that Shakespeare disavowed the prevailing division of male and female natures according to the vague but powerful influence of humoral psychology. My purpose is not, however, to dig up the old chestnut of humoral psychoanalysis of Shakespeare's characters but rather to outline a more cosmic, meta-humoral dimension to Shakespeare's confrontations of male and female "natures." Let us admit that Shakespeare points to a humoral basis for women's weeping: "Women are soft, mild, pitiful, and flexible" (*3H6*, 1.4.141); they have "melting spirits" (*JC*, 2.1.122), "waxen hearts" (*TN*, 2.2.30), and "waxen minds" (*Luc.*, 1240). Thus women's weeping is grounded in a poetic psychobiology. It is Shakespeare's way, however, not to dismiss women's tears as a weakness of soft spirits but to counter the dismissive view with one that taps vast reservoirs of catharsis and redemption associated with weeping.

Our tears not only share the powers of holy and remediate rain, in Shakespeare's view, they also betoken a microcosmic sea of all-sweeping flood. Shakespeare writes of "sea-salt tears" (*Tit.*, 3.2.20), "Seas of tears" (*3H6*, 2.5.106), "an ocean of salt tears" (*2H6*, 3.2.143, "tears as salt as sea" (*2H6*, 3.2.96), and of persons who "weep seas" (*Tro.*, 3.2.78). Like the feminine moon that governs its tides, the sea in Shakespearean drama naturally abounds with feminine and tearful associations: "sea-nymphs" preside over the "sea-change" described for Ferdinand weeping his father's wrack (*Tmp.*, 1.2.403); Perdita is wished a "wave o' th' sea" by her lover Florizel (*WT*, 4.4.141); Pericles weeps in reunion with his sea-born daughter, Marina (*Per.*, 5.1); and Juliet's father addresses her as she weeps: "thy eyes, which I may call the sea, / Do ebb and flow with tears; the bark thy body is, / Sailing in this salt flood" (*Rom.*, 3.5.132). Those who weep deeply in Shakespeare are changing, growing, and journeying, as are Juliet, Pericles, and Ferdinand. Thus all the disparaging sketchy remarks in the plays about women's weak, watery natures are cast into a corner of frivolity when set against the mighty arguments of action that introduce their heroes and heroines to medicinal weeping and far sea-journeys of the soul.

Lear embodies the male principle of resistance to tears even as he comes to admit their significance. In the first act, he says to Goneril (1.2.296): "I am asham'd / That thou hast power to shake my manhood thus, / That these hot tears, which break from me perforce, / Should make thee worth them." In the second act, Lear prays to the gods: "touch me with noble anger, / And let not women's weapons, water-drops, / Stain my man's cheeks!" (2.4.276). In the third act, Lear promises to "weep no more" (3.4.17), but in the fourth he preaches to the blinded Gloucester: "If thou wilt weep my fortunes, take my eyes . . . we came crying hither . . . we wawl and cry . . . we cry that we are come / To this great stage of fools" (4.6.176), and Lear asserts that his condition "would make a man of salt / To use his eyes for garden water-pots." To the end, however, Lear battles his own weeping: "mine own tears / Do scald like molten lead" (4.7.46); "The good-years shall devour them, flesh and fell, / Ere they shall make us weep" (5.3.24). Yet we came crying hither, and Lear's weeping, as we know, parallels the rain that drowns the heath or, as he puts it, "this tempest in my mind" (3.4.12). This is a play, as are all of Shakespeare's plays, in which men are "minded like the weather" (3.1.2). When Lear is finally found, mad as the sea and crowned with idle weeds, it is in the context of Cordelia's smiles and tears, the "sunshine and rain" that foster renewed life. Lear becomes a kind of nature spirit metamorphosed from the kingly demigod who swore "by the sacred radiance of the sun" (1.1.109) down through storm to the substances of cold wind, of standing pool and sea. Then he rises again to life through the idle furrow-weed to be humanized and nourished under the tears of his daughter who "redeems nature from the general curse" (4.6.206).

In the tragedy that precedes *King Lear,* the martial Othello moves from a realm of Venetian law and stability, from a time when he could speak to Desdemona to "beguile her of her tears" (1.3.156), away through tempestuous sea-journey to the Cyprian chaos that puddles his clear spirit (3.4.143) and makes him equate Desdemona's tears with guile: "she can weep, sir, weep . . . O well-painted passion!" (4.1.254). In the final two acts, both Othello and Desdemona weep copiously. Othello calls Desdemona the fountain from which his current runs (4.2.59), weeps before killing her, and again, or still, just before killing himself. He ends as "one whose subdu'd eyes, / Albeit unused to the melting mood, / Drops tears as fast as the Arabian trees / Their medicinable gum" (5.2.348).

Behind Shakespeare's tragic heroes and heroines rise up mythic, elemental figures, forces of male and female that intermingle in an erotic reality, a bipolar nature of hard and soft, vengeful and forgiving, thirsty and fluid. In Shakespeare's tragedies, often, male struggles with female, and, even as they both succumb, the male element learns (though too late and imperfectly) to yield to, accept, take on, some traits of the feminine. Like Lear and Othello, Hamlet first thinks himself superior to weeping, mocking his mother who wept "like Niobe—all tears" (1.2.149). But he is forced to consider whether certain horrific "things mortal" might not make milky the burning eyes of heaven (3.3.516), whether one who acts tragically may not justly weep (2.2.560). When the Ghost appears to him in Gertrude's chamber, Hamlet says to it with his characteristic sense of paradox: "Do not look upon me, / Lest with this piteous action you convert / My stern effects, then what I have to do / Will want true color—tears perchance for blood" (3.4.127). And in the following scene, Gertrude reports that Hamlet weeps for what was done (4.1.27). Then, as Othello entered a watery world of cruel and medicinable tears against a background of sea-journey and Desdemona's weeping (remember that Desdemona sings the "willow" song as she weeps: "The fresh streams ran by her, and murmur'd her moans . . . Her salt tears fell from her, and soft'ned the stones" [4.3.44]), so Hamlet's sea-journey and sea-change toward his particular "readiness" for death are set against the simultaneous actions of Ophelia who sings mad songs of weeping "true-love showers" (4.5.40) and of the grave into which is "rain'd many a tear" (4.5.167), of Ophelia who drowns by the willow in the "weeping brook" (4.7.175) and who becomes, like the sea-gowned Hamlet, "native and indued" unto the watery element (4.7.179) of mortality.

Shakespeare never tires of drawing out implications inherent in tales of ambition—dry, fruitless, dusty—brought up against an opposed force of acceptance and love—moist, fertile, maternal. Macbeth, who may once have been "full o' th' milk of human kindness" (1.5.17), is, like the sailor in the witches' song, drained as dry as hay (1.3.18) in company with his wife who would turn her milk to gall or pluck the nipple from her baby's gums and dash out its brains. The early Macbeth can imagine tears of pity drowning the wind, but he never comes within himself to the metaphorical rainstorm or sea-journey that might symbolize his access to remorse; instead he dries into "the sear, the yellow leaf" (5.3.23), while opposing forces rise not only in the green leaves of Birnam Wood but also in Shakespeare's image of purging, bloodlettings that "dew the sovereign flower and drown the weeds" (5.2.30). Lady Macbeth dies longing for the more than a little water that might clear her of the deed.

Antony and Cleopatra escape the Macbeths' desperate drought even though Antony is martial and ambitious and Cleopatra is the general's general who can wear his sword Philippan (2.5.23). The great drift of the play is through Antony's sea-journeys, his entrance to the world of the flooding Nile, his battles at sea, his authority "melting" from him (3.13.90), his making his soldiers weep (4.2.34), and through Antony, who, like water poured in water, "cannot hold this visible shape" (4.14.14), a Mars who would die calling for "Eros" (4.14), and who finally "melts" (4.15.63) in death in Cleopatra's arms. Shakespeare's golden heroes, when they fall, come not to dust but to another element, to a recognition that nature honors more than the glorious sun/son, that nature honors also the moon, the sea, the rain, and their human analogues. Coriolanus, to take a last example, finds that he is "not / Of stronger earth than others" (5.3.24) but must "melt" before his family's intercession "which Great Nature cries, 'Deny not'" (5.3.32). His wife and mother weep

(5.3.100), and finally he weeps, too (5.3.195), as he extends mercy to Rome. Though Aufidius says that Coriolanus betrayed him "for certain drops of salt" (5.6.92) and "at his nurse's tears / He whin'd away the victory," it was of course that hero's finest hour when he let himself be, for a moment, a "boy of tears" (5.6.100).

There are no doubt many, many more ramifications to the idea that Shakespeare gathers together weeping, pity, forgiveness, rain, redemption, nursing, nurturing, and sea-changes all into a realm of Nature that may be identified as feminine though it dictates no one human's nature. The milk of nursing that Shakespeare associates with concord and mercy, for example, connects as well to weeping and rain in the milky eyes of heaven mentioned in *Hamlet,* or in Perdita's intent to "milk [her] ewes and weep" (*WT,* 4.4.450), or when Parolles "weeps like a wench that had shed her milk" (*AWW,* 4.3.107). As Cleopatra takes the asp to her breast, Charmian cries, "Dissolve, thick cloud, and rain, that I may say / The gods themselves do weep!" (*Ant.,* 5.2.299). Soon after, Cleopatra calls the asp "my baby at my breast / That sucks the nurse asleep" (5.2.309).

Let the closing image of Cleopatra suckled to a lasting sleep stand for the collective image of Shakespeare's tragic women who take something infinitely precious out of life as they die (together with the male protagonists) and leave the stage to a comparatively lifeless society of male survivors: Lavinia killed by Titus and for whom his tears made him blind (*Tit.,* 5.2.49); Juliet sheathing Romeo's dagger in her bosom; the corpses of Ophelia and Gertrude succeeding each other onstage in the last two scenes of Hamlet; Desdemona smothered on the bed; Cordelia's body the object of Lear's final concern (*Lr.,* 5.3.311); Lady Macbeth in her nightgown exiting to suicide—"What's done cannot be undone. To bed, to bed, to bed" (*Mac.,* 5.2.68). The women die, often with postures and gestures reminiscent of their procreative function: kissing or kissed, on love beds, in night gowns, nursing mortality itself. The women die, but men remain. The women were all objects of intense masculine interest, often a mix of disaffection and affection suggesting male ambivalence between values of war and love, crown and queen, politics and familial generation. Shakespeare's tragic heroes hold on too long to their concepts of valor, pride of place, nobility. The current of the tragedies is to take the hot-blooded, egoistic, oratorical, appetitive male and run him away from an old code of heroism and out of the male-domi-nated court or city toward the embrace and entanglements of love, women, family, nature, storm, and sea, that is, to demasculinize the male endeavor, to move it from a kind of rigid, proud, tumescent striving to a climax that overflows toward a freer, more accepting, quieter, cooler, more "femi-nine" sense of the world's body. The male who thinks or wishes to be self-reflexive and self-sufficient gives in, yields toward, the female or is shown the folly of not doing so.

The reason I have concentrated here on weeping and the Shakespearean opposition of a hot, dry masculinity and a cooler, wetter femininity is not to advocate that we all might profitably weep much more (though it seems apparent that we might) nor to suggest that male submit to female, but rather to remind us of Shakespeare's in some ways conser-vative polarization of sexuality that bifurcates his entire uni-verse. Shakespeare did not write prosaic drama confined to vectors of social inquiry; he wrote poetic drama that explores humankind's relations to the cosmos as well as to itself. Shake-spearean drama owes its unique depth and power in part to the materializing tendency of Shakespeare's imagination, his capacity and will to find physical analogues for psychic events, his binding of human emotions and acts to forces in nature, and his perception and rendering of an erotic division in all things. Shakespeare charges every element in his plays with a kind of sexual tension, because he sees the basic ele-ments as sharing in that tension. The matter of dry and moist humors and of men learning meanings of women's weeping provides, I believe, an illustration that a feminist interpreta-tion of Shakespeare need not deny all divisions between male and female natures.[8] There should be a place for feminist interpretation that can admit and even cherish a few distinctions between masculine and feminine even as it seeks to separate creative distinctions from destructive inequalities.[9] Such an interpretation can help all of us respond to the form and force of Shakespeare's liberating art.

VII

SUITING THE WORD TO THE ACTION?
Scholarship and Stage Direction

> Strange is it that our bloods,
> Of color, weight, and heat, poured all together,
> Would quite confound distinction, yet stands off
> In differences so mighty.
>
> (*AWW*, 2.3.119–22)[1]

Recently, Donald Sinden, an actor for the Royal Shakespeare Company, was interviewed by J. W. R. Meadowcroft, who said:

before we get down to specifics, perhaps you'd tell me how you go about preparing a Shakespeare role, one that you haven't previously done.

DS Well, you mustn't take this personally, Bob, but I never read any authorities; and the first thing I do is go through my text and cross out all stage directions.

. . . .

JWRM You say you don't read literary criticism.
DS No, no, I don't read any.[2]

Scholars don't suit their words to this actor's actions. Not only does he avoid literary criticism of Shakespeare and cross out editors' stage directions, he even crosses out their text. He resents "editors getting between" him and Shakespeare. When the scholar asks him, "What text do you use?," he replies:

For *Lear* we used—not because of its value as a text—we used the New Penguin Shakespeare, merely because of its size.
JWRM I think it's a very good text.

94

DS Is it? Well, I mean, it's easy to slip into the pocket and have around. My only source books that I ever use are the facsimile of the First Folio, the Norton—you know, the one that they did at the Folger—and the *Oxford English Dictionary.* They're the only two things I want to know about.

JWRM Not the thirteen-volume *Oxford*?

DS The thirteen-volume, yes, Robert Graves put me on to that some fifteen years ago. (p. 81)

More vehement than his dismissal of criticism is his dismissal of the edition. Where, then, do his words come from? He reveres "Shakespeare in the First Folio": "we're getting back to something there, aren't we?" (p. 81). He gets back to freedom of choice. He does not suit his action to an editor's word; he edits the word to suit his action:

In 1946, when I was playing William in *As You Like It,* I noticed that the word "ay" was spelled "I." I thought how fascinating, and so I changed it to an "I" meaning the first person, whereas all the modern texts have "ay." (p. 81)

Because Shakespeare editors silently emend the Folio spelling, the actor can reconsider the matter only by reading the Folio itself. No matter that the actor was shaky in refusing the emendation, at least he suited the word to his conception of character and action.[3]

Why does the actor resent the editor and the critic? Do scholars revere the *words* a little too much or in the wrong spirit, at least from the actor's point of view? Some scholars may think, for instance, that the words the actor speaks all should be distinct, as words and not just as tones or exclamation. But the actor may not see it that way. In the interview, Meadowcroft complained:

The lines are so beautiful. You want to hear the words; you don't want them thrown away.

DS Well, the director even had to stop me, because I was going too far on the lightning—trying to make it like when you put two live wires together: psst-tt-tt-t! . . . but the director said, "We're losing the words." (p. 85)

The actor would make the words actional; the scholar, backed by the director in this instance, says that it is throwing them away.

Editors direct the stage toward a clear text and a complete one. They direct, or at least so it seems to the actor, that the real play is the edited text. "Stage that," they say. "What?" says the actor, "don't you see how anti-theatrical your text is? Your emendations suggest a spurious clarity and fixity of meaning. The punctuation you insert limits my freedom of intonation. Your act divisions mistructure the experience. Your alterations of prose to verse hamper my choice and delivery. Your annotations make meaning tidy, a matter of a few synonyms, and they fail to stress how much tone, gesture, and movement count in the creation of meaning. In all this, your edited text constitutes unhelpful stage direction. No, thank you. I need something else for my text." To this diatribe, how can Shakespeare editors reply? Many editors probably would say, "Our editions are not directions, only suggestions. If you the actor wish to double check our work, well and good. Or if you wish to do your own work from the ground up, do it, and with our blessing." Yet still the actor may not be satisfied, for he may go on to complain that we are very much directing the stage when we direct readers who become audiences to expect, say, a certain emendation or certain pointing. The actor may mention further that expectations are conditioned by our practice of conflating Folio and Quarto texts or even by our spelling. These points are well taken. Scholars are now responding, however. They argue, for example, that the Folio *Lear* is Shakespeare's revision, for playhouse purposes, of the Quarto, so that it makes little sense to conflate the two.[4] Or they argue that some "bad" quartos tell us much about Shakespeare's theater.[5] They may deserve to be separately edited, even played.

The way scholars spell the text of a Shakespeare play presents a special case of stage direction. To the extent that modern spelling dictates the Received pronunciation of scholars, dictionary makers, the well educated in England, such spelling does not reflect pronunciations of most native speakers of English. Certainly few audiences in America speak the way American actors speak when they mimic Received pronunciation, a sound Shakespeare never heard. It makes Shakespeare sound classy, but we might do better to let the actors approximate an Elizabethan pronunciation that would be understandable, even to untrained ears, and would sound refreshingly (or depressingly if you take a conservative view) up-country, a little Appalachian, much nearer to a perhaps desirable Volk-speare.[6]

A defense of scholars directing actors to use modern spelling has been the argument that it provides an "experience closer to that of Shakespeare's contemporaries," who experienced the plays "in what was, for them, a modern form."[7] But if that is the aim, if we really want people to appropriate Shakespeare and not to worship from afar in dim comprehension, then should not editors and translators experiment with more phonetically accurate spelling (as in dialect dialogue in novels) that would reveal meter and soundplay (including puns and rhymes) now obscured by modern spelling? And should not modernizing editors change obsolete words into modern ones? Olivier's film dialogue for *Hamlet*, for example, changes *beaver* to *visor, let* to *stop, cataplasm* to *medicine*, and so on. Should scholars fault actors for changing words to fit the action of passing time? The actor in the interview said that at Stratford-on-Avon "ninety-five percent, if not more, of our audience are people who are seeing a Shakespeare play for the very first time, or that particular play for the first time" (p. 84).

What adjustment, then, between the preservation and the transmission of the old words will satisfy scholars, actors, and audiences? There is a problem here deeper than mutual adjustment of standards. Suppose that actors and audiences do try to satisfy the most conserving scholar-archaeologists. Suppose that the actors, as directed by scholars, speak the original words in the original way, and suppose that informed audiences understand them. Scholars still will complain, as they do now, that the actors by their actions distort the meanings of the words, that *tremor cordis* does not mean a breathless seizure, that nothing in the text directs Leontes to bump the pregnant Hermione or to pull her hair or to laugh frequently or directs Hamlet to lie on Gertrude in the closet scene. The scholar, typically, wants, directs, the actor's actions to be more modest and decorous, to suit and serve the word and rarely let the word serve and swerve to the creative demands of action.

Shakespeare saw this problem. When Hamlet, advising the players, reverses his formula—"suit the action to the word"— and shifts to suit "the word to the action," he then adds, "With this special observance, that you o'erstep not the modesty of nature." When word suits action, it risks becoming actional, physical, bare, immodest.[8] When words shift from silent, fixed notation to living intonation, then someone's freedom intervenes. Shakespeare (and Hamlet in his play within the play) wrote down letters that suggested only the very rudiments of sound for minds sensitized to much more, to the all-important tone (including all the elements of vocal modulation). The actors have freedom to intone those sounds in a variety of ways, to make them suit the action.[9] That freedom, moreover, is irreversible and irrepressible, never completely subject to the tonic controls of playwright, editor, critic, or director. The very constitutive nature of theater, then, demands that the actor wrench the pre-temporal word into time and make what was seemingly universal and general now concrete and particular. The actor uses, ab-uses, the primal, silent, written words to suit a specific time and place, the conditions of history.

No wonder then that playwright, director, and scholar would mistrust the materializing, reifying work of actors and would insist wishfully on a modesty and decorousness at the heart of nature, an art there in charge of subversive freedoms inherent in all action. Acting, theater, forever threatens modesty, as if subversively from below. Shakespeare makes modesty of speech partly a class issue. His aristocrats counsel it to low players the way mind might counsel body or conscience chastise will, as when, for example, in *Taming of the Shrew,* the

Lord counsels his servant players, "It will be a pastime passing excellent if it be husbanded with modesty" (Ind., 1.67).[10]

How the theater must resent, does resent, the advice of aristocrats and scholars that it behave itself! In *Love's Labor's Lost*,
the not unsympathetic Princess of France still coolly sums up
the pageant of the Nine Worthies: its "contents / Dies in the
Zeal of that which it presents" (5.2.517–18). What zeal is to be
left the theater? Is not a foolish immodesty of nature both its
shame and its glory? To an aristocrat, Shakespeare as speaker
in the sonnets complains of having to make himself "a motley
to the view" (sonnet 110), complains of his nature "subdu'd /
To what it works in" (sonnet 111), complains of the theater's
"public means which public manners breeds" (sonnet 111).
Public manners; the players cannot keep counsel; the actor
will "not shame" (*Ham.*, 3.2.145). The theater would drive
word into action, drive us out of mind into body: "off, you
lendings!" (*Lr.*, 3.4.108), just as the world would do the same,
asking maturity to note what lies beneath the cloak of culture:
"High and mighty, You shall know I am set naked on your
kingdom" (*Ham.*, 4.7.43). This is the theater's awesome drive,
to seek an immodesty of nature that challenges, teaches,
changes the rational word. "Is it not monstrous that this
player here . . . Could force his soul"? (*Ham.*, 2.2.551–53). Acting is ever monstrous as it violates the purely scriptural word,
making it a little soiled in the working.

No doubt the theater, in its great zeal for action, can unsuit
the word. But too many scholars have countered with their
own awesome tendency, to drive action back toward word,
looking for the fixed play, for central, original meanings—a
rationalist, antiquarian bias—cutting down the free range of
intonation, making Shakespeare a bit more bookish. quieter,
more modest, truer to a timeless truth. Despite their service to
theatrical study and even within that service, such scholars
quite habitually point to the rhetorical nature of Shakespearean drama, often subordinating movement to speech
and feeling to thought, as if the pauser reason could stay in
command, as if action had not its own creative impulse. The

scholar, like Hamlet, tends to doubt that he or she, too, is an actor and values instead the atemporal word as against historically conditioned action. Thus, many scholars feel more comfortable with the aesthetic approach, the formalistic approach, the universalizing approach to content in terms of basic moral themes, anything that leads away from too-pressing responsibilities to time, history, our own stage.

How, then, can scholarship look as it must back toward the original word, the old text silent and fixed, asking the theater to suit its action to that ideal, ordered word, but also look forward again conceding theater the vital place of intonation, a realizing energy? I believe that many scholars could more actively affirm their responsibility to help direct the stage through their writing and teaching. In addition to the actor who boasts of never reading authorities, there is another type, the "actor-scholar" who may find stage directions in much that we write about Shakespeare.[11] If we insist (questionably) that there was an inner stage, as indicated by a recent model (by C. Walter Hodges), then sooner or later certain directors and designers will follow suit. If we debate the nature of Elizabethan acting styles, so will the theater. If we highlight successful bits of rarely known stage business in the history of performance, the theater will take the hint. If we show wherein past productions failed, future directors and actors will take heed. If Shakespeare biography and Shakespeare exhibitions stress Gentleman Shakespeare, beloved by the nobility, and best treated in elegant, regal, glossy style, then the festival and big-money productions will translate this coffee-table Shakespeare to the stage.[12] If we remain open to a more egalitarian Shakespeare, an empathic soul who walked through a decrepit Paul's Church, a boarder's London, a plaguey England, who worked in the public theater primarily in love and not in complaint, whose nobles often find that our bloods "confound distinction," whose women often beckon men toward their own humanity, then, again, our stage may make its Shakespeare more humane and more genuine, as well.

Lastly, even as we grant that feminist, Marxist, Christian, and other programmatic scholars can hardly decline to consider their influence on the players, so we should grant that scholars of less overt ideology, the close readers and the "just plain teachers," share a responsibility to suit their words to our stage. Not just as editors but more generally as interpreters, many of us subscribe to a kind of formalism—a humanist/rhetorician's interest in words for their own sake and in life as play—that would seem to deny much responsibility for giving purpose to the stage in our time. When I look at Hamlet's advice to the players—"suit the action to the word, the word to the action"—I hear, as Shakespeare and Hamlet probably did, a rhetorical device, antimetabole, or as Puttenham puts it, the "Counterchange."[13] But what does it mean? The play is rife with this mirror figure where what comes out from the middle is the reverse of what went in: "heaven hath pleas'd it so / To punish me with this, and this with me" (3.1.174–75). Sometimes the counterchange draws attention to the words as words, the repetition trivializing them by suggesting that word order means nothing: "'tis true 'tis pity, / And pity 'tis 'tis true" (2.2.97–98)—a "foolish figure" indeed. Or the device may suggest interchangeable personalities: "Thanks, Rosencrantz and gentle Guildenstern . . . Thanks, Guildenstern and gentle Rosencrantz" (2.2.33–34). In Hamlet's mouth the counterchange becomes a kind of restless habit, a way of searching back over a phrase to question it, to reveal paradox beneath simplicity: "The body is with the King, but the King is not with the body" (4.2.27–28); "What's Hecuba to him, or he to Hecuba, / That he should weep for her?" (2.2.502–3). The actor might feel sorrow for that "mobled queen" (2.2.502), but what could she ever have felt for him? That kind of inquiry underlies Hamlet's own cue for passion: he may find his father in images of Hercules and Hyperion (as well as "poor Ghost"), but what is he to his father or to the Ghost that demands he murder and possibly be damned for it? The ethic of revenge suggests perfect counterchange, a tautology of acts: if he hurts you, you hurt him. Then all is equal, static; the circle is closed.

And if the father is killed, he kills back through his son. They are equal. Time means nothing. The son has no freedom to intone his own life. This is the machine in the Ghost.[14]

In life, however, the counterchange is rarely so neat, so circular. Only a Player King can so equalize our differences: "Grief joys, joy grieves, on slender accident" (3.2.199); "For 'tis a question left us yet to prove, / Whether love lead fortune, or else fortune love" (3.2.202–3). If the terms are interchangeable, then the result is loss of will to keep distinction, loss of purpose and creativity in time. Fortune, in that view, leads love. The Player King, perhaps speaking Hamlet's twelve or sixteen lines, does indeed decide that fate binds the will. He is passive, ill, a sleeper, poisoned in his ears before and after the speech. But Hamlet is both more poised and more active than that. Out of the counterchanges he wins choice, distinction, decision. He knows about the poisonous word wounding the ear, quartering thought out of action, repeating only the timeless first word, but he goes on to intone the word freshly for himself, shifting from sheer lexical denotation to examined life, working the Ghost's selfish "revenge" into his own just act, the actor's freedom to voice new meaning from a given text. We are not condemned to mere repetition. Brother cannot really replace brother, nor the son the father. To repeat lines is to change them, inevitably: "Who's there? / Nay, answer me. Stand and unfold yourself" (1.1.1–2). We seek answers from the unknown, and it asks us to look within. "If the man go to this water. . . . But if the water come to him . . ." (5.1.17–19). In *Hamlet*, both are happening. Hamlet proves that a fated man can still act. His final verbal counterchange sounds fatalistic: "If it be now, 'tis not to come; if it be not to come, it will be now" (5.2.220–21). He even begins another counterchange—"if it be not now, yet it will come"— but he breaks off with "the readiness is all." True, this "readiness" mixes with references to "providence" and to "letting be." Is this a fatalistic Hamlet who stops devising plays and yields to the superior play of divine authorship? A scholar, who concludes that there are no politics in *Hamlet*, says

Hamlet learns that "all of life is a play in which man is an actor, not the playwright, playing out a part he did not choose in a plot not of his own making." Shakespeare, then, is content to show the "structure of life itself prior to any particular form it may take or any particular moral it may illustrate. . . . He withdraws from the position of moral propagandist."[15]

This is to make Hamlet and all of us puppets. The Player King may find that "our wills and fates do so contrary run" (3.2.211), but Hamlet wills his fate in a very significant sense. Even after saying "let be," he enters the counterchange of the duel, and then he kills Claudius. Even after saying, "But let it be" (5.2.338), as he is dying, he insists that Horatio tell his story. Still, ever suiting word to action, even as he expires he says that Fortinbras has his dying voice. Even after "The rest is silence" (5.2.358), we hear that Horatio will speak as if from Hamlet's mouth, "his mouth whose voice will draw on more" (5.2.392). The wounded ear signifies greatly in *Hamlet*, yes, but the dying voice, too, and in a distinctly political act. As a scholar once said, concerning committed theater: "Even to make a very little difference can be a very big achievement, necessary to a social cause as well as to one's personal honour."[16]

In poetic patterns, words spirit us away, but then they deliver us back to action.[17] Let actors and directors intone the counterchange in *Hamlet* so as to reveal repetition and renewal, mirror and movement, play and afterplay. Let scholars write so as to celebrate Shakespeare for himself, for his words, but also to enact a Shakespearean vision of life, one that knows the world to be a stage yet shows the swordplay real, the statue warm, the magician's books all drowned behind departures from his fabled isle.[18] Not to lose the name of action: we all owe that much.

SHAKESPEARE AND THE
NEXT GENERATION

"Where lies your text?" says Olivia to Viola/Cesario who has come to plead on her master's behalf.[1] The answer: "In Orsino's bosom." We have long known that texts are not just in pages but in persons, too. Yet in times like these, new and opposing texts seem to inhabit/inhibit each human breast. We think that our precursors believed in external, objectified texts such as matter, nature, historical evidence, books, authors, heroes, traditions, gods, and ideals, whereas we see those texts made relative, subjective, ironic, deconstructed, depth-charged out of meaning. We wonder, can the text be broken and not the heart?

Will a new generation *take* heart and create new texts? Like ours, Illyria was a late state, its revels almost ended, the man's house divided from the woman's, before Viola came like a spring flower to intensify and question the old wintry divisions as if with a single attractive will. But she proved to be not just a woman/man. She was also a twin. She and her brother made up a family and could make a society. No division without relation. No man an island. Or, every island a text-isle, webbed in words to every other.

Where lies the I(s)-land of Shakespeare's text? Start with the example of his name. Is it "William Shakespeare" as in the First Folio? Or is it "Will Shakespeare"? Or, pronounced more authentically, "Shakspere"? He never signed his name, so far as can be proved, as we spell it, nor did he pronounce it as we do. One text died with him; another lives with us, in our bosom. Indeed, the name appeared first in the spent Latin of parish records: "*Gulielmus filius Johannes Shakespeare.*"[2] An "absolute Iohannes fac totum," Robert Greene named Shakespeare, "the onely Shake-scene in a countrey." Did the playwright do all for Johannes his father, or for the warlike family name that he tried to gentle into the rebus on his coat of arms, the falcon shaking the spear?[3] Where now is that name, Shakespeare? Will's Will shows that he keenly wanted a male heir to succeed him, as if to flesh out his will, to be his "best piece of poetry." His sonnets show that he mistrusted his textual progeny. "Do not so much as my poor name rehearse / But let your love even with my life decay" (sonnet 71). Still, his name remains its own rehearsal, the actor—is he hero or extra?—preparing to brandish his crude pike, forever forecast into a future where murder and dying become the final act, WILL SHAKE SPEAR. His name text, then, is neither documentary signatures nor conventional spelling but what from these we can carve or create.

The name text "Will Shakespeare" points to the actor's art and to the will to wound. Shakespeare tells us that his actor's art wounds his name (sonnet 111): "Thenceforth comes it that my name receives a brand." But the "poor wounded name" to which Shakespeare so often refers—along with speaking wounds—comes not merely from scandals of public, gossipy, aggressive interpretation but even, in his view, from private attempts to reverence his text:

> O, lest your true love may seem false in this,
> That you for love speak well of me untrue,
> My name be buried where my body is,
> And live no more to shame nor me nor you.
>   For I am sham'd by that which I bring forth,
>   And so should you, to love things nothing worth.
> (sonnet 72)

Is the interpreter's love false because the text of Shakespeare is neither good nor true, is nothing, pure will?[4] In a different mood, Shakespeare found his name's "nothing" to be "something," after all: "*Will*, / And *Will* to boot, and *Will* in overplus;

/ More than enough am I that vex thee still" (sonnet 135); "For nothing hold me, so it please thee hold / that nothing me, a something sweet to thee. / Make but my name thy love, and love that still, / And then thou lovest me, for my name is *Will*" (sonnet 136).[5]

Today the theorist wonders whether we love the name and not the thing? Can we speak of Shakespeare's text in willful, spear-shaking ways and still speak well and true? Let him be Shake-spear as threat, or Shake-spear in Falstaffian feint or faint, or Shakes-peer as anti-elitist, or, entering the phonemic core-text, shake-ear, ache-ear, ache-spear, speak-share, and onward to silence.[6] Is it not hurtful and helpful thus to disintegrate the text? Is it not both degenerating and generating, overpowering the next generation with our explosive energy yet clearing a space for the next generation's own work, that of regeneration?

Surely our principal Shakespeare texts, our collected editions, deserve such rework. They are too collected, the product of limiting professional association that has made its purpose to interpret and teach something fixed, measurable, objective, communal in too tight a sense. Our collected editions take the welter of past texts—quartos, folios, three *Hamlets*, two *Lears*, the autograph section of *Sir Thomas More*, parts of *Love's Martyr*, perhaps *The Passionate Pilgrim*, snatches from sources, commentary, stage-history—and then reduce them to digested regularity as if the main thing to do with Shakespeare is to own his text, consume it, and explain it away, as if we could best learn and teach the text's agreeable meaning. Think how these editions socialize, acculturate, or deny the strangeness, the hooded beckoning, of the plays: conflating, respelling, emending, annotating, repunctuating, stage directing, act-dividing, line-numbering, cast-listing, and introducing so that the composite text announces itself as something that asks for and should yield to definitive analysis, scientific observation, conceptual generalization.

True, such devices as act-division and lists of dramatis personae pop up sporadically in the First Folio, but the very tentativeness of the appearances there might caution us against extending and generalizing their use. Why, for example, shift the list of dramatis personae from after the text to before it? Do editors assume that readers will want to prepare a grid in mind so that social, familial, and sexual hierarchies will be reassuringly established before the play can unfold its own relations? Even though the Folio may occasionally append a list of dramatis personae to a play, it still may put the person of highest rank elsewhere than first (*Othello*), or it may scatter women among men. The Folio list for *The Winter's Tale* divides the characters by country, not rank or sex, and so places Hermione, Perdita, Emilia, and Paulina "ahead" of Polixenes and company. But the modern Riverside edition, while asserting in its textual note that its list of dramatis personae is "as given in F1,"[7] actually regroups all the women, whether from Sicilia or Bohemia, at the end of the list, after the men and just before the unnamed characters such as servants.

In preparing the texts for general readers and in teaching them to students, do we not underestimate the power of our ranked and sex-divided lists of dramatis personae to put characters in their places, to make us see male leaders as most important, women as less important, commoners as featureless?[8] Think how greatly our texts conflict, moreover, with stage experience where nameless citizens, soldiers, sailors, guards, servants, messengers, musicians, and players become as palpable as kings. The "etceteras and the and so forths who do the work" (*Ballad for Americans*), while their betters take time to flounder, often ground the tense societies in Shakespeare's plays in quiet service, health, right functioning, much as the waste of a tragedy is grounded in the living, creative skill of the actors or as deconstructive ironies are grounded in the critic's searching wit and the likelihood of later reconstruction and further destruction.[9]

In Shakespeare studies, that ever likely reconstruction of an assumed coherence for reinterpretations now threatens a premature establishment in the so-called performance approach. Shakespeare critics who may be disappointed with failures of the editorially reconstituted text to generate agreement about meaning, themes, or content may seek the apparent integrity of "action," stage life, as a more objective locus of experience. Reacting in part against the silence of the text and its consequent indeterminacy, the performance approach substitutes the directors' and actors' tendencies toward concreteness and unity in stage production. But the stage, which depends for its life on hordes of decisions the text cannot make for it—decisions about casting, blocking, tone, technical resources—promotes as many interpretations as the page promotes. Given, moreover, the distinctly marginal significance of theater today, the typical contemporary production of Shakespeare— whether RSC, BBC, ACT, or "festival"—is likely to suggest not only an aura of aesthetic indeterminacy but also a lack of any real social function beyond consumption of an evening.[10]

The performance approach encourages us to explore ways in which Shakespeare's text participates in a life larger than attempts to appropriate editions and their contents. It resembles in this respect the approach through authorial intent, presence, or voice, that is, an approach to another locus of knowing and being (such as nature, god, history, society) outside our own mentation. Yet to seek an intent or authorial voice in Shakespeare's or any dramatist's text would seem a hopeless enterprise. Intent is a dark hole that soaks up the prismatic lights of interpretation. As for Shakespeare's voice, literally it must be that of an actor or else of our own varied speech. Shakespeare did write, however, for particular companies—Chamberlain's Men, King's Men—and he often knew who would speak the parts. We need to sharpen our assumptions about Shakespeare's methods of composition. Do we assume that he wrote in his own voice? Did he imagine particular actors? If so, did he hear the voices of the characters as distinct men, women, children, fairies, ghosts, witches? Could he forget that all the feminine parts would receive masculine voice from male actors (as if a novelist imagined women characters to be male transvestites)? When, as a result, he wrote or we read, say, Cleopatra's part, might not imagination or the stage resurrect a boy exploring how far things feminine may unfold from within his nature or character? To seek Shakespeare's voice, then, might initiate a journey toward precincts of his boarding room or the Globe theater where a genius and a pride of players together with hushed thousands worked at sounding the man in woman, the woman in man.

The search for authorial voice or intent in order to save the text from our disintegrative appetites and overcorrosive ironies is like the search for historical context to limit the play of modern attitudes that supposedly reach beyond the text and read in what never could have been intended. In the case of an author such as Shakespeare, however, few of us will be confident that we know the limits of his own intended meanings and ironies. In the first place, part of authorial intent should be to have readers and audiences take from the text meanings that suit the receptive context. Thus, for example, we may in our day appropriately stress how much of Shakespeare shows men either tragically denying the full humanity of women or else comically coming to understand it. Indeed, judged by the central characters and concerns evident in Shakespeare's tragedies versus his comedies, his tragedy is male and his comedy female. Our era presents a fine opportunity to recognize the many ways in which Shakespeare presents men and women talking and walking toward shared paths, a recognition perhaps denied earlier and more uniformly patriarchal times. That Shakespeare would have intended us *not* to pursue the insights and conversations we find most germane to his plays seems unthinkable. Since Shakespeare holds the mirror up to each succeeding age, one delineation of his intent will always be the response that wins the most sustained, coherent, and vigorous dialogue or action from each generation.

A second reason why the search for Shakespeare's intent cannot relieve us of creative responsibility for our interpretations is that Shakespeare's capacity for skeptical and creative ambiguity appears greater than our own capacity. Beyond the point that language and particularly literary language may lend itself to paradox and deconstruction much more deeply than heretofore suspected, Shakespeare gives evidence of exceeding even the most radical skeptics, and ironists of his day and ours. When I last taught *Henry V,* I showed my students Olivier's patriotic film of the play and then showed them the longer and, arguably, quite opposed text. We wondered, for example, why it was funny, or whether it was, to hear Macmorris say: "I would have blowed up the town, so Chrish save me" (*H5,* 3.2.91), or to hear Pistol say, "O Signieur Dew should be a gentleman" (4.4.7), then to hear the French swear, "*O diable. O seigneur*" (4.5.1–2), and then to hear Fluellen say of Henry that "he be as good a gentleman as the devil" (4.7.137). Some students found here and elsewhere in the play only the qualifying ironies most typical of New Criticism; some saw Henry as a hero/villain; some declared themselves beyond such complementarity and pronounced a deep skepticism truer to the play than Olivier's film is true; some, finally, denied coherent meaning to the play: the play is not what Olivier did with it, it is not skeptical; its main significance is rather its disintegrating quizzicality, its humorous detachment from any need to make sense. (I argued, this time, for a post-ironic, re-illusioned response, authenticating styles of honesty and honor partly through but largely beyond or below Henry.)

Shakespeare's text and its significance lie most clearly in the present and future lives of all who study the text. I imagine that only part of the next generation will doubt truth to be a liar or want poetries of self-cancellation or silence. The coming age, however, even if it should specialize in entropic images of cancer, holocaust, silent spring, ice age, psycho-babble, and future shock may still make Shakespeare its spokesman; the past four centuries give reason to think he can interpret almost any age. But barring the end of time, a further generation will ensue and will look for greener pastures, perhaps in Shakespeare's many scenes of regeneration, of women waking or throwing off disguise for fresh life and love, or youth, the next generation, coming back from foreign lands to regenerate its homeland. Indeed, in his four romances Shakespeare chose stories all showing children raised away from home and then returning like spring to the earth, embodying in their strangeness and hope whatever it is that makes a generation new.

But if we ask a new generation of Shakespeare critics to take heart from Shakespeare's youths and to bring into our society like qualities of saving grace, we must admit that our text is foolish. For, in the late plays themselves, the children only tenuously give promise of supplanting their elders. Their mothers and fathers remain in charge or else are seen launched on darker, longer journeys far surpassing youthful heroism. The young ones hardly stand for what the play and its auditors have become. We both celebrate and scorn, therefore, the next generation's archaizing influence.[11]

When, in other words, a new generation of critics and hence of texts enters the ken and domain of elder associated scholars, the established group is likely to yield the field somewhat snipingly, taking consolation at the last in old fellowship. Still, our future association in Shakespeare promises to become global, if it is not so already, extending beyond our own generation, sexual division, class, or culture. What text and association we see in and want from Shakespeare remains an abiding question, one that eases us out of individuated thoughts and into social re-creation. "For society, sayeth the text, is the happiness of life" (LLL, 4.3.162).

IX

AARON MURDERS THE NURSE

Shakespeare shows many women dying. But there are few natural deaths. Are there seven or eight suicides? Seven or eight murders? Does only one woman murder another? Goneril poisons Regan. Men—Aaron, Titus, Othello, Iago—murder women. And Claudius, does he murder Gertrude? In what sense did Shakespeare choose these stories? Why these patterns? What did such murders mean to him? To us? Start with the first probable murder. Imagination means as it moves.

Aaron stabs the Nurse of his baby son, ostensibly to keep her from telling that Aaron committed adultery with Tamora:

> Shall she live to betray this guilt of ours,
> A long-tongu'd babbling gossip?
> *(Tit.,* 4.2.149)[1]

This reference to woman's betraying tongue may be no idle metaphor. The play centers on Lavinia's tongue cut out by Tamora's sons, who then are served up to their mother's tongue. Like the Nurse, Lavinia with her tongue would betray illicit sex. She could still reveal her rape in some other way, as she soon does with a stick between her stumps. To live is to make signs. The deeper rape attacks her tongue not for its potential harm but for its charm. Her uncle Marcus (himself the "sign," "Mark, Marcus, mark!" 3.1.143) says of her attacker:

112

. . . had he heard the heavenly harmony
Which that sweet tongue had made,
He would have dropp'd his knife, and fell asleep,
As Cerberus at the Thracian poet's feet

(2.4.48)

Lavinia's tongue had orphic powers, could invade the earth and sing food, a sop to make the rude dog sleep. Her tongue's power to betray sexual guilt mingles with its power to raise love from the underworld, from the lower elements of water and earth, "unsounded deeps" (*TGV*, 3.2.77–80). Ophelia dies beneath death's willow chanting "old lauds," "her melodious lay" (4.7.177–82). Desdemona sings the willow song on her deathbed and dies trying to pray. Cordelia's "voice was ever soft, / Gentle, and low, an excellent thing in woman" (*Lr.*, 5.3.273). Yet Lear forced that tongue to say "nothing," to "love and be silent" (1.1.62). He tells Cordelia, "Mend your speech a little" (1.1.94). He had hoped to set his rest on her kind "nursery" (1.1.124), but she refused the trap of becoming the hypocrite, the "long-tongu'd nurse." She insisted, instead, "My love's / More ponderous than my tongue" (1.2.77).[2]

Titus stabs Lavinia at his banquet (Shakespeare's second murder of a woman) to kill her "shame" (5.3.46), the sexual shame she finally had revealed with the long-tongued "shaft in her mouth" (4.1.77s.d.). Lavinia's comic twin is "Katherine the curst" (*Shr.*, 1.2.128; 2.1.186), who was fathered by Shakespeare probably within a year of Lavinia. Kate's "tongue will tell the anger" of her heart (4.3.77), but she seems to chasten her speech at the closing banquet. The two plays, tragedy and comedy, tell of taming women's tongues—Lavinia's, Tamora's, Kate's—and deflecting woman's speech to food, the upper element to the lower. Shakespeare's comedy often subdues word-powered women—"curst" Kate or Rosalind who cannot be overcome "unless you take her without her tongue" (*AYL*, 4.1.173) or Beatrice "my Lady Tongue" (*Ado*, 2.1.275)—women who let their wild hearts be tamed (*Ado*, 3.1.112) and their mouths "stopped" with men's kisses (*Ado*, 5.4.98; *Shr.*, 5.2.180). The theme darkens in darker plays, as when Angelo fears how Isabella "might tongue" him (*MM*, 4.4.25) or when Leontes fears Paulina as "callat / Of boundless tongue" (*WT*, 2.3.91). Hamlet says to Gertrude, "Go, go, you question with a wicked tongue" (*Ham.*, 3.4.12). Iago half-jokingly complains of Emilia's tongue (*Oth.*, 2.1.101), and later he silences it, "Go to, charm your tongue." She responds, "I will not charm my tongue; I am bound to speak" (*Ant.*, 5.2.182). He stabs her. Men attack, even as they demand, many "charms" in women's tongues.

The Nurse feeds the baby's tongue and, in Shakespeare's view, teaches speech. Pleading with Henry to excuse Aumerle's fault, York's Duchess fancies an overpowering relation: "if I were the nurse, thy tongue to teach" (*R2*, 5.2.113; cf. *AYL*, 4.1.172–76). But to Shakespeare, the Nurse may be cursed, "long-tongu'd" (*Tit.*, 4.2.150) and snake-like, in speaking of guilty sex. Juliet's Nurse, like Aaron's Nurse a go-between, a "bawd" (2.4.130), tells of putting "wormwood" on her nipples to wean Juliet (1.3.26, 30). Juliet finally denounces the Nurse:

> Ancient damnation! O most wicked fiend!
> Is it more sin to wish me thus forsworn,
> Or to dispraise my lord with that same tongue
> Which she hath prais'd him with . . . ?
>   (3.5.235)

"Wormwood," "Ancient damnation," "sin," "fiend," with double praising and dispraising "tongue": the Nurse is likened to the Serpent in Eden, just as Aaron's Nurse is imaged as long-tongued and snake-like. Shakespeare seems to connect nursing and serpentry, nursing the tongue and cursing the tongue. There's poison at the breast. Lady Macbeth would chastise Macbeth with the "valor" of her "tongue" (1.5.27) and would teach him to bear false welcome in his "tongue; look like the innocent flower, / But be the serpent under't" (1.5.65). She, too, is imaged as horrific nurse of galled milk and death to the sucking babe (1.5.48; 1.7.58).

Shakespeare joins nurse and serpent visually on stage when Cleopatra, herself a "serpent of old Nile" (1.5.25), dies from the "worm," "my baby at my breast / That sucks the nurse asleep" (5.2.309). In this image of a snake-nurse feeding and being fed upon, Shakespeare's materializing, substantiating imagination and his pervasive skepticisms drive all human appetites—for honor, wealth, power, sex, or love—down to the domain of food, the original will. The Clown wishes Cleopatra "joy of the worm" (5.2.260), but at the same time he says, "There is no goodness in the worm" (5.2.267). The phallic snake-mouth "is not worth the feeding" (270). Cleopatra responds, "Will it eat me?" No, "the devil himself will not eat a woman"; she "is a dish for the gods, if the devil dress her not" (271). The Clown complains, however, that "the devils mar" half the women (276).

Thus Shakespeare connects women's tongues with sexual desire, nursing, the snake, the devil, and food-appetite. As early as *I Henry VI*, he fused the same trace-images in his portrait of Joan of Arc. Promiscuously pregnant, she appears in the fifth act, summoning her familiars, "fiends," whom she feeds with her blood (5.3.14). York enters and says, "Fell banning hag, enchantress, hold thy tongue!" Joan of Arc replies, "I prithee give me leave to curse a while" (42). Her father enters, to damn her:

> Now cursed be the time
> Of thy nativity! I would the milk
> Thy mother gave thee, when thou suck'dst her breast,
> Had been a little ratsbane for thy sake!
> Or else, when thou didst keep my lambs a-field,
> I wish some ravenous wolf had eaten thee!
>
> (5.4.26)

Joan is led to her death.

In Shakespeare, the nurse and bawd who taint motherhood are seen as cursed, devilish, over-appetitive, consumed or self-consuming. Goneril, who has only contempt for her husband "milk-liver'd" Albany (*Lr.*, 4.2.50), who disbranches from her "material sap" (4.2.35), is also a "gilded serpent" (5.3.84) striking Lear "with her tongue, / Most serpent-like, upon the very heart" (2.4.160). She is condemned, ultimately, to prey on herself (4.2.49) in suicide. The long-tongued snake-woman at once suggests and ingests, curses and eats, and lastly consumes herself.[3] Snaky Goneril and Regan in their insane lust for Edmund and for power have brought a "curse" on nature (4.6.206). Always in the background lies the original Edenic sin, as Richard's Queen notes: "What Eve, what serpent, hath suggested thee / To make a second fall of cursed man?" (R2, 3.4.76).

To imagine the lust-woman consuming herself is to take a defensive response. To picture the helpless babe at the worm-wooded, galled, ratsbaned nipple is to suggest a need for un-nursed appetite. Aaron murders the Nurse and declares, indeed, that he wants his son never again to nurse a woman:

> I'll make you feed on berries and on roots,
> And feed on curds and whey, and suck the goat.
>   (4.2.187)

"As though a man were author of himself," are the words used by Coriolanus as he tries to deny his own mother. But to attack woman bodily, stopping her talk and milk at once, is to assert man's superior appetite, stronger hunger. Through his murder of the Nurse, Aaron converts her to food:

> Go to the Empress, tell her this I said.   *He kills her.*
> Weeke, weeke!—so cries a pig prepared to the spit.
>   (4.2.145)

The threatening speech of the Nurse becomes "weeke"/weak as she metamorphoses into bacon.

If the digestive struggle between the sexes were kept at the oral, mouthy, above-waist level, it might be handled humorously, as for example in Shakespeare's punning on the name "Kate" as food: "my super-dainty Kate, / For dainties are all Kates" (Shr., 2.1.188). And Hotspur says, "Swear me, Kate . . .

a good mouth-filling oath" (1H4, 3.1.253). Or consider the words of Henry V: "You have witchcraft in your lips, Kate; there is more eloquence in a sugar touch of them than in the tongues of the French council" (5.2.275). That is, women should fill men's mouths even as men stop women's mouths, converting words to food; unless the Kate/cate is *too* tart: "none of us cared for Kate; / For she had a tongue with a tang" (*Tmp.*, 2.2.49). Such comic Kate-baiting may be relatively easy. "Shutting up" women in the tragedies, however, proves a deeper assignment. Often, a dying woman is silenced by being literally stopped up: Tamora dies with her sons' flesh in her mouth; Portia swallows fire; Ophelia swallows "too much of water" (*Ham.*, 4.7.185); Gertrude swallows poison; Desdemona is smothered; Regan swallows lethal "medicine" (*Lr.*, 5.3.96); Cordelia chokes from the cord. The literal attack on women's mouths is horribly excessive.

Sometimes in reality or else in unsweetened imagination of tragic men, the mouths of women stand for their lower appetite: "that ravenous tiger Tamora" (5.3.195) or Lear's "simpering dame" with "face between her forks" (4.6.118). Women "eat lords; so they come by great bellies" (*Tim.*, 1.1.106). Shakespeare joins women and men in an appetitive combat that degrades and debases them downward to animality and literal earthiness, consumption, the pit. "Lechery eats itself" (*Tro.*, 5.4.35), as does the snake, whose mouth is closest to the dust. Shakespeare sees sex in terms of anatomical portioning. To descend in appetites is to reach Centaur-woman (*Lr.*, 4.6.124), god-like above the waist, fiendish below: "there's hell, there's darkness" (4.6.127). As if the upper body were elemented in heavenly air and fire and the lower body were consigned to water and hellish earth. So we walk.

In Shakespeare's tragedies, to be sure, certain degraded men rival the hellish natures of fiendish women and share their deadly earth-appetite. In *Titus,* one of the men who rapes Lavinia is named Chiron, that is, Centaur. Shakespeare's Chiron kills by means of the "blood-drinking pit," that "fell devouring . . . mouth" of the grave (2.3.224–36). In the same play, Aaron is buried "breast-deep in earth" where he is to cry for food (5.3.180).[4]

Shakespeare, then, in these tragedies of lust tends to materialize all appetites toward basic food-hunger. He thinks, however, of the Moor's hunger as especially earthy, snakelike, and dark. Emilia says:

> They are all but stomachs, and we all but food;
> They eat us hungerly, and when they are full
> They belch us.
>
> (*Oth.*, 3.4.144)

Othello's "bosom" is burdened with "aspics' tongues." His "black" "hell" vengeance will "swallow" Desdemona (3.3.446–60); he will "chop her into messes" (4.1.200), bits of food. He has "stomach for them all" (5.2.75). Aaron sees the rolled snake and feels like an uncurling adder (2.3.13–35) in his greed for vengeance. The Moor in Shakespeare is most terrible. When women come down to darkly feed on sex, the Moor waits to receive them. Hamlet asks Gertrude, "Could you on this fair mountain leave to feed / And batten on this moor?" (3.4.66).[5] What loathing of sex appetite lurks in Shakespeare's punning on Moor/moor/more (cf. *MV*, 3.5.40). Shakespeare makes Moor-lust most deadly. He shows men striking down women *only* in the Moorish plays. "*Integer vitae . . . non eget Mauri jaculis*" (*Tit.*, 5.2.20). The pure man needs no weapon of the Moor. Call it Shakespeare's racism, or merely conventional symbolism for black desire, or a partial stimulus from the psychic geography of England's dark-pitted moors and London's rank sewer of Moor-ditch (*1H4*, 1.2.78). Whatever its sources, Shakespeare's attention to the sex-murderous Moors (and Tamora) remains sensational, a palpable ground for his display of foul appetites.

In Shakespeare's tragedy, women often die by bringing their fertility to earth. Shakespeare realigns the old polarity of womb and tomb into a parallel; he drives difference to identity. Womb and tomb meet in several ways. The womb may bear a murderous offspring: "From forth the kennel of thy womb hath crept / A hell-hound that doth hunt us all to death": (*R3*, 4.4.47). Or the grave, the earth-pit, may be seen as "the swallowing womb." As Juliet's Friar puts it:

> The earth that's nature's mother is her tomb;
> What is her burying grave, that is her womb.
> (*Rom.*, 2.3.9)

The Duchess of York thinks of her womb issuing a cockatrice: "O my accursed womb, the bed of death!" (*R3*, 4.1.54). In Shakespeare, the *bed* becomes, obsessively, the site or context for both womb and tomb. Shakespeare chose plots that would allow him to stage this image. Beds of sex and dying join in Juliet's tomb: "my grave is like to be my wedding-bed" (1.5.135); "the bridal bed in that dim monument" (3.5.200); "I descend into this bed of death . . . to behold my lady's face" (5.3.28). Ophelia, too, sings of the "death-bed" (4.5.153) before going to her grave where Hamlet comes, declaring his love for her. Desdemona and Othello both become the "tragic loading of this bed" (5.2.363). Lady Macbeth exits to suicide with her final words the sleepwalk summons of her husband: "To bed, to bed, to bed" (5.1.68). Antony runs to death "as to a lover's bed" (4.4.10) and dies in Cleopatra's tomb where she, too, dies on her "bed" (5.2.356).

In Shakespearean tragedy, dying women merge their own appetitive wombs with the deeper womb-mouth of earth. Romeo opens the tomb where Juliet lies sleeping:

> Thou detestable maw, thou womb of death,
> Gorg'd with the dearest morsel of the earth.
> (5.3.45)

There he finds both death and life, as the Friar earlier intimated. Allied as they are with earth, the "common mother, thou / Whose womb unmeasurable and infinite breast / Feeds all" (*Tim.*, 4.3.177; cf. sonnet 3), Shakespeare's dying women often die ambiguously, die into a not-quite-deadness:

Juliet, / Why art thou yet so fair . . . unsubstantial Death is amo-
rous. . . . (*Rom.*, 5.3.101)

And will 'a not come again / No, no he is dead, / Go to thy deathbed
. . . 'Tis for the dead, not for the quick . . . Now pile your dust upon
the quick and dead . . . Be buried quick with her, and so will I. (*Ham.*,
4.5.191–5.1.279)

Still as the grave . . . I think she stirs again . . . my lady's voice. . . .
(*Oth.*, 5.2.94–119)

She's dead as earth . . . This feather stirs, she lives! . . Look her
lips. . . . (*Lr.*, 5.3.262–311)[6]

All dead . . . but she looks like sleep. (*Ant.*, 5.2.329–46)

Shakespeare's tragedies search for the inmost life, relentlessly
killing down from air to earth, from light to dark, from lust to
death to find if there be any unquenchable spark. They often
end in bed and grave, with women felled, at the time of "tiring
day and heavy night" (*Tit.*, 5.2.24) when the sun recedes and
the "error of the moon" (*Oth.*, 5.2.109), "the visiting moon,"
"the fleeting moon" (*Ant.*, 4.15.68; 5.2.240) asserts itself, gov-
erning all the "great ones, that ebb and flow by the 'moon'"
(*Lr.*, 5.3.19). This is what we must mean by elemental sadness.
Shakespeare in his sonnets seems overwhelmed with "the
dull substance" of flesh, "so much of earth and water
wrought" (sonnet 44), his nature "subdu'd" to what it worked
in (sonnet 111) or as on a "death-bed," "consum'd with that
which it was nourished by" (sonnet 73). He tries to find some
lasting principle of life—"the earth can have but earth" (sonnet 74), "But ah, thought kills me that I am not thought" (sonnet 44)—knowing himself "the prey of worms" (sonnet 44),
perhaps doubting the soul itself. He seeks a life principle in
woman, tracing her down to water and earth, the common
matter, mater, and he finds her death ambiguous—even in the
most chilling damp. Why not? In the last line of the sonnets we
read: "Love's fire heats water, water cools not love" (sonnet

154). In Shakespeare's grave-bed deaths of women, did he not suggest a chance of such lingering heat?[7]

When Shakespeare died, he left a Will commending his soul to his Creator and his body "to the Earth whereof yt ys made."[8] Then he tirelessly conditioned bequests to his daughters on their producing issue of their bodies. Finally, after conceding the possible default of all such issue, he inserted the bequest to his wife of their second-best bed, perhaps their love-bed and bed of both their dyings. In the next sentence, he bequeathed to his daughter his "gilt bole." Though they may die leaving no issue of their bodies, tragic women still must sleep, still eat, still carry the bowl of "gilt" until the end. So Shakespeare provides, provides. Shakespeare, hunting and haunting issue, from Aaron and his victim to Cleopatra and her "baby." Shakespeare, our dark, amouring nurse.

TEACHING SHAKESPEARE IN AMERICA

Stand by and mark the manner of his teaching.
(*Shr.*, 4.2.5)[1]

In 1932, Henry W. Simon, a Columbia Ph.D., brought out *The Reading of Shakespeare in American Schools and Colleges*, surveying the history of Shakespeare's presence, or absence, in American education. Simon traced a curve indicating that Shakespeare was only minimally present during the first two hundred years, that selected passages were then introduced to teach elocution and morality, that whole-play teaching emerged in the latter half of the nineteenth century, and that the first third of this century witnessed a shift from rhetorical and philological study toward dramaturgic and interpretive study. Based, apparently, on his perception that the college boards were de-emphasizing Shakespeare, that the plays did "not deal so well with contemporary problems," and that Shakespeare did not appeal to the interests of modern students, Simon closed his study with a prophecy that "in another half century Shakespeare in the high school curriculum [will] have gone the way of Greek and Latin."[2]

Seven years later, Esther Cloudman Dunn, a teacher at Smith College, reviewed Simon's materials and arrived at a different conclusion:

What our own twentieth century education is likely to do about Shakespeare is still uncertain. Probably the method of studying him, or the complete omission of him, will follow the curves, depressions and changing prejudices of our world, exactly as they followed the needs, partialities and limitations of the nineteenth century. The genius of Shakespeare is extraordinarily sensitive to the hour and the age. Into his book, each age has peered, as into a mirror, to see its own face. The images in that mirror fade and are replaced as the decades go by. But the mirror is not discarded. There is a strange compulsion to look into it, to scrutinize this Shakespeare, no matter how cramped and dated the era may be. He responds by showing only so much of himself as is comely in the eyes of the particular world which reads him.[3]

Whereas Simon approved the attempt to broaden the understanding and appeal of Shakespeare while yet seeing the canon, ultimately, as an *object* too antiquated and difficult to hold the attention of the democratic masses, Dunn, while recognizing Shakespeare's "cramped and dated" nature, saw Shakespeare as a *subject* responsive to our own "strange compulsion" toward scrutiny. Her book closed with an image of Shakespeare "inviolate" but nevertheless "yielding" to "the manipulation, the form and pressure of each succeeding era" (p. 306).

When compared in this way, the surveys of Simon and Dunn suggest a tension between two views of Shakespeare's place in American education, and perhaps between two views of education itself. Simon presents evidence for an early colonial distrust of formal, nonpractical education, and the audience he depicts is dominated by gentlemen in both the North and the South who could not have read Shakespeare "in the privacy of a library without a guilty conscience." "Shakespeare thus shared, together with lesser dramatists, the holy horror of good Americans" (p. 7). This, despite the likelihood that members of the Virginia Company were friends of Shakespeare's. Dunn, on the other hand, imagines a John Harvard growing up thinking of Shakespeare as an "old Stratford family friend of his mother's" (p. 18).

Simon says that Shakespeare had to enter American schools "anonymously through the back-door in the form of short passages to be declaimed" in elocution texts (p. 9) and notes that such texts were advertised as "Education for the Young

Nobility and Gentry" (p. 17). Dunn argues that the elocutionary school readers were a part of the "new democracy" that
offered upward mobility to strong speakers "in pulpit or on
campground" or "on the campaign platform" (p. 225). "It is no
wonder," she says, "that the secondary school began at once
to work on a system which should give every girl and boy the
necessary training for these ends" (p. 226).

Simon reminds us that Shakespeare was almost tamed in
the nineteenth century by such teachers as Henry Hudson
and W. J. Rolfe, who issued ennobling texts and eschewed low
utilitarian teaching in favor of the high universal road of "the
true, the beautiful, and the good" (p. 109). One can infer from
Simon's book, however, that the introduction of whole-play
texts (described by Harry Levin as "badly edited, ineptly
glossed, and inexcusably bowdlerized"[4]) created difficulties
for the mass of high-school students and teachers, who felt
that the ideals to be promoted through literary study were
more clearly presented in books by American authors. No
matter how proudly the Shakespeareans might declare their
subject one of exalted grandeur, the rewards of study seemed,
to many high-school teachers and students, hardly worth the
effort. Dunn, writing from a college teacher's perspective,
apparently, about college students, worried less about this
problem. She cited James Russell Lowell's argument to the
Modern Language Association in 1889 that students bored
with Greek and Latin would take interest in Shakespeare as
nearer to their modern modes of thought. She cheerfully
endorsed a rosy future for the teaching of Shakespeare in a
post-philological style.

Simon shows teachers wary of Shakespeare because his
texts are "difficult," only partly tamable—dark, other, and
suspect because they are not susceptible to full domestication.
Simon suggests that English teachers found themselves
bedeviled by hundreds of "utterly bewildering" objectives (p.
132), by "chaotic opinion" (p. 139), and by the absence of any
"real agreement as to the specific objectives and methods of
teaching Shakespeare" (p. 140). Dunn remains much more

relaxed and confident about our relations to Shakespeare. Though she opines that "Shakespeare in the schools and colleges reached a peak of importance at the end of the nineteenth century" (p. 304), she insists that Shakespeare need not be pinned down to objective and unvarying meaning or "smothered" by overliteral interpretation: "Those lines were cunningly devised to evoke from the audience a contributing share toward the realization of the situation" (pp. 305–6).[5] For her, Shakespeare is continually reinvigorating and reinvigorated.

Through Simon and Dunn may be identified two basic and opposed "readings" of Shakespeare in the schools: one forecasting his demise, the other forecasting his continuance. Simon shows how American teachers have tended to *use* Shakespeare to teach elocution and morals, and he suggests that the full texts may be too difficult for democratic understanding. Dunn expresses more confidence that Shakespeare's strangeness may converse fruitfully with our own.

Within the husks of these opposed hypotheses lie genetic promptings for mutation, reversal, decay, and—it may be—renewal. In what follows, I wish to question certain assumptions implicit within past, present, and prospectively advocated ways of teaching Shakespeare in America.

How Shakespeare Was Taught

> But pardon me, I am too sudden bold;
> To teach a teacher ill beseemeth me.
> (*LLL*, 2.1.107)

There are focal or pressure points in the history of American responses to Shakespeare that may help us perceive what Shakespeare has meant at various times in American schools and colleges. To begin at the beginning, it seems likely that some of the Jamestown colonists not only had heard of Shakespeare but even had been in the Globe Theatre. Some Plymouth colonists may have known of Shakespeare, too, but perhaps fewer would have attended or read his plays. At any rate, among the early settlers there must have been a wide range of opinions about Shakespeare and the stage. But if so, such preoccupations soon became constricted by the harsh environmental conditions of the early settlements. For well over a hundred years, the people of the New World seem to have had little or nothing to do with Shakespeare. Our country was founded without him. There were not only religious prejudices against playwrights and the stage. The conditions of labor, the absence of leisure and urbanities, and the class divisions of the colonies all militated against Shakespeare. Where would one find in the colonies of the seventeenth and early eighteenth centuries such equivalent admirers of Shakespeare as Dryden, Milton, Rowe, Addison, and Pope? What colonist edited Shakespeare? When Shakespeare was gradually reappropriated in stage performance and gentlemen's reading during the later eighteenth century, it was after a much greater time lapse than that experienced in England during the mother country's interregnum. And of course the later eighteenth century in America was a period of increasing hostility toward England. By the time Shakespeare began to be introduced to the mass of American students in elocutionary readers, he was no longer regarded as a dramatist but rather as a writer of lofty moral tags, many of which were quoted approvingly by American presidents. And this approval was largely a trickle-down from the bardolatry that had migrated with the upper classes from England in the later eighteenth century. To a significant degree, in other words, America was independent of Shakespeare until well after it had declared itself independent from England.

In the second half of the nineteenth century, the snippety Shakespeare of elocutionary school readers was slowly supplanted by the Shakespeare of school texts presenting nearly complete versions of accepted plays. Beginning in the 1850s, Henry Norman Hudson brought out a series of school editions. Simon and Dunn are cloudy on the point, but it seems probable that the texts and writings of Hudson, William J. Rolfe, and others were responsible for insertions of Shakespeare into secondary school curricula *before* pressure to include Shakespeare began coming from the colleges' entrance examinations.[6] Hudson argued for a non-philological style of secondary-school teaching that stressed character analysis and the enjoyment of Shakespeare's truths. At the college level, meanwhile, Shakespeare was conscripted into courses on rhetoric and philology by Francis James Child at Harvard and by others at Yale, Princeton, Cornell, and Columbia. As Simon explains, the philological emphasis slowly backwashed into the schools (p. 113), but the more literary, moral/aesthetic emphasis of Hudson and Rolfe may also have seeped upward, encouraging the development of broader interpretive approaches in college courses.

It is worth speculating on the Hudsonian influence in Shakespeare teaching, because one interpretation of academic Shakespeare is that the playwright has been used primarily as an instrument of class oppression, as a tool for "the imposition of white Anglo-Saxon Protestant civility from above."[7] This reading depends for its cogency on the argument that the college entrance examinations, once they "assumed a knowledge of Shakespeare," began to shape the curricula of the secondary schools. If so, "the direction of control is clear: it moved from the top down, and from the Eastern colleges and universities to those of the Middle and Far West" (p. 231). Whitman had questioned the relevance of Shakespeare to democratic vistas. But as Stephen J. Brown has argued,

Whitman's vision was not shared by the American upper class of his day; as one of its modern descendants, the eminent sociologist E. Digby Baltzell, has amply shown in his book *The Protestant Establishment*, this class after the Civil War gradually withdrew from contact with, if not from control of, the ever-growing alien masses—into their summer and winter resorts, into their country clubs and metropolitan clubs, into their Eastern boarding schools, and (of especial concern to us) into their universities such as Harvard, Yale, and Princeton, which they owned (and still own) and operate. As we have seen, through dominating the new College Entrance Examination Board, these Ivy League universities in turn firmly shaped the

English curriculum throughout the American educational system, and placed Shakespeare at the center of that curriculum. (p. 235)

I respect the general tenor of this argument, but I question whether the colleges really imposed Shakespeare on the schools. Hudson and others were there well before the creation of the College Entrance Examination Board in 1901. Hudson's school editions can be seen, of course, as another arm of the upper classes and of the university-inspired imposition of a "noble," "gentle" set of ideals for Shakespeare and his teachers.[8] But this thesis becomes somewhat less credible when one recognizes that Hudson himself was from a poverty-stricken background, and was thus hardly a representative of upper-class ideology. Though he became a preacher and later a private-school teacher, he seems to have retained his own democratic vista:

I suspect that our American parents have become somewhat absurdly, and not very innocently, ambitious of having their boys and girls all educated to be gentlemen and ladies; which is, I take it, the same as having them educated to be good for nothing.[9]

As examined by Simon, Hudson's admission that many students aimed at acquiring gentility through their schooling contrasts with his own dedication to a semi-classless aspiration to form "character," to converse with "the truth of things," and yet "to teach or learn Shakespeare and not to use him as a means of teaching or learning something else" (pp. 109–10).

From quite early on, then, it seems that Shakespeare's position in the schools was as problematic as the functions of the schools themselves. Were the schools and colleges there, and was Shakespeare there, to acclimatize diverse peoples to upper-class conceptions of civility as wealth, gentility as class-standing, and nobility as economic and political power? Or were the academies and Shakespeare there to inspire a democratic populace toward visions of the classless nobility and "stainless gentility" potentially available to every person through a radical, egalitarian humanism?[10] That such deep ambiguity has long pervaded the teaching of Shakespeare in America (as it has pervaded the performance of Shakespeare in America) appears from the historic dialogue among teachers that has accumulated since the era of Hudson and Rolfe.[11]

Our Teachers at Work

O, let me teach you how to knit again
This scattered corn into one mutual sheaf,
These broken limbs again into one body.
(Tit., 5.3.70)

To search out what American teachers have exhorted about the teaching of Shakespeare is to delve into an enormous record of heterogeneous materials. Only gradually do patterns appear.[12]

Around the turn of the century, the trend was to teach Shakespeare's "art" primarily in terms of how plot and scene construction contributed to revelations of character and message.[13] A little later, some of the teachers seem to have become a trifle restless with aesthetic and moral appreciation, as if the First World War made more problematic the Bard's civilizing authority.[14] Yet still, amid all the calls for student performance, visual aids, and dramatic readings by teachers, we find promptings to struggle against the coarsening and sex-haunted tastes of youth in the Jazz Age.[15]

In the 1930s, there was a noticeable split between teachers who began to doubt that Shakespeare, though valuable, could be made suitable for democratic education of the masses and teachers who persisted in arguing that the Bard offered excitement and uplift for all. Whether or not to teach Shakespeare was much discussed, and much of the counsel had to do with ways of making Shakespeare livelier for students.[16] Criticism was launched specifically against the philological method that had been propounded for years at Harvard under George Lyman Kittredge and had achieved wide influence. Kittredge

(1860–1941) taught Icelandic, Old Norse, Chaucer, and Shakespeare from 1888 until 1936.[17] In his principal Shakespeare course, as Levin demonstrates, he explicated the text line by line and rarely completed six plays a year: "his chilling distrust of all interpretation, save what he chose to echo from his forerunners, frightened most of his graduate students into becoming editors, collectors, compilers, and writers of notes and queries" (p. 19). From all accounts, Kittredge was a vain and pompous martinet who "never tired of ridiculing" attempts to inculcate morality through teaching Shakespeare.[18] As early as 1913, Stuart P. Sherman and others had complained in print that Kittredge over-emphasized medieval philology at the expense of more modern literature, and in 1941 Oscar Cargill renewed the attack on the word-by-word method of teaching Shakespeare.[19]

Though Kittredge had defenders, the time came for reconsideration of his teachings. His successors at Harvard, including Alfred Harbage and Harry Levin, helped promote the New Critical shift from mainly philological explication of Shakespeare's *language* toward broader rhetorical and interpretive study, and they encouraged renewed interest in Shakespeare's theatrical and intellectual backgrounds. During the 1920s, 1930s, and 1940s, moreover, largely beneath Kittredge's notice and contrasting with his decline, occurred that remarkable flowering of Shakespearean interpretation represented in the work of E. E. Stoll, T. S. Eliot, William Empson, G. Wilson Knight, L. C. Knights, Caroline Spurgeon, Wolfgang Clemen, Derek Traversi, Cleanth Brooks, and others, all promoting fresh interest in the vitality and accessibility of Shakespeare's language, ideas, and theater. From the 1940s onward, collected editions used as student texts—editions such as Neilson and Hill's, G. B. Harrison's or Harbage's—bypassed Kittredge's style of extensive glossarial annotation. Harbage encouraged the general reader to believe in the "simplicity" of Shakespeare, to believe that annotations should not be daunting, that Shakespeare's linguistic "difficulties can be exaggerated," that abstract criticism should be avoided, and that the good teacher will "defend readers from that criticism" by encouraging a direct and "close knowledge of the works themselves," a "noticing mood," "attentive reading."[20]

Here was a redefinition of reading, a shift no doubt inspired by I. A. Richards and a host of New Critical influences. And the consequence was that the dissective parsing and paraphrase of the Kittredge school gave way to a different system of linguistic analysis focusing on word patterns, images, metaphors, ironies. If Caroline Spurgeon could adduce discrete image clusters, the method could also be adapted by high school teachers; if Cleanth Brooks could unlock patterns of metaphor and symbolism in Shakespearean tragedy, other teachers could follow suit; if Harbage could write of Shakespeare as dramatist as well as poet, high school teachers would take the hint. A new confidence in the interpretability of Shakespeare swept over both high school and college teaching.[21]

In 1932, Henry Simon had doubted whether the teaching of Shakespeare could persist in the schools, given an increasingly widespread recognition of the "difficulties" Shakespeare's language presented to the democratic mass of students. But the new close-reading approaches developed by Harbage and others led to a revised image of Shakespeare as an "affable," "tolerant," "modest" writer with a "unique gift for responding to life as Everyman."[22] The poet was eulogized and universalized and mythologized in this era as "Shakespeare for Everyman."[23]

To link Shakespeare with Everyman is both to democratize him and to place him within a moral spectrum congenial to teachers. John Holloway argues that the new linguistic analyses of Shakespeare that were stimulated by Eliot, Leavis, Richards, and Knight mingled with the main intellectual and philosophical currents of the period:

> But here one must notice a distinction of absolutely first-rate importance. While linguistic analysis in philosophy went on the whole with a sceptical temper of mind, it was linked in criticism with an emphatic stress on the place of moral values; or at least a sense

that complexity resulted from no mere self-contained skill with words, but rather from a richer development of the whole self of the poet, a fuller capacity on his part to receive experience in all its range, variety, and difficulty, and to order and master it without omission or crudification. Verbal complexity was thus an index of superiority of character, a superiority of not the aesthetic but the moral life. To put the point briefly and in the key terms of this school of criticism, the complex was the moral, and the moral was the mature.[24]

Holloway's is an accurate summary of the philosophy embodied in the school of Harbage. According to Harbage, *Hamlet* "has been interpreted for centuries, and will be interpreted for centuries to come. It invites us to collaborate with its author in 'forging the conscience' of mankind." At the close of *Macbeth*, Harbage says, "We feel that we have been witnesses of the continuing creation of moral law."[25] With the arrival of Harbage, the hounds of morality, so mercilessly held at bay by Kittredge, had returned with a vengeance.

The morality that Harbage attributed to Shakespeare— seemingly middle-road, middle-class, timeless, universal, safe, and sane—was sure to attract many teachers. Harbage authorized them to teach Shakespeare as "a person friendly, humorous, kind. Surely this is what it means truly to be a man."[26] Shakespeare was "noble and good" (p. 58).

The safest generalization about the actors as people is that those who have risen to the top of the profession have tended to be superior people. (pp. 40–41)

To correspond to his soldierly, scholarly, honest man, his ideal woman had to be gentle, chaste, and fair.[27]

Shakespeare's ideal man borrows virtue from the aristocracy, of course, but from other social strata as well: the man possesses middle-class honesty and even a clerkly regard for the well-furnished and active mind. (p. 137)

Whether or not they were directly influenced by the kinds of aesthetic-to-ethical interpretation associated with Harbage and Levin, other teachers of the 1950s and 1960s echoed their sentiments.[23] "*Close* reading" sounded almost as objective as scientific, inductive scrutiny; but it, too, remained subservient to ideology. Take, for example, the matter of Shylock. Harbage had argued that "Shylock's accent is not 'Jewish' but the universal accent of money-lenders." He assured us that Shylock's characteristics "might well appear in a member of any persecuted minority." And so, he said, "In reading the play we must discount the sectarianism, and concentrate upon the values in themselves. In the cognate stories it tells, mercy and love triumph over vindictiveness and hatred."[29] Harbage's tendency to trade historical contingencies for universal aesthetic and moral values was reflected by others of his time, among them Alan Downer in *Teaching Shakespeare*: "Shylock happens to be a Jew, but his dramatic function lies in his profession as a usurer. . . . Shylock's famous self-justification is not a defense of his race but of the principle of revenge."[30]

A few teachers of Harbage's generation found it more problematic to shake off the "Jewish question": "A Jewish student cannot question the prevailing critical view of the non-anti-semitism of *The Merchant of Venice*," said Hans Guth, "without rattling all the skeletons in the academic closet."[31] And as the 1960s drew to a close, teachers began to question, more and more seriously, the primacy of a stainless Shakespeare objectively interpreted through "close" readings promoting approved values.[32] Yet few things are as difficult, it seems, as teaching a capacity for genuine criticism—or imagining a Shakespeare unresolved in the conflict between ruling and subversive ideologies.

Half-Teaching Performance, Un-Teaching Texts

> You do ill to teach the child such words.
> (*Wiv.*, 4.1.65)

"This is not the place to pursue modern theories of sensory perception, only to urge that whenever the classroom ceases to insist upon the same means of communication as that intended for the play, it risks its distortion and death. The direct method aims to create a live experience in a dead classroom." So wrote J. L. Styan ten years ago in an issue of *Shakespeare Quarterly* devoted to the topic of teaching Shakespeare.[33] Since then, the "play way," advocated persistently by Thomas Baker, H. C. Cook, A. K. Hudson, J. L. Styan, Homer Swander, Hugh Richmond, and others, has grown apace.[34] Why? In the 1970s, the breakup of New Critical orthodoxies and the drive "beyond formalism" promised a revival of interest in ways of teaching that might allow students to reappropriate their response-abilities for the perception and creation of literary/dramatic meaning. Thus, the essays in *Teaching Shakespeare* were said to

share a particular concern for developing students' interests and skills beyond strict formal analysis—a concern which seems characteristic of the present moment in Shakespeare studies and in literary criticism in general. The kind of close reading that we identify with New Criticism remains a foundation for most of the methods of teaching described here, but this book also exhibits new or renewed attention on the part of Shakespeare teachers to the affective and historical dimensions of literature. All of the essays raise broad questions about the relationship between the text and its audience. Does "close reading" preempt the emotional experience of a play? What are the significant differences between the responses of a reader and the responses of a theater audience? . . .

The last section . . . addresses the question most disputed throughout this book: what should the teacher do about the specifically theatrical aspect, the performability, of Shakespeare's texts? . . . The teacher of literature should be warned that to conceive of drama as performance may mean to shift his fundamental assumptions about the stability and integrity of the literary text.[35]

Implicit in the essays comprising the volume was a good deal of indirect debate over "the ontological place of the play." This was also true of the teaching issue of *Shakespeare Quarterly*, referred to above, in which Jackson Barry attacked Maynard Mack's critiques of several *Lear* productions as assessments based on the mistaken notion that they were "reproductions

of an independently existing original, the script or 'text.'"
Barry argued that "it is in the possibility of these physical real-
izations that the play itself' lives" (pp. 162, 168–69). But in the
Princeton volume on *Teaching Shakespeare*, Bernard Beckerman
cautioned against an approach such as Barry's:

> strong feeling exists among many theater directors that the text is
> merely a point of departure for the creation of a new event, that there
> is no *a priori* form beyond what is currently performed. My argu-
> ment is quite contrary. The shape of a potential event inheres in the
> text. A director may choose to alter that shape, but he cannot assume
> that it does not exist. . . . Form is embedded in a Shakespearean
> text, and though it permits, even more invites, variation, it also has a
> primary integrity of its own. (p. 310)

And indeed Barry himself had conceded that it is "futile" for
classroom teachers of Shakespeare to attempt instruction
through student performance; teachers, he said, can do little
more than offer "explication of the texts" (p. 167). While there
was considerable lip-service, therefore, to the idea of getting
beyond formalist study of "the" text, actual testaments to successful use of the "play way" were weak and isolated.[36]
Undoubtedly, the vast majority of Shakespeare teachers today
would still approve the sentiments of Edward Partridge in the
Shakespeare Quarterly teaching issue:

> I want to make clear that I am not suggesting that our students work
> out elaborate promptbooks or act out scenes in class. . . . Our busi-
> ness is finally critical and scholarly and analytic, not technical or pro-
> fessional. . . . We recover [the play] through long hours of critical
> analysis and long years of living with it as an object of contemplation
> until we see it in its total design and possess it. . . . (pp. 206–7)[37]

At the present moment, teachers of Shakespeare might do
well to consider critically the concept of "the text itself" and
the many lingering appeals for "close" reading of it. I believe
that the search for and the appeals to Shakespeare's "text" are
too often based on desires for authority and ownership, or
"possession," desires inappropriate to student-centered
teaching. Too often, today's texts of Shakespeare are edited

and taught as if they were fixed and objective containers of meaning to be scientifically studied for authoritative results. Editors seek ever more definitive texts, and teachers debate the definitiveness of readings and professional productions. But now these models of authority should be and are being questioned. The major classroom texts of Shakespeare, for instance, the collected editions (Pelican, Signet, Riverside, Scott-Foresman, Xerox—all, incidentally, the products of Harvard-trained general editors), are remarkably similar in format and in their underlying assumptions and are vulnerable to objections. By presenting eclectic, conflated mixtures of Folio, Quarto, and editorial emendations, they claim to honor Shakespeare's authorial intention, as if that itself were not a problematic concept. In fact, the various early texts give evidence of innumerable authorial revisions and indecisions; and not only these, but also working cuts and additions suggesting that the various texts bear witness to collaborative ventures to produce varied plays. One can no longer teach *the* play of *King Lear*: there is now a widespread recognition that there are two of them![38] Nor can one any longer dismiss memorial reconstructions ("bad" quartos) or other "contaminations" without recognizing that they help us understand what a Shakespeare play might be— and most particularly when they suggest that the plays were really "composed" by prompters, actors, and scriveners, as well as by Shakespeare. This principle of refracted intention compels us to question the collected editions, to see them as exercises in editorial second-guessing and simplification that deny students the opportunity to choose their own responses. Failing in their efforts to find Shakespeare's authority, modern editors frequently substitute their own.[39]

A second issue concerns the treatment of spelling. The usual rationale for modernizing the spelling in Shakespeare's texts is that modernization rarely affects meaning and that, since the old-spelling texts had an up-to-date appearance to their first readers, modern readers deserve the same advantage (though that rationale is not applied to the texts of Shakespeare's contemporary, Spenser, not to mention the texts of

Chaucer). But spellings point toward historically conditioned *sounds* and not just Platonic essences of meaning. To modernize is to prevent the reader from hearing what Elizabethan auditors heard, just as to modernize the spelling of *Uncle Remus* or *Huckleberry Finn* would prevent our hearing their Southern (and dated) accents.

Why, moreover, do we *stage* Shakespeare in Elizabethan costumes, employ Elizabethan facades and staging, use old instruments for their old sounds, and yet cancel the old sounds of the voices? How much of their music is lost? And how much of the datable, contingent, historic meaning is lost, too? We not only lose puns such as bile/boil, death/debt, fool/full, goat/Goth, haven/heaven, hour/whore, jakes/Jaques, nothing/noting, pistol/pizzle, reason/raisin, steal/stale, travel/travail, and so on; we also obscure Shakespeare's mesh between the dialogue that he wrote in special dialects or foreign language sounds and the dialogue that he wrote in his and his company's Elizabethan sounds. Sometimes editors ignore evidence of words and phrases that Shakespeare's audience actually heard the actors speak. In *Henry V* (2.1.119), for example, editors have Mistress Quickly describe Falstaff as shaking of a fever, a "burning quotidian tertian," as the passage is rendered in the Folio version. But in the Quarto version, the actors' memories supplied "tashan contigian," which may very well reflect Shakespeare's choice *after* the Folio version and which may also be what the actor/actress of Quickly really said (as well as being funnier, with the pun on "contagious"). Why ignore the memorial version? Or, for another example, why not make use of our knowledge that Shakespeare spelled and pronounced "sheriff" as a one-syllable word: "shreve"? Why distort the metrics of verse lines by substituting two-syllable spellings for Shakespeare's one-syllable spellings? At the very least, modern editors should experiment with conventional and unconventional phonetic spellings of texts, just as actors should experiment with varied pronunciations.

The many secondary-school translations, comic books, and other versions of the plays that radically simplify Shakespeare

are to me no more objectionable than Lambs' tales—indeed less so, if they help students to see the explosive violence and ungentleness of the plays. The major collected editions purport to equip us to teach Shakespeare *whole*; yet their excessive regularizing and "clarifying" of spelling, punctuation, verse lineation, speech prefixes, and stage directions prematurely solve problems that students need to consider. Or worse, they hide the very existence of such problems. The annotations, moreover, are often worse than nothing. They lead students to think that there can be single-word synonyms and single-phrase equivalents for Shakespeare's complex language, and too frequently they ignore innuendo and other dimensions of language that students desperately need to be aware of in order to consider the text carefully. As the situation stands now, students who wish to investigate the bawdry at the opening of *Julius Caesar* or at various points in *Twelfth Night* must resort to the less-than-impeccable scholarship of Partridge, Rubinstein, and others, which may serve only to reinforce the entirely reasonable suspicion that the Shakespeare of their collected editions has been "set up" in objectionable ways. In most school editions, sex-ranked and power-ranked lists of dramatis personae precede each play— thus predetermining the students' sense of social structure and emphasizing the relative invisibility of unnamed characters such as the many Citizens, Guards, Messengers, Attendants, Servants, Jailers, Shepherds, Sailors, Thieves, Clowns, Musicians, Players, Gardeners, Heralds, and the like who are equally present in the society displayed on Shakespeare's stage and who in their numbers and generally humane actions continually show us another face for "Everyman" in the societal substructure of the plays. The bulk of the people we *see* in Shakespearean drama are not prideful nobles but the plain-speaking plebeians who do the world's work.

Because of their brevity, the introductions in the collected editions implicitly advise students to think of Shakespearean interpretation in short-essay terms, and such introductions usually endorse over-simplified, high-moralizing "appreciations" of each play. The regularizing of act and scene divisions is yet another feature of collected editions that imposes a false sense of order. They encourage a satisfaction in architectonic neatness that is totally foreign to the early texts. Finally, the much-vaunted apparatus of General Introductions, with their stage histories, histories of criticism and the like, tend toward vapid generalities. They say too much too quickly, and they are written, most often, in bardolatrous or mainline styles that fail to acknowledge the dubieties endemic to nearly every area of discussion.

In their total impact, then, the collected editions currently being used as school and college texts perpetuate the Harbagesque image of gentle Will, the ennobling, not-of-an-age, universal, uncriticizable genius. And, in so doing, they resist the often-dissenting but often-persuasive claims not only of anti-eclectic editors but also of the feminists, Marxists, deconstructionists, and New Historiographers who have much to say that might inspire students toward an exercise of fresh judgment, fresh will, in their responses to Shakespeare.

Looking Forward

We'll teach you to drink deep ere you depart.
(*Ham.*, 1.2.175)

Shakespeare, at this moment in our cultural life, is being critically re-examined in our academies and beyond and, along with many another canonical monument, would be by some critics destabilized, decentered, and displaced, at least partially and for a time. Though the reasons for such decentering are many, I return to Henry Simon and Esther Dunn, with whom I began, for one dramatization of the vectors.

Some fifty years ago, it seemed to Simon that Shakespeare would prove too "difficult" for an increasingly democratized system of education. But the relentless drive of New Critical pedagogy toward objective, autonomous, unconditional, and ahistoric meanings preserved Shakespeare for the kinds of renewed glorification now provided by the generalizing, moralizing school editions. One of the paradoxes of our time, however, is that the drive of the (curiously male-dominated) editors to establish Shakespeare's definitive, authoritative intent and to settle on ever more close(d) readings has led to a strange new myopia. Far from having isolated the single textual object and its refraction, we now find ourselves confronted with ever more variable expressions of newly problematic "intention." Ironically, the "scientific" search for the authoritative Shakespearean object has brought us to the point where we are now turned back on our own will to choose among infinite textual choices. The Other has turned out to be the Self. "Shakespeare" is once again our creation.

Conversely, for those who would follow Esther Dunn's humane and confident vision of our democratic age finding "its own face" in the Shakespearean mirror, the process of projecting on Shakespeare a persuasive liberalism, or a radical humanism, or a Marxist egalitarianism, or a feminist reinterpretation, or a deconstructive openness has proved daunting indeed, for there always seems to be something there, a recalcitrant *other* Will of stubborn and perverse particularity that responds by showing a little *more* of itself than is comely in the eyes of the beholder. So that now, many teachers of Shakespeare who would like to take advantage of his pervasive ironies and skepticism in order to question the ruling ideologies—patriarchal, capitalist, elitist—present in his plays may find themselves forced instead to question whether Shakespeare's irony and skepticism are not finally dependent, even parasitic, on the objectionable ideologies they perhaps ineffectively attack.

Teachers of Shakespeare who would encourage their students to challenge the over-universalized and ennobled Bard endorsed by their texts face formidable problems. In part, such teachers are asking students to question or even doubt an ideology that has long seemed not only true, beautiful, and good, but also authoritative and powerful.[40] Such students may not *want* to know that Shakespeare's language is much more dark and explosive in its sexuality and violence than their texts indicate, or that "the myth of a sweet and gentle Shakespeare must be challenged."[41] And what is more, the students who are willing to consider such possibilities may not wish to consider that Shakespeare's capacity to question militaristic, patriarchal, or providential ideals was likely to have been geographically and historically limited.[42] Still, it is an absolutely primary function of high school and college education—is it not?—to enhance the student's willingness and ability to reconsider received ideologies, of whatever persuasion.[43]

Students, teachers, and school authorities can, of course, undermine and subvert the most determined calls for genuinely critical thinking about Shakespeare:

where independence of mind is demanded by authority, its forms can be mastered and "handed in" while the spirit remains obediently conformist. As a student said of his performance on an examination, "Well, I decided to be in favor of that book they asked about, but I did not forget to be balanced."[44]

But because of the notorious and even frightening ambiguity, complementarity, and indefinition in Shakespeare, which forever beckons us beyond belief in timeless inclusiveness, teachers of Shakespeare face the special responsibility of teasing students away from the temptation to accept anyone's formulations of a Shakespearean balance, fairness, or centrality that may turn out to be illusory. Shakespeare disturbs more dust than he settles.

How, then, to proceed? In my view, even the turn to performance methods of teaching Shakespeare will yield only minimal gains if, instead of experimenting continually with student-centered performance, Shakespeare teachers settle into the more convenient, less challenging orthodoxies to be found in comparative reviews of television, film, and stage productions. While such comparatist study mentally suggests the creative willfulness required in genuine Shakespearean interpretation, it has a greater tendency to leave students less than fully engaged with the possibilities of full participation—

ideological, emotional, sensuous, kinetic, somatic—in Shakespearean drama. It is depressing to hear a staunch advocate of
the study of Shakespeare in performance concede, "All such
work should stop far short of [student] performance: a student needs a cool mind to assess what is happening and is not
equipped to cross the frontier between going through the
motions of a play and actually performing it."[45] I have found,
on the contrary, that students need very warm minds to create
the happening of a play and that they are fully equipped and
often surprisingly ready to go beyond the motions of critical
"assessment" and monotonic readings to "actual performance."

We must reckon, admittedly, with the depth and complexity
of teacherly and societal resistance to such "corporeal" teaching.[46] But we are beginning to hear tentative advocacy of such
an approach even within the establishment forum.[47] Such
advocacy notwithstanding, however, the teaching of Shakespeare shows little promise or significant change in this direction until the teaching of English *per se* begins to be
reconceived as a "literary-expressive discipline" in which the
teacher is encouraged "to relate the creative act of [the stu-
dent] to the great creative acts of the received culture . . . to
encourage a living experimentation with the forms in the
culture."[48] That such a development will not come soon
seems manifest, given our all-too-human reluctance to risk
authorizing the kind of student "experimentation" that might
easily turn toward expressions of qualified acceptance, satire,
parody, rejection, and other rebellious appropriations of our
interpretive powers as teachers. Perhaps it is best that only a
minority of us should experiment with the radical transfer of
interpretive/creative authority I am advocating here. After all,
such teachers run a frightening risk:

> in these cases
> We still have judgment here, that we but teach
> Bloody instructions, which, being taught, return
> To plague th' inventor.
>
> (*Mac.*, 1.7.7)

Still, despite what their generally right-minded fellows think are intolerable dangers to be expected when one sets the magician playwright free, those teachers who do release Shakespeare to their students' own hands may sometimes discover untold rewards.

SHAKESPEARE'S BOMBAST

Shakespeare's bombast as aggressive and false pride in the inflated speech of males

> We have receiv'd your letters full of love;
> Your favours, embassadors of love;
> And in our maiden council rated them
> At courtship, pleasant jest, and courtesy,
> As bombast and as lining to the time:
> But more devout than this in our respects
> Have we not been, and therefore met your loves
> In their own fashion, like a merriment.
>
> (*LLL*, 5.2.777)[1]

The Princess, I think, gives a fine prescription for how we might take much of Shakespeare in our time: as a kind of merry bombast. Have we better choices?

Bombast is padding, "lining," in clothes. Transferred to speech and to writing, the term suggests grandiloquence, pomposity, inflation, an overreaching or pride. Bombast enters the language of love when that language becomes over-full. The men's "favours" to the women were bombast, too, because they were ultra copious, aggressive, threatening, producing "a lady wall'd about with diamonds" (5.2.3). Too much lining makes the clothes, the man, the falsely impressive, oppressive. Bombast is fat language, stomach talk. Falstaff is a "sweet creature of bumbast" (*1H4*, 2.4.326), sweating in swollen ego-talk that argues all others frail, naked, undressed in comparison. Iago tells how Othello "unsuited" the "off-capp'd" mediators:

he (as loving his own pride and purposes)
Evades them with a bumbast circumstance
Horribly stuffed with epithites of war . . .

(1.1.12)

Stuffed, prideful circumlocution, an act of going around, wal-
ling, lining the subject, making it bigger than it should be,
need be, long and loud material language: this is bombast.
This is Shakespeare.

The Princess, Hal, and Iago are Shakespeare's only characters who use the term "bombast." This is strange company,
but they all want to cut the bombast figure down to size, to
show how horribly stuffed are the conventional (male) languages of courtship, fellowship, and war. Would they substitute, like the company of deconstructors, perhaps, their
own self-denying versions of pride?

Bombast As Latinate Amplitude

We must not forget that when Nashe speaks of the swelling bombast of a bragging blank verse the word was still vivid with metaphor. Bombast was stuffing—the material and the process by which
unaccommodated man was endowed with bulbous curves. Nashe
and his circle were perfectly familiar, by first-hand experience, with
the analogous literary process and, with their usual disregard of *tu
quoque,* were always ready to hurl the term at a rival. Greene's gibe at
Shakespeare's bombasting out a blank verse expresses as much envy
as criticism. It was the writer's business to dress and deck his subject,
even to inflate it, if this was done with "art." No hollowness or
redundancy was felt, because language itself was loved and pursued
as a great and urgently delightful reality. The chronicle plays, Shakespearian and other, are excellent examples of this nation-wide satisfaction in *bene dicere*.[2]

"No hollowness" was felt by *whom*? It is true that the men's
bombast poetry in *Love's Labor Lost* was reprinted admiringly
in *The Passionate Pilgrim*. Shakespeare's contemporaries then
saw this bombast as straight Shakespeare, did they not? They
also accepted as Shakespeare's the bombast of his dedication
for *The Rape of Lucrece*:

The loue I dedicate to your Lordship is without end: wherof this Pamphlet without beginning is but a superfluous Moity. The warrant I haue of your Honourable disposition, not the worth of my untutord Lines makes it assured of acceptance.[3]

Shakespeare's bombast thus escapes the safe confines of criticized characters in his plays. Indeed, its romance-ic, Roman-sick fullness becomes one of its main claims to fame.

Shakespeare was introduced into American education in order to teach elocution through such arguably bombastic speeches as those of Richard II on the vanities of kingship, Othello explaining his marriage, or Henry V exhorting his men to war.[4] Even twentieth-century teachers have endorsed and promoted the Shakespearean drive to inflate English in the name of wealth, power, and supremacy in expression. The rhetorician above, who equates inflation with the pursuit of "language itself," elsewhere approves an Elizabethan impatience with the "monosyllabic small change of which the native part of our language so largely consists":

The educated Englishman became critically and linguistically self-conscious; he acquired standards and powers of comparison. He was compelled to consider England's place in the Republic of Letters. In the phase of expansion, fine words, racy phrases, exuberant sentences appealed not only through novelty and contrast, but also as ammunition; it was as patriot that the Elizabethan developed his linguistic sense.

Shakespeare's plays not only harvest the linguistic wealth of this period of expansion, but . . . .[5]

Do you hear it here? The jingle of the jingo, the tingle of the lingo? Shakespeare, once again, interprets his interpreter who would discount our native, colloquial small change in favor of linguistic wealth, the Republic of Latinate letters. Poetry becomes a supreme diction. This attitude is endemic still:

Hamlet as a "character" may be confused, but his poetry is not; he is less a "character" than a poetic voice, speaking from a height over-looking his problems. That is our primary fact. It may be untrue to life; people do not speak like that, but there it is, and we have to make what we can of it. If we succeed, we end up by having a supreme experience.[6]

Instead of reducing Shakespeare to the vernacular, you have done the reverse; you have begun with the vernacular and found its parallel in the lines of the play. You are ascending toward Shakespearean language, poetry, and imagery; you are not descending from it. . . . Allow the Shakespearean version to soak in for some minutes. A considerable minority, at the least, will assert that the Shakespearean version presents the same idea in greater depth, with more overtones, and with greater power.[7]

Teacher: Prove that Shakespeare's plot is inferior but his poetry memorable.
Student: This play haunted my soul—it sank in the quicksand of my mind.[8]

Shakespeareans often encourage us to shortchange the vernacular, but for what reward? For the wealth, the power, of a nonvernacular language? Shakespeare's poetry becomes "memorable," "supreme," precisely because "people do not speak like that"? Because they have Roman "ammunition"? Perhaps the outstanding linguistic trait of Shakespeare's most secure bombaster, Pistol, is his egregious, aggressive Latinism: "What? shall we have incision? Shall we imbrue" (*2H4*, 2.4.196); "His heart is fracted and corroborate" (*H5*, 2.1.124). But, once we leave the company of Pistol, Fluellen, Don Armado, Holofernes, Osric, and all the other plainly comic bombasts, are we sure where to stop? What character in *Titus* can escape the charge? What Prince in *Troilus* runs free?[9] What history play is untainted? How Latinate is Othello?:

> I therefore beg it not
> To please the palate of my appetite,
> Nor to comply with heat (the young affects
> In me defunct) and proper satisfaction.
>   . . . No, when light-wing'd toys
> Of feather'd Cupid seel with wanton'd dullness

My speculative and offic'd instruments,
That my disports corrupt and taint my business . . . .

(1.3.261)

How Latinate is Macbeth?: "the multitudinous seas incarnadine" (2.2.59). Or Lear?: "By all the operation of the orbs, /
From whom we do exist and cease to be; / Here I disclaim all
my paternal care, / Propinquity and property of blood"
(1.1.111). And so on. Not just the regal or noble characters—
Hamlet, Timon, Leontes, Prospero, Posthumous Leonatus,
Coriolanus, Caesar, and the rest—but the men generally of
their class speak this enriched, Latinate language. To what
effect is it spoken if not bombast?

The usual defenses of Shakespeare's ornate, Latinate style
are that we should like it because it "enriches" an otherwise
limited Germanic word-horde, that inkhorn terms have
become acceptable, that double epithets, Latinate and Germanic, provide admirable plenitude, that Latinate, osten-
tatious language is free and witty, and that copious
ornamentation and not "meaning" is the true end and pleasure of Shakespeare's art.[10] Nowadays, if you question Shakespeare's Latinate copiousness or inflation, you may be
regarded as a killjoy, an anti-esthete, a lugubrious meaning-
monger, or an undeconstructed "interpreter." You may be
assigned to the ranks of such misunderstanders of Shakespeare as Greene or Jonson (wishing that Shakespeare had
blotted out a thousand lines) or Dryden (complaining of
Shakespeare's "serious swelling into bombast") or Pope (fault-
ing Shakespeare's "verbose and bombast expression") or
Arnold (despairing that Shakespeare's language is "so
artificial, so curiously tortured") or Bradley (decrying passages "obscure, inflated, tasteless") or Tolstoy (hating Shakespeare's "pompous volubility") or G. B. S. or certain
feminists. Or you may be referred to the work of those who
deny that Shakespeare strays from the "diction of common
life," though such denial makes a mockery of the vast range in
levels of diction from the predominating ones in Shakespeare
that are relatively Latinate, ornate, amplified, and copious to

the rarer examples of plain style and low diction, most often employed by women, children, and the uneducated.[11] And even if it is argued that the diction of common life may include "an elaborately patterned, euphuistic style of speaking and writing, full of classical allusions as evidence that one was not a member of the herd" because "in court, legal, and aristocratic circles, there were people who talked and wrote in this way,"[12] still the argument distorts the meaning of *common* toward a silly tautology: Shakespeare's Latinate, bombastic diction was the diction of common life because Shakespeare, lawyers, and aristocrats commonly used it.

Never quite common enough, the persons who wrote and talked in the Latinate style were almost all males trained in an intensive, sex exclusive, and limited educational system that fostered a language of male-oriented oratory, forensic aggression, "bombast." Consider their schools.

Bombast and the Latin Grammar School

At the grammar-school an Elizabethan schoolboy's lessons, enforced by not infrequent "jerks of the breech," continued from seven in the morning until five in the afternoon. The curriculum consisted chiefly of Latin, and its hard core was Lyly's *Grammatica Latina*, which by royal decree was the sole authority for use in schools. Having mastered the rudiments of grammar, the pupils went on to read certain approved works and authors, such as the fables of Aesop, the maxims of Cato, the eclogues of Virgil and Baptista Spagnolo (the "good old Mantuan" beloved of Holofernes), Cicero, Sallust, Horace, Ovid and the *Copia Rerum et Verborum* of Erasmus. They learned little else.

. . . If Shakespeare did not receive this discipline at the Stratford school, it is surprising. His plays and poetry seem to reveal an intimate familiarity with the whole process of education as it existed in his youth. . . . He seems to be always giving indications of having in the first instance acquired his Latin and little Greek at the feet of Holofernes himself, and of having failed to relish the experience.[13]

When will we begin to take seriously the implications of the near certainty that Shakespeare studied Latin ten hours a day for ten years and under the conditions of "a brutality towards

boys which not only, and not surprisingly, reflected the violence of personal life which remained part of the Tudor scene,
but also found a new sanction in the Calvinistic insistence of
the essential depravity of man"?[14] Shakespeare, spending the
first few years of his life at home in a predominantly oral, vernacular culture, with parents who may well have been non-
literate in important ways, abruptly began the study of Latin,
the phenomenally intensive study of Latin *in* Latin, for most of
his waking days for a decade. What a way to be driven (as
most of us may be in growing "up") out of the body and into
the mind! And what were the effects of such training?

Since the student had read and imitated almost exclusively Latin
authors, the style of his expression was necessarily Latinate, complex in form and vocabulary if not completely Ciceronian. . . .
Othello's "round unvarnish'd tale" is set in a strictly patterned *exor-
dium* or introduction which comes straight out of the textbook.
　Furthermore, the study of rhetoric gave the most diverse literary
genres a more or less oratorical case, largely because the dominance
of oratory in ancient culture had never been effectively challenged.[15]

The stuffing of bombast is, then, not solely Latin. It is
school-talk and oratory, the weaning of English not only away
from vernacular vocabularies but also away from vernacular
"small-talk," from languages of privacy, intimacy, reciprocity,
conversationality. Ciceronian techniques of composition produce Ciceronian discourse. "These techniques, comprising
the core of grammar school discipline, were applied to both
composition and the reading of classical Latin literature in a
manner which formed the Renaissance creating and responding mind."[16] That is, Latin grammar school *forced* Shakespeare
to write ornate, Latinate, inflated, oratorical discourse.
Shakespeare's bombast, in this sense, merely betrays an
accentuation of his tendency toward oratorical inflation and
forensic aggressiveness throughout his texts. Whether Latinate in diction or not, his bombast is the pervasive and unlov-
ing language that reveals and revels in its power to order,
encadence, manipulate, persuade, assert the will, not in reci-

procity and willingness to fall silent for listening but in
prideful dominance:

> Now by my mother's son, and that's myself,
> It shall be moon, or star, or what I list,
> Or ere I journey to your father's house.
>   (*Shr.*, 4.5.6)

We are the makers of manners, Kate; and the liberty that follows our
places stops the mouth of all find-faults, as I will do yours, for
upholding the nice fashion of your country in denying me a kiss;
therefore patiently and yielding. [*Kissing her.*] You have witchcraft in
your lips, Kate; there is more eloquence in a sugar touch of them
than in the tongues of the French council; and they should sooner
persuade Harry of England than a general petition of monarchs.
(*H5*, 5.2.270)

Bombast makes war on the peaceful speech of heart's ease, of
plain trust and affection, on language that *could* be calm, mild,
relaxed, private, quiet, a listening language, and converts it to
bragging, lying celebration of will. Bombast charges and over-
charges not only grand words but also mundane ones into
self-aggrandizing power play. All words.

Because we today think of the Elizabethan period as an age of bombast we tend to think that only the heavy words are significant. In
fact, many of the more ordinary words were charged with meaning
through the controversies of the time, and it is important to pay
attention to them.[17]

The example is "nothing," a fair thought to lie between maids'
legs. Who, what men, charged that word with meanings of
their own angry fear?
   But bombast in Shakespeare associates itself most often
with a Latinny attitudinizing of male speakers, Roe-men.
Why? Shakespeare, educated like the rest of his fellows in a
boys-only Latin Grammar school, endured a puberty rite
there, and "in helping to maintain the closed male environment the psychological role of Latin should not be underesti-
mated. It was the language of those on the 'inside,' and thus

learning Latin at even the infra-university level was the first step toward initiation into the closed world."[18] Latin language study with its emphasis on flogging, fear, and treasured initiation into realms of manly virtue, courage, and civic accomplishment, was essentially an initiation *rite*, an entry into ranks of manhood, a male world of Roman power.

Those who were initiated, as Shakespeare was, into the "Roman" temper tended to write according to the resultant extra-vernacular, "classical" ethos:

This Latin orientation of formal literary training gave to all literature a curiously public, and formal, although not necessarily an unemotional cast. This was because Latin was no longer a vernacular language. The vernacular enters into areas of life where other languages cannot enter—the family, intimate personal relationships, and, most of all, the depths of the individual consciousness initially opened and permanently occupied by the terms and the concomitant concepts through which the individual first becomes conscious of his own existence as he learns to think and talk. . . .

The result of this dominance of a nonvernacular language on criticism is marked. Literature tends to be judged as somewhat doggedly public, free from intimacy, exterior. . . . Habituation to nonvernacular modes of expression tended to strengthen and make more virile the intimate note in communication when these did appear, inevitably, in vernacular productions.[19]

Doggedly public, virile, and so never-for-long vernacular Shakespeare. So. Long.

Bombast and Intimacy

As the extreme of a tendency found throughout Shakespeare, bombast amounts to an attitude of mind, an ideology of language and desire. Shakespeare's language, with one *new* word in every ten and with more than five hundred presently dead words, with more than six hundred Latin neologisms,[20] with its recurring Latinate diction, its ornate rhetorical flavor, its brocaded, figured, baroque, or even mannerist cast, is definitely *not* the language of common life, not the language of women, or children, or the poor, or the non-urban or urbane, or Jews, or Ethiopes, or Indians, or anyone but one educated as its author was educated. The language of Shakespeare is a curiosity, not a model, certainly not a model for the language of democratic education, nor for intimate communications among diverse peoples seeking reciprocal understanding.[21]

Indeed, Shakespeare himself adverts to the barriers of his own non-intimate, virile, raised-diction styles that form the staple of his dialogue when, in his sonnets and plays such as *Titus, Love's Labor's Lost, Othello,* and *Troilus and Cressida,* he questions the very capacity of such language to express or to kindle pity, affection, trust. Many of the plays, in fact, depict Latinate, oratorical, forensically powerful males—generals, princes, rich men, proud men—facing a need to communicate intimately with persons out of their element—wives, children, plebeians—and with the deepest humanity of their colleagues and their inmost selves, and finding themselves unable to do it successfully, lacking, it might be said, a language of equality, reciprocity, and genuine connection, a language of a nonbombastic self:

> if they did hear,
> They would not mark me; if they did mark
> They would not pity me; yet plead I must,
> And bootless unto them
> Therefore I tell my sorrows to the stones,
> Who, though they cannot answer my distress,
> Yet in some sort they are better than the tribunes,
> For that they will not intercept my tale.
>
> (*Tit.,* 3.1.33)

> O, never will I trust to speeches penn'd
> Nor to the motion of a schoolboy's tongue,
> Nor never come in vizard to my friend,
> Nor woo in rhyme, like a blind harper's song!
> Taffeta phrases, silken terms precise,
> Three-pil'd hyperboles, spruce affection,
> Figures pedantical—these summer flies
> Have blown me full of maggot ostentation
> I do forswear them, and I here protest,
> By this white glove (how white the hand, God knows!),

Henceforth my wooing mind shall be express'd
In russet yeas and honest kersey noes.
And to begin, wench, so God help me law!
My love to thee is sound, sans crack or flaw.
   Ros. Sans "sans" I pray you.
   Ber.   Yet I have a trick
Of the old rage. Bear with me, I am sick;
I'll leave it by degrees.

                      (*LLL,* 5.2.402)

To the end, Shakespeare's men betray a trick of the old rage. As Hermione says to Leontes, "You speak a language that I understand not" (*WT,* 3.2.80).

Relentlessly, Shakespeare's plays tease our attention onto what is absent: Lear's wife, Othello's mother, Macbeth's children, Timon's friends, Leontes's youth. Just as relentlessly, they note by its absence a language of intimacy, one that is not speechifying, too long drawn, interested mainly in its own being. But can we say persuasively that the internal contradictions of the plays, the bombast pointing to a language of reciprocity, receptiveness, and intimacy, is sufficient to allay our mistrust or to dispel our sense that the aggressive ethos lingers? Within the intercepting rage of Shakespeare's male speech, can we hear women speaking "in a different voice"?[22]

Bombast and Ill Will

To come at the problem in another way, we may note that Shakespeare dramatized failures of bombast orators to achieve personal, domestic, or affectionate communication, but we should doubt whether Shakespeare's conception of the nature of language led him to ask whether language itself may be self-corrupting and whether language per se denies deep integrity, at-one-ment. The speech of his characters generally becomes less Latinate as it "descends" to women, children, the uneducated.[23] And Shakespeare seems consistently to have associated a plain style with deep communication, deep feeling. In his sonnets, "he exploits the emptiness and grandeur of the high style to establish his own sincerity and seriousness."[24] But is Shakespeare's "plain" style really so plain? And, even if you judge it to be occasionally so, of what *relative* significance are the occasions? Even colloquial language may stiffen: "the colloquial language of one century may be the formal language of the next."[25] Shakespeare may, to be sure, have identified the speech of certain women in his plays with a language of integrity, but the question remains whether he ever found or endorsed a style of nonsentimental "directness and utter candour": "The linguistic problem is acute, perhaps even beyond the range of the mature Shakespeare."[26]

We may be tempted to reinhabit alleged Elizabethan uncertainties as to whether human will could ever become so free from infection as to work "the salvation of language from sophistry": "On the one hand, the new eristics coupled with a renewed skepticism had called all in doubt; on the other hand, without language the center, human reason cannot hold."[27] Despite his skepticism (only sporadic?) toward languages of status, power, and colonial bearing, and toward the chance of democratically disseminating our language—

> You taught me language, and my profit on't
> Is, I know how to curse. The red-plague rid you
> For learning me your language!
>
> > (*Tmp.*, 1.2.362)

—Shakespeare never thoroughly explores attractive alternatives. Unlike Samuel Daniel, Shakespeare seems hardly to have "envisioned a maturing English as the future language of colonial responsibility,"[28] though Cranmer's prophecy of James I (*H8*, 5.5.51) that "the greatness of his name / Shall be, and make new nations" might suggest otherwise. We are left with a question: in how many senses does the language of the closed male environment reflect an ill Will?

Shakespeare was of an age, and not for every time, at least not equally. The generally orotund, loud, rapid, lengthy speaking in his plays is too proud, too rhetorical, for the needs and interest of our day when the many virtues of nonverbal communication, of ethnic, street, and children's eloquence, of writing as discovery, and of participatory art forms, are being explored. Yes, Shakespeare uncannily explores moments of quiet recognition and reconciliation in his plays and makes the verbal magician drown his book, but that is not, proportionately, what the plays are about. Much more they concern our whirled, whorled world of words, the prison of our grammar, and its willing cost. Some of our strongest critics see that in Shakespeare:

The whole play [*LLL*], much as it questions linguistic artifice, is constructed in terms of linguistic artifice, and leaves no room for alternatives other than linguistic.

At this play's [*Oth.*] heart lies a critique of the artificiality built into stylized language and behavior which that language permits and even encourages.

In this play [*Tro.*], Shakespeare shows us—unflinchingly, since words were his livelihood and his life—the dangers in words, in their "mereness," their automatic substitution for real response and engagement, and in their tricky grandiloquence as well.[29]

But how easily such seeing is blinked aside:

What at first sounds like bombast in Antony's speech is naturalized in the course of the play, until his way of speaking becomes a standard against which other men are judged. . . . At the play's start, Philo had called a spade a spade, or even a shovel; in contrast, Antony and Cleopatra spoke in love's arrogant, idealized overstatements. By the end of the play, Philo's linguistic practice is blocked out by Antony's hyperbole coming true, until we too believe that "the nobleness of life" is for such lovers to embrace.

. . . .
Such an exercise in "undoing" allows us to see, even more clearly than without its contrasts, Shakespeare's customary habits of "doing," of examining and enriching traditions.[30]

Is there, then, no belief or relief beyond formality? and beyond "enrichment"? Can Shakespeare's or any public drama tell? What experience, what wisdom, what integrity can break the grip of learned, learn-ed language? None? "Curiously, Shakespeare has presented Hamlet as a university student. But each time it is the knowledge of a learned grammarian which is displayed."[31] Hamlet, the ultimate bombaster, genius-victim of child abuse at the endless grammar school, trapping the critic grammarians of each later day. One such, whose book speaks of *Redeeming Shakespeare's Words*,[32] thinks he sees *Hamlet*, at the last, canceling the wordy absence of presence:

Though "words," as Gertrude says, "be made of breath," truth must be made of life. And although words can continue temporarily an almost independent existence, life will ultimately show through.

In his own spiritual pilgrimage, Hamlet moves from a world filled with words, words, words, to a place where the rest is silence. He did not, happily, know that generations of scholars would reverse the process.

"Life," apparently, shows through by means of death, silence. Some life. And scholars succeeding Hamlet have hardly been able to re-verse the process any more than, or as well as, Shakespeare could himself—leaving no play of rest or silence.

Opposing Argument

To oppose an essentially Shakespearean language of power or bombast to a language of "intimacy" absent from or unrealized in Shakespeare is to embark on a fallacious enterprise. The concept of bombast—beginning with uses of the term in Shakespeare, all of which are highly suspect as either lying or distorted or inapplicable, all themselves bombastic—quickly expands from the likes of Pistol and Don Armado, who are from the outset *under*-privileged, comically *de*-flated characters, to privileged male speakers such as Hamlet or Lear whose assertions of personal power may be all the more effective and frightening as they self-consciously abandon claims to linguistic force. That is, the heralded "language" of reciprocity and intimacy in no way escapes the masks and projections of power or manipulation inherent in all human intercourse. In this sense, non-bombastic language, while accorded a privileged position vis-à-vis bombast (just as private, domestic, youthful, and feminine are being privileged over against public, political, mature, and male), must itself be rife with subtler versions of competition, status moves, and power plays: always already "the privileged terms in such hierarchical oppositions are inhabited by their opposites."[33] Intimacy, after all, is the very breeding ground of difference, even violence. Most arguments (inevitably bombastic?) of great violence, like most murders, involve intimates, inmates. Conversely, standard forms of bombast are comically self-declaratory, purgative, exhaustive of the will to fight, substituting words for wounds, talking the talk in order not to walk the walk. And, of course, a hallowed social function of drama itself is to allow us a moment's bombastic topsy-turveydom in order to proceed a trifle more freshly with enduring conventions, structures, and intimacies that permit the great ongoingness of life.

What, furthermore, could possibly be dramatic about the never-exampled but allegedly nonbombastic language of reciprocity and peaceful intimacy so lauded in the preceding argument? Shall Shakespeare be faulted for not showing mothers and babes cooing together? Or for not showing our murmurs over a quiet game of chess? Miranda knew better. Or some imagined bubbly babble over the feast of fellowship? Is there not, moreover, a further confusion in equating a language of intimacy with informality, quietness, calmness, relaxation, and so on, as if the rigid declamations of marital, familial, clan, and societal strife were not the very condition and appropriation of true intimacy? Must the language of love be singularly colloquial, spontaneous, sleepy, vague, groping, unthoughtful, documentary, grained with pause, snuffle, and *uh*?

As for the specific complaints of Latinism, the argument has wholly failed to recognize, or at least to concede, the degree to which conventions of high diction, ornate syntax, class-conscious grammar, and speechifying, power-grabbing delivery may be nullified by context and tone. When Hamlet says, "Absent thee from felicity a while," no audience in the world becomes offended, or should be so, at the dying actor's diction. All attentive energy is absorbed in Hamlet's intimacy with Horatio, the man who is not passion's slave yet whom Hamlet is filching from suicide. When Macbeth says that his bloody hand will "the multitudinous seas incarnadine," the essential linguistic transaction with the audience is an apprehension of the spreading, staining power of a little blood, or "so much blood," necessarily evoked in the complexifying vocalics of ornate speech (followed here by the whole-world unity of "one red").

And as for the complaint that Shakespeare's habits of diction smack too much of the closed male environments of grammar school (if not also his acting company and patriarchal society in general), the point would seem vitiated by the fact that so many generations of women have now read, watched, and acted the plays without noticeable strains of incomprehension, boredom, or sense of assault. Unless you will argue that women's historically proved interest in and praise of Shakespeare's language is but patriarchal puppetry, you must concede it strange that women have shown such satisfaction with Will.

Really the argument against "bombast" amounts to an anti-intellectual, anti-verbal prejudice in theater criticism. Once one begins asking for shorter, quieter, more intimate, and more direct speeches, where will one stop before demanding pure body language, nonverbal communication, as a guarantee of sincerity and truth in feeling? We may grant what Shakespeare certainly knew: "The physical part of language is naturally forceful, it is universal and affective, and it speaks particularly to the vulgar."[34] But since exploration of the powers of language is our past and destiny why not celebrate what it reveals rather than revile what it celebrates?

Bombast, finally, has been equated with aggressive male Will (spear-shaking), as suggested by intonations thought dictated by contexts in the passages selected. Such intonations,

issues as excessive average speech-lengths and play-lengths (most directors through time have cut substantially), overly dense wordplay (many "fatal Cleopatras" here?), and mentalized emotion (characters and, of necessity, their actors who seem to be thinking their feelings instead of feeling them), but such querying will, probably, meet with vigorous opposition. Once an author is deified for those most timeless qualities of writing we think to call aesthetic or literary, then any judicial criticisms of our very reasons for spotting such literary divinity may easily appear to work too far this side of idolatry.

It may not be precisely the "Bottom" line, but it is polemically useful to remind oneself that Shakespeare was a white, Christian, literate, middle-class male who lived four hundred years ago on an island off the northwest coast of Europe. He studied Latin for ten years, married, fathered three children, became sharer in a company of players, wrote plays and poems, acquired money and property, and died at the age of fifty-two. Shakespeare was a man of his times. Much of the language in his plays sounds, by today's standards, highly Latinate. Many of the words are obsolete. Many of the ideas perhaps should be obsolete. There is, arguably, little in Shakespeare's works to suggest that non-Europeans, non-whites, non-males, and non-Christians are of much historical importance in the world. Shakespeare lived in a repressive society that accepted slavery of non-whites, exploitation of non-Europeans, especially inhumane treatment of women and children, attacks on non-Christians, judicial torture, capital punishment, censorship, brutal working conditions, state religion, vast inequalities of wealth, ruinous wars, exploitive colonialism, suppression of homosexuals and atheists, formal education only for men, no vote for women or for unpropertied men, in short an undemocratic police state. There are, naturally, few protests in Shakespeare's works against these (to us) undemocratic and inhumane assumptions as to how society should be structured and should function.

Shakespeare often presents men scheming competitively for power, wealth, or women, and these activities are often viewed as glorious, sometimes as humorous, occasionally as regrettable, rarely as avoidable. Shakespeare almost never portrays what a modern psychotherapist would call mature and loving reciprocity among intimate friends: a combination of Shakespeare's apparent fears, the interactive styles of his day, the drive toward incessant debate in his drama, and the ornately self-conscious language effectively prevent such a portrayal.

Shakespeare shows us who we have been. He affects a heady skepticism toward many of our pretensions and ideals, but, given the course of world and cosmic history toward standards of freedom, equality, and toleration undreamed of in Shakespeare's day, Shakespeare's skepticism may be remarkable more for its limitations than for its wide embrace. Shakespeare shows us how families fight, how friends fume and fret, how love is lost and ambition brutalized, and to us those things seem deeply universal in human nature and society. Stated so abstractly, the themes of Shakespeare's art, like the themes of anyone's art, must appear to be universal and enduring. But what if the substance of the themes becomes indifferent, irrelevant, boring? What if we come to feel that the demands, say, of Shakespeare's fathers on their children— Capulet's on Juliet's loyalty, Hamlet's father's on Hamlet's avenging energies, Lear's on his daughters' gratitude, Prospero's on his daughter's virginity—are too stale to be tragic, too childish to command mature concern? What if we no longer take so seriously those bunches of men standing about to argue their "honor"? What if, instead of seeing in the plays women who can be spirited for a time and still submit to inevitably patriarchal husbands, we see in the plays a man's projection of such women and see playing those women, moreover, boy actors whose spirited defiance for a time merely spices their submission as apprentices to their masters? What then? What stage have we reached for Shakespeare?

Over the past ten years, interpreters of Shakespeare have come closer to admitting the full relevance of history, culture, ideology, gender, and self to ascriptions of meaning, signifi-

cance, and aesthetic valuation. If we are coming to acknowledge, furthermore, that much of the self is the body and much
of the mind works in the body, too, then we may need to
accept more completely the degree to which abstractive and
generalizing language masks a moment's desire, a communal
dream, or the life myth of a particular body. If secondary or
unconscious process nudges at our most considered words,
then writers and readers, playwrights and spectators, need to
accept a timeful mystery of reasons for seeing what they see,
feeling what they feel, or for seeing, in Gloucester's phrase,
"feelingly."

The first six or perhaps seven chapters herein feel, to me,
tied to a time past, to a sense of relative innocence and of
institutional enclosure. Only in the final three or four essays
do stronger hints of ideological self-awareness and somewhat
increased sophistication concerning institutional contexts of
Shakespeare study enter the discourse. To some degree, the
changes in my approach and methods may reflect more general changes in literary discourse during the past few years. I
employ more sexist language, for example, in the earlier chapters than in the later ones. I never really abandon "close reading," yet I think the closeness becomes less a matter of so-
called logical or objective rigor and more a matter of closeness
to immediately affective and even somatic responses. But
whether the body and the unconscious provide only freshly
false frontiers for seemingly pre-acculturated or what I would
call "closer" readings remains to be explored.

More and more, when I encounter Shakespeare or any artist
as Proteus (now bombastic, now plain, now sexist, now not,
now afraid, now accepting), I let go of my restraining grasp
and work simply to pace the changes. I am certainly much less
interested than I used to be in controlling a stable meaning or
winning a gleaming, long-term truth from the texts. If I can
find and cherish for a minute what's partial, vulnerable,
needy, wishful, and alive in my or anyone's response to a
word, line, scene, character, or issue, then I tend to feel a little
more present in the gift of this present.

I still see, read, teach, and act out my version of Shakespeare because I still accept that "he" (or the culture that
speaks through him) knows and feels an important part of
what I want to know and feel. But I also see that Shakespeare
or the culture that speaks through him seems in rather puffed
and unathletic condition, much in need of question, testing,
contest, refinement. In our schools and "festival" theaters,
just now, Shakespeare tends to appear in paternal or millin-
ery guise. Yes, Shakespeare is of more than one age, but
Shakespeare also inhabits a process, as does each of his interpreters, a patterned motion of change. Our collective process
in Shakespeare now incorporates many subliminal tics and
chronic dis-eases. To know any process, one wakes to the
waking moment (though sleep moves it onward, too). One
becomes aware of awareness, but one stays grounded in the
baffling and energizing moment as well. Teaching, studying,
watching, acting, editing, and generally "producing" Shakespeare in America all invoke much more than traditional liter-
ary/aesthetic issues. Profoundly political and ethical issues
are invoked, corporeal and medical issues are invoked, and
they deserve our attention and respect.

Notes

Notes for Chapter I: Shakespearean Interpretation

1. Thomas McFarland, *Shakespeare's Pastoral Comedy* (Chapel Hill: University of North Carolina Press, 1972), p. ix. Compare Mark Rose, *Shakespearean Design* (Cambridge: Harvard University Press, 1972), p. vii: "Shakespeare has been studied and written about for so many hundreds of years that it must appear foolish to suppose there can be anything very novel left to say about him. Shakespeareans tend to be suspicious—and rightly so—of claims to novelty. Anything that is very 'original' in this field is likely to be merely perverse."

2. *Shakespeare 1971: Proceedings of the World Shakespeare Congress*, Vancouver, August 1971, ed. Clifford Leech and J. M. R. Margeson (Toronto: University of Toronto Press, 1972); *Shakespeare: Pattern of Excelling Nature*, ed. David Berington and Jay L. Halio (Newark: University of Delaware Press, 1978); *Shakespeare: Man of the Theater*, ed. Kenneth Muir, et al. (Newark: University of Delaware Press, 1983).

3. Citations of Shakespeare are taken from *The Complete Signet Classic Shakespeare*, ed. Sylvan Barnet (New York: Harcourt Brace, 1972).

Notes for Chapter II: The Sweetest Rose

1. John Evans, *The Progress of Human Life: Shakespeare's Seven Ages of Man: Illustrated by a Series of Extracts in Prose and Poetry. For the Use of Schools and Families: With a View to the Improvement of the Rising Generation* (Chiswick: Charles Whittingham, 1818), p. 43. *As You Like It* is quoted from the new Arden edition of Agnes Latham (London: Methuen, 1975).

2. Hugh M. Richmond, *Shakespeare's Sexual Comedy: A Mirror for Lovers* (Indianapolis: Bobbs-Merrill, 1971), pp. 138, 145.

3. Some of these problems are usefully discussed by, among others, Agnes Latham, Introduction to Arden *AYL*, pp. lxix–lxxxii, and John Russell Brown, *Shakespeare's Dramatic Style* (New York: Barnes & Noble, 1971), pp. 82–94. On Helena Faucit's Rosalind, compare Helena Faucit Martin, *On Rosalind* (Edinburgh: Wm. Blackwood, 1884), and Charles H. Shattuck, *Mr. Macready Produces As You Like It; A Prompt-Book Study* (Urbana, Ill.: Beta Phi Mu Chapbook 56, 1968), pp. 55–57. Elisabeth Bergner's performance may be seen in the 1936 film produced by Paul Czinner. Vanessa Redgrave's Rosalind may be heard on the recording by the Royal Shakespeare Company (Caedmon 210).

4. An old tale such as the fourteenth-century romance of *Gamelyn*, which contributed to Lodge's source story as well as to legends of Robin Hood.

5. For the notions of "bitter Arcadia" and desires for androgyny, see Jan Kott, *Shakespeare Our Contemporary*, trans. Boleslaw Taborski, rev. ed. (London: Methuen, 1972), pp. 217–36. The unromantic Arden of hostile competitiveness is that of Ralph Berry, *Shakespeare's Comedies: Explorations in*

Form (Princeton University Press, 1972), pp. 175–95. See also James Smith, *Shakespearian and Other Essays* (Cambridge University Press, 1974), pp. 1–23.

6. "In the songs of Shakespearean comedy, the grimmest facts of human experience are transmuted by the lyric art, relegated to their proper place in the natural scheme of things, and thereupon dismissed, their sting having been drawn." Cyrus Hoy, *The Hyacinth Room: An Investigation into the Nature of Comedy, Tragedy, & Tragicomedy* (New York: Knopf, 1964), p. 37.

7. I exclude romances, such as *Cymbeline* and *The Two Noble Kinsmen*. See Marvin Spevack, *The Harvard Concordance to Shakespeare* (Cambridge, Mass.: Belknap Press, 1973).

8. See Marvin Spevack, *A Complete Concordance to the Works of Shakespeare* (Hildesheim: Georg Olms, 1968), vol. 1.

9. Lane Cooper, *An Aristotelian Theory of Comedy* (New York: Harcourt, Brace, 1922), p. 137.

10. On classical and Christian perspectives in the play, see Richard Knowles, "Myth and Type in *As You Like It*," *ELH* 33 (1966): 1–22, and René E. Fortin, "'Tongues in Trees': Symbolic Patterns in *As You Like It*," *Texas Studies in Literature and Language* 14 (1973): 569–82. Reassurance amid perturbation is Alfred Harbage's general concept of As They Like It. See *Shakespeare and the Rival Traditions* (1952, rpt. Bloomington: Indiana University Press, 1970), p. xiii. Harold Jenkins, "As You Like It," *Shakespeare Survey* 8 (1955): 45, and Latham, Introduction to Arden *AYL*, p. lxxxv, *inter alia*, get at larger views engendered of contradictions. See also David Young, *The Heart's Forest: A Study of Shakespeare's Pastoral Plays* (New Haven: Yale University Press, 1972), esp. pp. 71–72. On elegant outrage, see E. M. W. Tillyard, *The Nature of Comedy and Shakespeare*, The English Association Presidential Address, 1958 (London: Oxford University Press, 1958), pp. 14–15. To critics impressed with the play's religious dimension must be opposed one who sees "nothing in it of our relation to powers suprahuman—nothing of astral determinism, nothing of any divinity." Warren Staebler, "Shakespeare's Play of Atonement," *Shakespeare Association Bulletin* 24 (1949): 103. Young, *Heart's Forest*, p. 71, says: "*As You Like It* is, in fact, almost all style"; Staebler, "Shakespeare's Play," p. 105, says there is "little playing with words and no playing with words solely for the play as in other comedies." Yet a recent critic insists with regard to *As You Like It*: "Readers may differ among themselves as to the exact tone of the play, but the areas for interpretive disagreement are small." Michael Jamieson, *Shakespeare: As You Like It* (London: Edward Arnold, 1965), p. 68.

11. The opposition of Jonsonian satire and Shakespearean humor is a commonplace. See Helen Gardner, "As You Like It," originally in *More Talking of Shakespeare*, ed. John Garrett (London: Longmans, Green, 1959), rpt. in *Twentieth Century Interpretations of As You Like it*, ed. Jay L. Halio (Englewood Cliffs, N.J.: Prentice-Hall, 1968), p. 58, referring to Nevill Coghill's well-known essay "The Basis of Shakespearian Comedy" in *Essays and Studies* 3 (1950), pp. 145–67, and esp. p. 166. Dover Wilson, *Shakespeare's Happy Comedies* (London: Faber & Faber, 1962), pp. 21–23, says that Shakespearean comedy lacks social criticism. Allan Rodway, *English Comedy* (London: Chatto & Windus, 1975), p. 98: "Generally speaking, Shake-

speare seems to promote integration with nature, Jonson with society. In the one a *sharing* is offered, in the other a *warning*. Shakespeare relies not on one comic view but on a comic sense of relativity. Consequently he creates characters whom one may laugh *with*, who are funny in themselves." See also Elder Olson, *The Theory of Comedy* (Bloomington: University of Indiana Press, 1968), p. 89.

12. Tillyard, *The Nature of Comedy and Shakespeare*, p. 15: "For all its apparent ease no play of Shakespeare includes more or masters its content more magnificently." To Albert Cirillo, "*As You Like It*: Pastoralism Gone Awry," *ELH* 38 (1971): 39, *As You Like It* suggests an ideal that "can only exist in the impetus for a conversion of the will that lets us see things, not necessarily as we like them, but as they should be, and as they are." For Young, *Heart's Forest*, pp. 71–72, the play offers its audiences a "remarkable widening of judgment, a new tolerance," something close to an "Olympian amusement and understanding." Notice that none of these testimonials suggests much of a call to action. Sixteenth-century theory of comedy was, to be sure, didactic, but it was not really incitory. Thomas Lodge saw the intent of comedy to be praise of God as well as the "imitation of life, the mirror of custom, the image of truth." (From Lodge's *Defence of Poetry* [1579] as quoted in Marvin Herrick, *Comic Theory in the Sixteenth Century* [Urbana: University of Illinois Press, 1950], p. 223.) Yet it has been well argued that comedy, concerned as it is with formal limits, tends to be more revolutionary than tragedy. See James Feibleman, *In Praise of Comedy: A Study in Its Theory and Practice* (London: George Allen and Unwin, 1939), p. 200.

13. Anne Baron, "'As You Like It' and 'Twelfth Night': Shakespeare's Sense of an Ending," in *Shakespearian Comedy*, Stratford-upon-Avon Studies 14, ed. Malcolm Bradbury and David Palmer (London: Edward Arnold, 1972), p. 162.

14. In this sentence I am following Allardyce Nicoll, *An Introduction to Dramatic Theory* (New York: Brentano's, 1923), pp. 178–79.

15. For the idea of "voices of maturity" in *As You Like It*, see R. A. Foakes, "The Owl and the Cuckoo: Voices of Maturity in Shakespeare's Comedies," in *Shakespearian Comedy*, ed. Bradbury and Palmer, p. 124.

16. Kenneth Muir, "Didacticism in Shakespearean Comedy: Renaissance Theory and Practice," in *Review of National Literatures* 3 (1972): 52.

17. *Samuel Johnson on Shakespeare*, ed. W. K. Wimsatt, Jr. (New York: Hill and Wang, 1960), p. 29 (emphasis supplied).

18. G. K. Hunter, *Shakespeare: The Later Comedies* (London: Longmans, Green, 1962), p. 32, referring to *As You Like It*. M. A. Shaaber, "The Comic View of Life in Shakespeare's Comedies," in *The Drama of the Renaissance: Essays for Leicester Bradner* (Providence: Brown University Press, 1970), pp. 176–77: "Shakespeare's comic view of love is based on the acceptance of it— on the acceptance of all of it, its component of folly as well as its component of glory." As William Empson puts it, speaking of love's truth and feigning in *As You Like It*, in *Some Versions of Pastoral* (1935, rpt. New York: New Directions, 1968), p. 139: "Two ideas are united which in normal use are contradictory, and our machinery of interpretation so acts that we feel there is a series of senses in which they could be more and more truly combined."

19. Vernon Hall, Jr., *Renaissance Literary Criticism: A Study of Its Social Content* (New York: Columbia University Press, 1945), pp. 180–85.

20. On the "crisis of degree" in Shakespeare, see René Girard, "Levi-Strauss, Frye, Derrida, and Shakespearean Criticism," *Diacritics* 3 (1973): 34–38. In Shakespeare's pastoral romance, particularly, we find the move from Fortune's City to nature an escape in part from a patriarchally dominated world to one in which women such as Rosalind, Marina, Imogen, Perdita, and Miranda are enabled to gain a more independent footing and to assert on other court expatriates an influence that redeems nature and restores civility. Shakespeare's later comedy thus shares with much of his tragedy (*Lear, Othello, Macbeth, Antony and Cleopatra*) the theme of lusty, proud, martial male ego confusing and humbling itself through woman's love but at the same time rising to a higher nature and civility.

Notes for Chapter III: Interpreting *The Winter's Tale*

1. G. Wilson Knight, *The Sovereign Flower* (London: Methuen, 1958), p. 240. Knight's essay, "The Shakespearian Integrity," in which the quotation appears, was published in 1939.

2. Helena Faucit, Lady Martin, *On Some of Shakespeare's Female Characters* (Edinburgh: W. Blackwood and Sons, 1891), p. 390.

3. Knight, *The Sovereign Flower*, p. 288.

4. "On the Principles of Shakespeare Interpretation," in *The Wheel of Fire*, 4th ed. (1949; rpt. with corrections, London: Methuen, 1965), pp. 1–16.

5. Ibid., p. 6.

6. William H. Matchett, "Some Dramatic Techniques in *The Winter's Tale*," *Shakespeare Survey* 22 (1969): 103.

7. Adrien Bonjour, "The Final Scene of *The Winter's Tale*," *Essays and Studies* 33 (1952): 201.

8. Mary L. Livingston, "The Natural Art of *The Winter's Tale*," *Modern Language Quarterly* 30 (1969): 354–55. See also, Kenneth Muir, "The Conclusion of *The Winter's Tale*," in *The Morality of Art*, ed. D. W. Jefferson (New York: Barnes & Noble, 1969), p. 101.

9. G. Wilson Knight, *The Crown of Life* (1947; rpt. with corrections, London: Methuen, 1958), p. 127 (emphasis supplied). In later works, Knight may have retreated somewhat from his uncompromising theoretical stand against literary analysis of theatrical values: see, for example, *Shakespeare's Dramatic Challenge: On the Rise of Shakespeare's Dramatic Heroes* (New York: Barnes & Noble, 1977), p. 19.

10. Northrop Frye, *A Natural Perspective: The Development of Shakespearean Comedy and Romance* (New York: Harcourt, Brace, 1965), p. 9. Cf. Frye's *Anatomy of Criticism* (Princeton University Press, 1957), pp. 27–28: "critical terminology . . . can never recapture or include the original experience. The original experience is like the direct vision of color, or the direct sensation of heat or cold, that physics 'explains' in what, from the point of view of experience itself, is a quite irrelevant way. . . . The attempt to bring the direct experience of literature into the structure of criticism produces . . .

aberrations of the history of taste. . . . The attempt to reverse the procedure and bring criticism into direct experience will destroy the integrity of both." But cf. Frye, *The Educated Imagination* (Bloomington: Indiana University Press, 1964), p. 104: "This critical response, with practice, gradually makes our pre-critical responses more sensitive and accurate, or improves our taste, as we say."

11. Frye, *A Natural Perspective*, p. 116.

12. Frank Kermode, Introduction to *The Winter's Tale* (New York: New American Library, 1963), p. xxxv. Compare Frank Kermode, *William Shakespeare: The Final Plays* (London: Longmans, Green, 1963), p. 39: "The greatness of the play is self-evident; it does not need the prestige of covert meanings."

13. F. R. Leavis, *The Common Pursuit* (London: Chatto & Windus, 1952), p. 175.

14. David Grene, *Reality and the Heroic Pattern: Last Plays of Ibsen, Shakespeare, and Sophocles* (University of Chicago Press, 1967), p. 37. Compare Barbara A. Mowat, *The Dramaturgy of Shakespeare's Romances* (Athens: University of Georgia Press, 1976), p. 2: "Every account that I have read that has attempted to reduce the plays to thematic statement, to express what they say in words other than the words of the plays themselves, has, indeed, *reduced* the plays. Rich with meaning, these plays reveal that meaning to us only through the experience of the play as a whole, or through glimpses, fragments, or lines and images which haunt us. The flame of meaning is there, but we may not approach it directly." Norman Rabkin, *Shakespeare and the Common Understanding* (New York: The Free Press, 1967), pp. 213–14: "In a large sense it is superogatory to look for 'themes' in the romances, for the meaning is built into the simple structure of the plot." Kirby Farrell, *Shakespeare's Creation: The Language of Magic and Play* (Amherst: University of Massachusetts Press, 1975), p. 62: "Only by entering into the 'play' of *The Winter's Tale*, guided to see that our imagination of it *is* the play, can we fully appreciate the transcendence figured by Hermione's 'resurrection.'"

15. See, for example, E. A. J. Honigmann, *Shakespeare: Seven Tragedies: The Dramatist's Manipulation of Response* (New York: Barnes & Noble, 1976), pp. 1–3, "Shakespeare and the Study of Response." Compare Bernard Beckerman, "Shakespeare and the Life of the Scene," in *English Renaissance Drama*, ed. Standish Henning, et al. (Carbondale: Southern Illinois University Press, 1976), pp. 44–45: "To my mind scene-analysis must precede interpretation. The active-reactive scheme is only one feature of drama. There are many other features that need definition and illumination. Drama is an extremely complex art, complex not only in its construction but in the responses it evokes in an audience. Yet ironically, our descriptive language for drama is pathetically simple, virtually childish. As a result, our observations on drama remain primitive. Because we have no commonly recognized form of discourse, we cannot go beyond elementary discussion among ourselves. And if this inarticulateness affects drama as a whole, how much more does it affect Shakespeare's drama, which is simultaneously complex and simple, poetic and dramatic. Until

we can speak a language of drama more fluently than we do, we shall only half understand Shakespeare's art." Also compare J. Hillis Miller, "The Antitheses of Criticism," in *Velocities of Change,* ed. Richard Macksey (Baltimore: Johns Hopkins University Press, 1974), pp. 151–52. Finally, "The search for *the* meaning in a work, interpretation in the riddle-solving rather than the performing sense of the word, falsifies a largely affective experience by over-emphasizing its rational, hermeneutic element" (Peter Bilton, *Commentary and Control in Shakespeare's Plays* [Oslo: Universitets forlaget, 1974], p. 11).

16. Robert B. Heilman, *Magic in the Web: Action and Language in Othello* (Lexington: University of Kentucky Press, 1956), p. 13.

17. Robert B. Heilman, *Tragedy and Melodrama: Versions of Experience* (Seattle: University of Washington Press, 1968), p. 248. And see Jackson G. Barry, *Dramatic Structure: The Shaping Experience* (Berkeley: University of California Press, 1970), chapter 10, "Structure and Thematic Analysis: The Shakespeare Criticism of Robert Heilman," pp. 174–89.

18. I juxtapose Frye, *A Natural Perspective,* p. 9, and J. V. Cunningham, *Woe or Wonder: The Emotional Effect of Shakespearean Tragedy* (1951; rpt. University of Denver Press, 1964), p. 90. On multidimensional interpretation, compare Elder Olson's three "levels" of dramatic criticism: "The first is that practised by any reader or theatre-goer: it involves nothing more than taking in the work and judging it as pleasing or displeasing. The second is that practised by most literary critics in their technical analysis. . . . The third kind of criticism . . . involves an assessment of the effect, as effect, or, in other words, of the experience which we have in responding to the work precisely according to its value as an experience" (*Tragedy and the Theory of Drama* [Detroit: Wayne State University Press, 1966], p. 157).

19. John Holloway, *The Story of the Night* (Lincoln: University of Nebraska Press, 1963), p. 19. Compare Arnold Berleant, "A Note on the Problem of Defining 'Art,' " *Philosophy and Phenomenological Research* 35 (1964): 240: "A language of experience is far more appropriate in dealing with experiences than is a language of things." Put another way, "the idea of a work of literature as 'a linguistic fact' or an 'integrated symbol' is comparable to the notions of 'a concept' in philosophy or 'behavior' in psychology in being the manifestation of an irresistible demand for discrete, coherent and enduring objects of investigation" (F. Cioffi, "Intention and Interpretation in Criticism," in *Collected Papers on the Aesthetics,* ed. Cyril Barrett [New York: Barnes & Noble, 1966], p. 183). Art tends to become what critics can talk about, at least for critics trying to "escape into objectivity." See John W. Dixon, Jr., "The Ontological Intransigence of the Aesthetic Fact," *CLS* 3 (1966): 257.

20. Unsigned review, the *Scotchman* (Edinburgh), 3 March 1847, in Horace Howard Furness. ed., *The Winter's Tale,* 6th ed. (1898; rpt. New York: Dover, 1964), pp. 392–93.

21. Burton Rascoe, "*The Winter's Tale* Takes Its Place with Bard's Best," a review of a production at the Court Theatre, New York, in the *New York World-Telegram,* 16 January 1946, rpt. in *New York Theatre Critics' Reviews* 7 (1947): 487.

22. Eric Bentley, *The Life of the Drama* (New York: Atheneum, 1964), p. 145. The quotations that follow are from pp. 145–47.

23. Brents Stirling, *The Populace in Shakespeare* (New York: Columbia University Press, 1949), p. 5.

24. Compare Kenneth Burke's description of form as the creation of psychological appetites in an audience and as the satisfaction of those appetites through eloquence. *Counter-Statement*, 2d ed. (1952; rpt. Berkeley: University of California Press, 1968), pp. 29–44. And see Burke's "Antony in Behalf of the Play," in *The Philosophy of Literary Form*, rev. ed. (New York: Vintage Books, 1957), pp. 279–90. See also Raymond Williams, *Drama in Performance* (New York: Basic Books, 1968), pp. 170–88.

25. Benedetto Croce, *Aesthetic*, trans. Douglas Ainslie, rev. ed. (1922; rpt. New York: Farrar, Straus, and Giroux, 1966), p. 146. Compare Paul Weiss, "The Being of the Work of Art," in *The World of Art* (Carbondale: Southern Illinois University Press, 1961), p. 170: "It takes a sensitive man to know that every art object is a created substance having distinctive features not to be found in any other kind of substance."

26. Bernard J. F. Lonergan, *Insight: A Study of Human Understanding*, rev. ed. (New York: Longmans, 1965), p. 185. As Gaston Bachelard puts it, in *The Poetics of Reverie*, trans. David Russell (1960; rpt. Boston: Beacon Press, 1969), p. 190, "We are always coming upon the maxim of our admirative critique of poets: admire first then you will understand." The work itself, moreover, responds to precedent questions. Indeterminate pressures of meaning help to generate the play. We may, indeed, criticize "the effort to conceive of meaning in terms of a posteriori structures built up around it, whereas meaning lays claim to understanding in terms of its own genesis, indeed can only be understood as the generator of language rather than as generated by language." Philip E. Lewis, "Merleau-Ponty and the Phenomenology of Language," in *Structuralism*, ed. Jacques Ehrmann (Garden City, N.Y.: Anchor Books, 1970), p. 24.

27. Susan Sontag, *Against Interpretaion* (New York: Farrar, Straus, and Giroux, 1966), p. 14.

28. Francis Fergusson, *The Human Image in Dramatic Literature* (Garden City, N.Y.: Doubleday, 1957), p. 143.

29. See, for example, Stanley Glenn, *A Director Prepares* (Encino, Calif.: Dickson Publishing Co., 1973); H. D. Albright, et al., *Principles of Theatre Art*, 2d ed. (Boston: Houghton Mifflin, 1968); James Roose-Evans, *Directing a Play* (New York: Theatre Arts Books, 1968); W. David Sievers, *Directing for the Theatre*, 2d ed. (Dubuque: W. C. Brown Co., 1965).

30. John Russell Brown, *Shakespeare's Plays in Performance* (London: Arnold, 1966), p. 105. And see F. R. Leavis, "The Criticism of Shakespeare's Late Plays: A Caveat," *Scrutiny* 10 (1942): 341.

31. *The Winter's Tale*, ed. J. H. P. Pafford, New Arden ed. (London: Methuen, 1963), 5.3.98.

32. These complaints occur in reviews of three modern productions—respectively: 11 May 1966, Oxford Playhouse (Oxford University Dramatic Society), unsigned review in *The Times* (London), 12 May 1966, p. 6; August 1963, Delacorte Theatre, Central Park, New York (N.Y. Shakespeare Fes-

tival), reviewed by Alice Griffin, in *SQ* 14 (1963): 443; 30 August 1960, Mem. Theatre, Stratford-on-Avon, unsigned review, *The Times* (London), 31 August 1960, p. 11.

33. Unsigned review in *The Times* (London), 28 June 1951, p. 8, of Phoenix Theatre production by Peter Brook with John Gielgud as Leontes.

34. Eric Johns, "Gielgud in a New Role," *Theatre World* 47 (1951): 7, reviewing the Phoenix Theatre production.

35. Brown, *Shakespeare's Plays in Performance*, p. 15.

36. See Maynard Mack, *King Lear in Our Time* (Berkeley: University of California Press, 1965), p. 78.

37. *An Apology for Actors* (1612), in E. K. Chambers, *The Elizabethan Stage* (Oxford: Clarendon, 1923), 4:251.

38. James Shirley, Preface to the First Folio of Beaumont and Fletcher (1647), quoted by Maynard Mack, "Engagement and Detachment in Shakespeare's Plays," in *Essays on Shakespeare and Elizabethan Drama in Honor of Hardin Craig*, ed. Richard Hosley (Columbia: University of Missouri Press, 1962), p. 272. But see Theodore Shank, *The Art of Dramatic Art* (Belmont, Calif.: Dickson Publishing Co., 1969), p. 181, arguing that audiences do not, unless bored, become so detached as to think discursively during a dramatic performance.

39. Sucharita Gamlath, "Indian Aesthetics and the Nature of Dramatic Emotions," *British Journal of Aesthetics* 9 (1969): 382.

40. See "How to Read a Shakespeare Play," in Wolfgang Clemen's *Shakespeare's Dramatic Art* (London: Methuen, 1972), pp. 214–27.

41. John Lawlor, "Continuity and Innovation in Shakespeare," in *The Elizabethan Theatre III*, ed. David Galloway (Hamden, Conn.: The Shoestring Press, 1973), p. 135. One should respect, as well, a need for dramatic criticism that is not only judicious in its comparisons among productions but also enthusiastic in its celebration of idiosyncratic details. See Norman Marshall, "Shakespeare and the Dramatic Critics," in *More Talking of Shakespeare*, ed. John Garret (London: Longmans, Green, 1959), pp. 104–15. Such a need, however, is not easily satisfied, and one must wonder whether it ever will be possible to say with much conviction: "The relationship between criticism and theatrical interpretation has blossomed to maturity" (Joseph G. Price, "The Interpretation of Shakespeare in the Theatre," in *Directions in Literary Criticism*, ed. Stanley Weintraub and Philip Young [University Park: Pennsylvania State University Press, 1973], p. 73).

42. To one interpreter, the successive lines of a Shakespearean work "do not admit of evaluation within a single system of values. Shakespeare invites the reader to judge 'them' [the lines], but the implied standards for judgment change from phrase to phrase and from word to word. The reader's essential experience of the lines is the experience of his own mind in flux" (Stephen Booth, *An Essay on Shakespeare's Sonnets* [New Haven: Yale University Press, 1969], p. 165). But cf. Paul J. Alpers, *The Poetry of the Faerie Queene* (Princeton University Press, 1967), p. 14, saying of this equally multivalent work: "*The Faerie Queene* . . . is best described as a *developing* psychological experience" (emphasis added). Booth's "flux" smacks of Heraclitean amorphousness, and, indeed, he praises Shakespeare's art for

never straying far from our "experience of random nature" and from the "intellectual discomfort of the human condition" (p. 171). But if *The Winter's Tale*, as process and product, stands for anything, surely it is that the human condition offers growth and development through intellectual discomfort toward experience of a creative, not random, nature.

43. See Howard Felperin, *Shakespearean Romance* (Princeton University Press, 1972), pp. 211–45; Hallett Smith, *Shakespeare's Romances* (San Marino: Huntington Library, 1972), pp. 95–120; Douglas L. Peterson, *Time, Tide, and Tempest* (San Marino: Huntington Library, 1973), pp. 151–213; Mowat, *The Dramaturgy of Shakespeare's Romances*; David Young, *The Heart's Forest: A Study of Shakespeare's Pastoral Plays* (New Haven: Yale University Press, 1972), pp. 122–45; Alan R. Velie, *Shakespeare's Repentance Plays* (Rutherford, N. J.: Fairleigh Dickinson University Press, 1972), pp. 91–113; Joan Hartwig, *Shakespeare's Tragicomic Vision* (Baton Rouge: Louisiana State University Press, 1972), pp. 104–36.

44. On language in *The Winter's Tale*, see, for example, M. M. Mahood, *Shakespeare's Wordplay* (London: Methuen, 1957), pp. 146–63; Jonathan Smith, "The Language of Leontes," *SQ* 19 (1968): 317–27; J. P. Thorne, "The Grammar of Jealousy: A Note on the Character of Leontes," *Edinburgh Studies in English and Scots*, ed. A. J. Aitken, et al. (London: Longman, 1971), pp. 55–65; Jay B. Ludwig, "Shakespearean Decorum: An Essay on *The Winter's Tale*," *Style* 8 (1974): 365–404; Carol Thomas Neely, "*The Winter's Tale*: The Triumph of Speech," *Studies in English Literature: 1500–1900* 15 (1975): 321–38. Among the psychological studies, see Barbara Melchiori, "'Still Harping on My Daughter,'" *English Miscellany* 11 (1960): 59–74; C. L. Barber, "'Thou that beget'st him that did thee beget': Transformation in 'Pericles' and 'The Winter's Tale'" *Shakespeare Survey* 22 (1969): 59–67; R. E. Gajdusek, "Death, Incest, and the Triple Bond in the Later Plays of Shakespeare," *American Imago* 31 (1974): 109–58; Murray M. Schwartz, "*The Winter's Tale*: Loss and Transformation," *American Imago* 32 (1975): 145–99; L. C. Knights, "'Integration' in *The Winter's Tale*," *Sewanee Review* 84 (1976): 595–613.

45. Such a focus on dramatic meanings heeds the advice of Richard David, who tells the interpreter of Shakespeare to "fix his eye upon the one unaltering star, the nature of theater itself. He will not, by concentrating exclusively on meaning and on verbal implications, over-simplify a structure that is maintained by a delicate balance between the three elements of sight, sound, and sense. He will not extract from the text subtleties so tortuous that they could never reach the consciousness of an audience through a medium as fast-moving and unhaltable as music, a medium that cannot even accommodate the double-take unless it is almost instantaneous. He will not forget that the material with which the dramatist works is as much the living personalities of his actors as the words he puts into their mouths" ("Shakespeare and the Players," *Proceedings of the British Academy* [London: British Academy, 1962], p. 158). And see Gerald Eades Bentley, "Shakespeare and the Readers of His Plays," in *Shakespeare and His Theatre* (Lincoln: University of Nebraska Press, 1964), p. 26.

46. The interpreter assumes prescriptive functions in the fashion of a drama critic: "The critic looks at this art object and then, with his own

experience, with his own intellect, emotional makeup, temperament, etc.—all those things that go to make him tick—he tries to take it apart, hopefully in a constructive way, and tries to demonstrate the way it might function, offer insights to the reader" (Clive Barnes, as reported in Judith Searle's "Four Drama Critics," *The Drama Review* 18, no. 3 [September 1974]: 6). Connections between the interpreter's "own intellect" and the way the play "might function" well for others lie in the belief that, "though we are operating in a region where the rules are uncodified and elusive and there is room for the play of irreducible temperamental differences, yet decisions and judgments are not arbitrary, but are subject to broad criteria such as coherent-incoherent, adequate-omissive, penetrating-silly, just-distorting, revealing-obfuscatory, disinterested-partisan, better-worse. Although such a mode of discourse is rarely capable of rigidly conclusive arguments, it possessses just the kind of rationality it needs to achieve its own purposes; and although its knowledge is not, judged by an alien criterion, certain, it must satisfy an equivalent criterion in its own realm of discourse, for which, in lieu of a specialized term, we use a word like valid, or sound." M. H. Abrams, "What's the Use of Theorizing about the Arts?," in *In Search of Literary Theory*, ed. Morton W. Bloomfield (Ithaca, N.Y.: Cornell University Press, 1972), p. 53. Attacks on the limiting subjectivity of any posited "ideal reader" often amount to arguments that "additional fields of knowledge are relevant to literary competence" and "are coded in the structure of language" in the play so that the interpreter's particular description of function and response appear inadequate. See Roger Fowler, "Language and the Reader: Shakespeare's Sonnet 73," in *Style and Structure in Literature*, ed. Roger Fowler (Ithaca, N.Y.: University Press, 1975), p. 122. That is, language in general and the play's language in particular constitute purposive systems of limited interpretive flexibility, having their own demands for response within them.

47. Clemen, "Shakespeare's Art of Preparation," *Shakespeare's Dramatic Art*, pp. 1–95, seeks a method of interpretation that will do justice to the play as generator of meaning and to the audience as catalyst of significance. "The study of Shakespeare's technique of preparation will constantly cause one to ask what is happening in the minds of the audience. Analyzing this process of accumulating impressions, expectations, and interests set in motion by the play as it is performed would shift the emphasis from mere textual explication towards another method of dramatic interpretation that has relatively seldom been tried out as yet." But Clemen hesitates to shift his emphasis, fearing the unresponsiveness of an audience ("of the many dramatic or tragic ironies woven into the texture of the tragedies only very few theater-goers will catch the premonitory meaning") or fearing an audience's subjective atomism ("These delicate effects . . . will differ from one theater-goer to another, according to the degree of his sensitivity and imaginative capability."). He believes, further, that preparation taken in a "wider sense as something not expressly stated in the text but suggested as it were 'between the lines' in a combination of stage-business, dramatic tempo, gesture, spectacle and atmosphere will be a concern of the producer rather than the scholar." Such wistful desire

with concomitant hesitation, on the part of the Shakespeare scholar, to expand concepts of text and play to include responses they promote is combated in the paradoxical argument of Norman Rabkin that a "concern with the response of the audience entails no less concern than before, perhaps more in fact, with the play itself." "Foreword," *Reinterpretations of Elizabethan Drama* (New York: Columbia University Press, 1969), p. viii. And see Rabkin's "Meaning and Shakespeare," in *Shakespeare 1971: Proceedings of the World Shakespeare Congress, Vancouver, August 1971,* ed. Clifford Leech and J. M. R. Margeson (University of Toronto Press, 1972), p. 104, insisting that a recognition of the "teeming multiplicity" of responses and interpretations is a precondition for examination of "the thing itself." "The play itself" is a mystical entity that refuses to stand still for inspection. Yet the play itself is properly apprehended through staged, silently imagined, and written performances, none of which are themselves the play but which may help point to the telling coherence and power the play permits to be advanced. Particular performances give audiences the chance to search back toward informing sources of the play's life.

48. This was the consensus reached at the Seminar, "Mutes or Audience: The Dynamics of Audiences' Response and Shakespeare's Control of Them," The Shakespeare Association of America, 9 April 1977 Meeting, New Orleans. Without attempting to impose an impossibly high standard on a production or an inevitably specious homogeneity on an audience, we are entitled in Hamlet's terms (3.2.24–28) to eschew real or imagined performances that make the "unskillful laugh." We should seek to find instead combinations of audiences and actors that together may interpret the play so as to make Hamlet's "judicious" interpreters not "grieve" but take delight. Otherwise, caught in the scholar's overreverence of theatrical flexibility, we will conceive of the Shakespearean spectator's role as infinitely multifaceted. Compare Robert Hapgood, "Shakespeare and the Included Spectator" and John Russell Brown, "The Theatrical Element of Shakespeare Criticism" in *Reinterpretations of Elizabethan Drama,* pp. 134, 186, and compare Kenneth Muir, "The Critic, the Director, and Liberty of Interpreting," in *The Triple Bond,* ed. J. G. Price (London and University Park: Pennsylvania University Press, 1975), p. 28, and Jane Williamson, "The Duke and Isabella on the Modern Stage," in *The Triple Bond,* pp. 149–69, as they reflect the current need for solutions to unproductive ambiguities in Duke Vincentio's character, as variously staged in this century. We will deny an interest in working toward more "definitive" performance or interpretation (see, for example, Ronald Watkins and Jeremy Lemmon, *The Poet's Method* [Totowa, N.J.: Rowman & Littlefield, 1974], p. 19). We will wander, lost in a funhouse of distorting mirrors, and the result will be that, if Shakespearean interpreters who are interested in the performed impact of a play give up seeking an agreed core of demands for production and response, if the common theme of such interpreters is only subjective multiplicity, then they will drive other interpreters back toward pseudoscientific searches for unchanging truths extracted from the imagined stability of texts with hypothetically objective existence and significance.

49. Clifford Leech, "On Seeing a Play," *The Dramatist's Experience* (London: Chatto & Windus, 1970), p. 216.

50. Murray Krieger, "Shakespeare and the Critic's Idolatry of the Word," in *Shakespeare: Aspects of Influence,* ed. G. B. Evans (Cambridge, Mass.: Harvard University Press, 1976), pp. 194–95, raises the question of whether Shakespeare shapes or is shaped by English empiricism. The reference to the antiphilosophical aesthetics of the English is from Geoffrey Hartman, "Literary Criticism and Its Discontents," *Critical Inquiry* 3 (1976): 213.

51. See, for example, Charles L. Barber, *"The Winter's Tale* and Jacobean Society," in *Shakespeare in a Changing World,* ed. Arnold Kettle (London: Lawrence & Wishard, 1964), pp. 233–52; Glynne Wickham, "Romance and Emblem; A Study in the Dramatic Structure of *The Winter's Tale,"* in *The Elizabethan Theatre III,* ed. David Galloway (Hamden: The Shoestring Press, 1973), pp. 82–99; Frances A. Yates, *Shakespeare's Last Plays: A New Approach* (London: Routledge & Kegan Paul, 1975).

Notes for Chapter IV: *The Tempest* and the New World

1. Citations are to Frank Kermode, ed., *The Tempest,* the Arden Edition (London: Methuen, 1954).

2. Richard Eden, *The Decades of the Newe World of West India* (London, 1555), p. 219v; Richard Eden, *The History of Trauayle in the West and East Indies* (London, 1577), p. 434v; the quotation has been modernized. Both Eden's account of 1555 and the expansion by Richard Willes in 1577 rely on short-ened versions of Antonio Pigafetta's narration of Magellan's voyage, a nar-ration that had been published by Ramusio and others and had been widely circulated in French and Italian versions. What scholar first con-nected Shakespeare's "Setebos" to the Patagonians remains a mystery. Richard Farmer cites Eden in correspondent's notes to the Johnson-Steev-ens editions of *The Tempest* (2d ed., 1778) but mentions others who made the connection of Setebos and Patagonia through sources (non-Elizabethan) other than Eden. Farmer does not mention Setebos in his famous *Essay on the Learning of Shakespeare* (Cambridge, 1767). Malone discusses connec-tions between *The Tempest* and the Jamestown adventures in his *Account of the Incidents from Which the Title and Part of the Story of Shakespeare's Tempest Were Derived* (London, 1808).

3. After Malone's *Account,* the subject was not treated exhaustively until Morton Luce edited the Arden *Tempest* editions of 1902, 1919, and 1926. Sidney Lee argued that Caliban resembled an American Indian and Pros-pero a planter in articles of 1907 and 1913 and in a revised edition of Lee's *A Life of William Shakespeare* (New York: Macmillan, 1923), pp. 428–31. Edward Everett Hale argued, in *Prospero's Island* (New York: Dramatic Museum of Columbia University, 1919), that Shakespeare probably met the adven-turers and read the narratives of Bartholomew Gosnold's voyage to the New England coast in May 1602. Henry Cabot Lodge, in the introduction to Hale's book (p. 15), mentions that Walter Raleigh, writing in the MacLehose

edition of *Hakluyt,* vol. 12, said, "'Shakespere, almost alone, saw the problem of American settlement in a detached light.'"

4. Gayley writes in this vein: Shakespeare "believed in the right of the individual to liberty, property and the pursuit of happiness; in equality before the law; and in law 'all-binding, keeping form and due proportion'; in even-handed justice; in duty to the common order in society and state; in fraternity of effort and patriotic allegiance. Like the best of them he affirmed right conscience as arbiter of internal issues; and he believed in a God overruling with justice the affairs of all nation." *Shakespeare and the Founders of Liberty in America* (New York: Macmillan, 1917), p. 161.

5. Adolphus William Ward, *Shakespeare and the Makers of Virginia* (London: Oxford University Press, 1919); Robert Ralston Cawley, "Shakespeare's Use of the Voyagers in *The Tempest*," *PMLA* 41 (1926): 688–726. Cawley followed this with two books, *The Voyagers and Elizabethan Drama* (Boston: D. C. Heath, 1938), and *Unpathed Waters: Studies in the Influence of the Voyagers on Elizabethan Literature* (Princeton University Press, 1940).

6. "Certain Fallacies and Irrelevancies in the Literary Scholarship of the Day," *Studies in Philology* 24 (1927): 487.

7. Kermode, ed., p. xxvii. *Narrative and Dramatic Sources of Shakespeare,* ed. Geoffrey Bullough (London: Routledge and Paul, 1975), 8:245.

8. *Shakespeare's Romances: A Study of Some Ways of the Imagination* (San Marino: Huntington Library, 1972), p. 143.

9. *The Stranger in Shakespeare* (New York: Stein and Day, 1972), pp. 238–39.

10. See, for example, E. P. Kuhl, "Shakespeare and the Founders of America: *The Tempest*," *Philological Quarterly* 41 (1962): 123–46; Philip Mason, *Prospero's Magic: Some Thoughts on Class and Race* (London: Oxford University Press, 1962); D. G. James, *The Dream of Prospero* (Oxford University Press, 1967); O. Mannoni, *Prospero and Caliban: The Psychology of Colonization,* trans. Pamela Powesland, 2d ed. (New York: Praeger, 1964). Cf. Stephen J. Greenblatt, "Learning to Curse: Aspects of Linguistic Colonialism in the Sixteenth Century," in *First Images of America: The Impact of the New World on the Old,* ed. Fredi Chiappelli (Berkeley: University of California Press, 1976), 2:568–76, who argues that *The Tempest* is the "profoundest literary exploration" in the Renaissance of the impact of a lettered culture on an unlettered one and that Caliban's rejection of language as taught him by Prospero has a "devastating justness."

11. "Shakespeare's American Fable," chapter 2 in *The Machine in the Garden* (London: Oxford University Press, 1964), p. 72.

12. Introduction to *The Tempest,* rev. Pelican ed. (Baltimore: Penguin Books, 1970), pp. 22–23.

13. *New Literary History* 6 (1974): 166. Bruce Erlich, in an unpublished paper presented to the Seminar on Marxist Interpretations of Shakespeare at the 1976 meeting of the Shakespeare Association of America, has argued, in somewhat more convincing fashion than the authors listed in note 10 above, that we may have a duty at times, and in our time, to play down the purely aesthetic or "beautiful" dimensions of *The Tempest* and recognize instead "how a work of profound social realism can be written in the mode of romance and 'sacramental allegory'" (p. 11).

14. *Magellan's Voyage, A Narrative Account of the First Circumnavigation, by Antonio Pigafetta*, translation of a French version, by R. A. Skelton (New Haven: Yale University Press, 1969), vol. 2, "Chapitre IX"; *Magellan's Voyage Around the World*, ed. James Alexander Robinson (Cleveland: Arthur Clarke, 1906), 1:64–65.

15. "Squama" may be found, for example, in Thomas Eliot's English *Dictionary* (1538), Thomas Thomas's Latin *Dictionarum* (1587), and John Florio's Italian lexicon, *Queen Anna's New World of Words* (1611). The *OED* lists "squamellate," and Littre's *Dictionnaire de la Langue Francaise* lists "squamelle."

16. *Magellan's Voyage*, ed. Robinson, 1:62–63, 231–34; *Magellan's Voyage*, trans. Skelton, "Chapitre IX."

17. *Magellan's Voyage*, trans. Skelton, "Chapitre IX." And see *Magellan's Voyage*, ed. Robinson, 1:62–63.

18. See, for example, Hugh Honour, *The European Vision of America* (Cleveland: Cleveland Museum of Art, 1975), pp. 2–5; J. H. Elliott, *The Old World and the New: 1492–1650* (Cambridge University Press, 1970), pp. 1–27; Howard Mumford Jones, *O Strange New World* (London: Chatto & Windus, 1965).

19. *The World Encompassed*, ed. Norman Mosley Penzer (London: The Argonaut Press, 1926), p. 111. The quotations that follow are taken from pp. 111–20 and are edited throughout. Henry R. Wagner, *Sir Francis Drake's Voyage Around the World* (San Francisco: J. Howell, 1926), p. 468, suggests that Fletcher may have lifted an account of the Patagonians and of Settaboth from some other source. The civility *vel non* of New World natives was a major topos not only in travelers' narratives but also in sermons on the New World (not to mention speculative essays such as Montaigne's). William Crashaw, in *A Sermon Preached Before the Lord Lawarre, Lord Governour of Virginia* (London, 1610), combined classical and Christian perspectives in arguing that the Virginia colonists would bring civility and Christianity to aid the savages in body and soul. See also J. H. Elliott, *The Old World and the New* (Cambridge University Press, 1970), pp. 41–53; and J. P. Brockbank, "*The Tempest*: Conventions of Art and Empire," in *Shakespeare's Later Comedies*, ed. D. J. Palmer (London: Penguin Books, 1971), pp. 392–93.

20. Regarding Cavendish, see *The Last Voyage of Thomas Cavendish: 1591–1592*, ed. David Beers Quinn (University of Chicago Press, 1976). The example of the Patagonian worshipers of Setebos is one of the best to illustrate how factual perceptions and fictional projections of Old World observers blended to create a Renaissance image of New World inhabitants. Pigafetta encountered the Patagonians in 1520, and his "grotesque portrait remained a legend for several centuries—a cliché and a stimulus for the inquisitive European mind. No less a philosopher than Vico made the *Patacones* the prototypes of a barbaric and heroic humanity" (Antonello Gerbi, "The Earliest Accounts of the New World," in *First Images of America*, 1:41–42). Cf. Joseph Hall, *The Discovery of a New World*, trans. J. Healey (London, 1609), sig. A4v, in *The Discovery . . .* , ed. Huntington Brown (Cambridge: Harvard University Press, 1937), p. 13: "If one of your *Patago-*

nian Giants should catch you and eate you quite vp, where are you then my fine discouerer?" And cf. Thomas Lodge, *A Margarite of America* (London, 1596), Dedication: "Touching the place where I wrote this, it was in those straits christned by *Magelan*; in which place to the southward many wonderous Isles, many strange fishes, many monstrous Patagones withdrew my senses; briefly, many bitter and extreme frosts at midsummer continually clothe and clad the discomfortable mountaines; so that as there was great wonder in the place wherein I writ this, so likewise might it be maruelled, that in such scantie fare, such causes of fear, so mightie discouragements, and many crosses, I should deserue or eternize anything." Such accounts as these help explain Shakespeare's wondrous island setting, his Patagonian Caliban, his references to "strange fish," "monsters," and men jostled from their "senses." These are the standard stuff of both travel narratives and romance.

21. *Newes from Virginia: The Lost Flocke Triumphant* (London, 1610), 2.59–64.

22. Theodor de Bry, ed., *Admiranda narratio fida tamen, de commodis et incolarum ritibus Virginiae . . . Anglico scripta sermone, a Thomas Hariot* (Frankfurt, 1590). This is part 1 of de Bry's *America* series. The title pages in other volumes refer to *"admiratione"* (part 5) and *"admiranda historia"* (part 4). The title page of the Harriot volume bears an engraving of a figure seated on an animal's skull that has a string of beads or, more probably, pearls above its eyes. "Full fadom five thy father lies; / Of his bones are coral made: / Those are pearls that were his eyes."

23. In his essay "Shakespeare's Brave New World" in *First Images of America*, 1:83–89, Paul A. Jorgensen appears terminally undecided about the possible influence of New World voyaging on *The Tempest*. Of actions and ideas in the play Jorgensen says, "All can be traced to conventions, literary and philosophical, independent of the new geography" (pp. 86–87). Yet he suggests at the same time that concerns of the play may have been stimulated by contemporary thought about the New World. Such confusion may be lessened if two observations are kept in mind. First, *The Tempest* should not be set off as fiction against the "new geography" or any historical phenomenon as fact. The term "new geography" tends to disguise the point, discussed above, that accounts of the New World cannot be dissociated from the projective, fiction-making, creative aspect of history-writing. Second, romance, like other kinds of literature, feeds on contemporary thought, on "history," and not merely on self-enclosed "conventions." Just as today's dominant forms of romance, such as science fiction and the detective story, explore contemporary notions of what it means to journey to outerworld or underworld, so Shakespeare's romances explore contemporary issues connecting Old World and New World.

24. The enthusiastic may see Shakespeare's interest in the romance voyaging mode opening up through *Antony and Cleopatra*, the sea-tossed Pericles first tempted by the "fair Hesperides," the travels and travails in *Cymbeline* between pastoral Wales in a "swan's nest" Britain and the old and intriguing but also law-giving world of Italy/Rome, and the sea voyage in *The Winter's Tale* from sophisticated Sicilia to rustic, golden age Bohemia. Cf. A. L. Rowse, *The Elizabethans and America* (New York: Harper, 1959), p.

190: "The influence of the voyagers speaks in them all, inciting the imagination to strange scenes and countries across the seas." More important, and deserving further exploration, however, is Shakespeare's habit of cross-qualifying romance and history as well as utopian and dystopian "strange scenes" ("strange" being the talismanic word of *The Tempest*). *Henry VIII*, written next after *The Tempest*, is obviously both history and romance as it matches the falls of Buckingham, Wolsey, and Katherine against Cranmer's providential vision of James: "Wherever the bright sun of heaven shall shine, / His honour and the greatness of his name / Shall be, and make new nations" (5.4.50–52). Thus the romances, especially *Cymbeline* and *The Tempest*, progress toward the colonial commentary of *Henry VIII*, portraying England as an actor in world history viewed as masque— that is, theatrical play acted by historical, non-play personages. Shakespeare shows that colonial history must not be too easily read in terms of providential romance. Insofar as *The Tempest* glances at the "new nation" of Virginia or any utopia via Gonzalo's "plantation . . . commonwealth," Miranda's "brave new world," or Prospero's isle itself, it suggests that the will to make a garden in the wilderness must not relax in assurance of divine guidance but must assert itself in discipline, freely accepted servitude, long learning, confinement, and labor all so repeatedly stressed in the play. This stress on the willed labor it takes to earn providential reward, in Caliban's terms to "seek for grace," is a crucial item in reports of voyagers and colonists. Cf. Edmund S. Morgan, "The Labor Problem at Jamestown, 1607–18," *American Historical Review* 76 (1971): 595–611. This stress helps keep the apt balance in *The Tempest* between romance and history, providence and human will, which is slighted by providentialists who fail to recognize the painful labor of those who would "insert a fictional career into the unfolding of time" (George Slover, "Shakespeare's Sense of History: Preface to an Analogical Reading of *The Tempest*," unpublished, p. 3) and slighted by antiprovidentialists who fail to recognize the prayerful praise echoing through the play that "frees all faults." Cf. Jorgensen's emphasis on the "rigorous testing" and "benevolent pessimism" of the play, in *First Images of America*, 1:87, or Jan Kott's notion that "*The Tempest* is the most bitter of Shakespeare's plays" because "nothing is purified" ("*The Tempest*, or Repetition," *Mosaic* 10 [1977]: 21, 36).

25. On connections beween utopian discourse (analogous to "romance") and travelers' narratives (analogous to "history"), see the suggestive, if opaque, essay by Frederick Jameson, "Of Islands and Trenches: Naturalization and the Production of Utopian Discourse," *Diacritics* 7 (1977): 2–21, especially 16–17, arguing that travel narratives often absorb description into narrative and nature into culture (for example, seeing the Patagonians as super-Christian in kindness or Caliban as noble savage), whereas utopias tend to absorb narrative into description and culture and history into timeless, ideal nature, so that utopias like More's and Prospero's threaten "to turn around into their opposite, a more properly dystopian repression of the unique existential experience of individual lives" (p. 17). Cf. Stephen J. Greenblatt, "More, Role-Playing, and Utopia," *Yale Review* 67 (1978): 517–36. In *The Tempest*, the central device for interpenetration of

timeless design and temporal human will is the masque that three times in the play presents magic spectacle but then reaches out, in "interruption" to its audience, so that men are made aware of acting against a background of divine/demonic drama, and so that, again, romance and history meet. All these perspectives on *The Tempest*—voyager's projections and perceptions, romance and history, utopia and dystopia, masque and anti-masque— help reveal reasons for the persistent balance of optimistic and pessimistic readings of the play.

Notes for Chapter V: Imperiled and Chastening Daughters

1. See also, for example, *Merry Wives of Windsor*, 4.6.23; *Othello*, 1.3.192; *Lear*, 1.1.113; *Cymbeline*, 1.2.131. Citations are from the *Riverside Shakespeare*, ed. G. B. Evans (Boston: Houghton Mifflin, 1974).

2. One may observe that in a tragedy where a daughter, such as Ophelia, *fails* to assert herself against her father's dictate, the sense of nature redeemed, of human nature and society revitalized, may be diminished, as when the relatively limited Fortinbras takes over at the end of *Hamlet*.

3. Just what portion, if any, of *The Two Noble Kinsmen* John Fletcher may be responsible for is as yet undetermined. Shakespeare is generally credited with scenes 1.1–1.2, 3.1, 4.1.34–173, and 5.3–5.4, which include the scene introducing the Jailer's Daughter and the addresses of Arcite, Palamon, and Emilia to Mars, Venus, and Diana. Paul Bertram, *Shakespeare and the Two Noble Kinsmen* (New Brunswick, N.J.: Rutgers University Press, 1965), argues at length that the entire play is by Shakespeare.

4. These plays are collected, together with *The Tempest*, in *Dramatic Romance: Plays, Theory, and Criticism*, ed. Howard Felperin (New York: Harcourt, 1973). I am indebted to Howard Felperin for the collocation and for thoughts it has fostered.

5. In discussing *Cardenio*, I refer to the plot of the Cardenio story as contained in the first part of Cervantes's novel, translated by Thomas Shelton in 1612. The Court Chamber Account and Court (Greenwich) account indicate the *Cardenio* was presented twice by the King's Men in 1613. On 9 September 1653, the publisher Humphrey Moseley registered "The History of Cardennio, by Mr. Fletcher and Shakespeare" in the Stationer's Register; see E. K. Chambers, *William Shakespeare: A Study of Facts and Problems* (Oxford: Clarendon, 1930), 2:343, 1:539–42. Lewis Theobald published a play, *Double Falsehood*, in 1728 and alleged that it was based on manuscripts of a play by Shakespeare that dealt with the Cardenio story. Opinions vary as to whether Theobald really could have adapted or did adapt his play from such a manuscript; see John Freehafer, "*Cardenio*, by Shakespeare and Fletcher," *PMLA* 84 (1969): 501-12, and Harriet C. Frazier, *A Babble of Ancestral Voices: Shakespeare, Cervantes, and Theobald* (The Hague: Mouton, 1974). Theobald's play excludes Don Quixote.

Notes for Chapter VI: Cordelia Weeping

1. Shakespeare citations are from *The Riverside Shakespeare*, ed. G. B. Evans, et al. (Boston: Houghton Mifflin, 1974).

2. Juliet Dusinberre, *Shakespeare and the Nature of Women* (London: Macmillan, 1975), p. 305. Cf., Inga Stina Ewbank, "Shakespeare's Portrayal of Women: A 1970's View," in *Shakespeare: Pattern of Excelling Nature*, ed. David Bevington and Jay L. Halio (Newark: University of Delaware Press, 1978), pp. 222–23, and Carole McKewin, "Shakespeare Liberata: Shakespeare, the Nature of Women, and the New Feminist Criticism," *Mosaic* 10, 3 (Spring 1977): 162.

3. Dusinberre, *Shakespeare and the Nature of Women*, p. 292.

4. *Doctrine for the Lady of the Renaissance* (Urbana: University of Illinois Press, 1956), p. 11, 26.

5. Ibid., p. 116.

6. Book 3, chapter 24, p. 243; cited in Kelso, *Doctrine for the Lady*, p. 27.

7. Kelso, *Doctrine for the Lady*, p. 22.

8. "Shakespeare considered, in play after play, the consequences to men and to the worlds they dominated, of undervaluing the fluid, insubstantial, and emotional dimension of experience." Marilyn French, *Shakespeare's Division of Experience* (New York: Ballantine, 1981), p. 348.

9. "Like the men, the women, too, respond to a variety of forces in their environment and are troubled by the world they see. But that world differs from the one perceived by men." Irene G. Dash, *Wooing, Wedding, and Power: Women in Shakespeare's Plays* (New York: Columbia University Press, 1981), p. 5. Cf. Linda Bamber, *Comic Women, Tragic Men* (Stanford University Press, 1982), p. 43: "the sexual other may be real and not projected. To each his own, to each her own: I have found in Shakespeare what I want to imagine as a possibility in my life."

Notes for Chapter VII: Suiting the Word to the Action?

1. Unless otherwise noted, all Shakespeare citations are taken from the *Riverside Shakespeare*, ed. G. B. Evans, et al. (Boston: Houghton Mifflin, 1974).

2. "Playing *King Lear*: Donald Sinden Talks to J. W. R. Meadowcroft," *Shakespeare Survey* 33 (1980): 81. Subsequent references to this work are cited by page number in the text.

3. When Touchstone asks William, "Art thou wise? (5.1.28; F1, line 2370), and William answers, "I sir, I haue a prettie wit," William repeats a formulaic "I sir" he used a few lines earlier to express assent; William, moreover, hardly need share Touchstone's egoism.

4. See Steven Urkowitz, *Shakespeare's Revision of King Lear* (Princeton University Press, 1980).

5. See, for example, Gary Taylor, *Three Studies in the Text of Henry V* (Oxford: Clarendon Press, 1979), p. 111. When scholars take more interest in the old texts as playhouse scripts, they may leave in more cues for actors, readers, audiences. Let us remember, for example, the stage direction "Enter young Osricke" as in the Folio (line 3586) and not "Enter a Courtier" or "Enter Osric" as in some modern editions. Here is a fourth son in the play, one whose announced youth may make Hamlet seem relatively

mature in the fifth act, and one who survives onstage to greet Fortinbras. Most editions, furthermore, direct that Hamlet wounds Laertes *before* Hamlet says to him, "Nay, come again" (5.2.304), but scholars who consult stage traditions as well as common sense may want to place the wounding *after* Hamlet's words to Laertes. See Horace Howard Furness, ed., *Hamlet*, New Variorum edition (Philadelphia: J. B. Lippincott, 1877), 1.448. In *King Lear*, F1 first presents Edmund in stage directions *and* speech prefixes as *Edmund*, but once he is identified as a bastard the speech prefixes consistently name him *Bastard* whereas stage directions generally name him *Edmund*. Editors who refuse to regularize the naming could open up the textual split in perspectives: internal, private, anarchic (*Bastard*) versus external, public, legitimated (*Edmund*). (My attention to possible consequences of editorial regularization of speech prefixes was first directed by Randall McLeod.)

6. To ask how English sounded in Shakespeare's day is to enter the murky thickets of phonology. Fausto Cercignani, *Shakespeare's Works and Elizabethan Pronunciation* (New York: Oxford University Press, 1980), discredits much of the work of Helge Kökeritz, *Shakespeare's Pronunciation* (New Haven: Yale University Press, 1953), but Cercignani fails to present a clear or comprehensive description of a rival pronunciation. What audiences and actors need are recordings. Kökeritz, at least, tried that. Should not others follow suit? Randolph Quirk, "Shakespeare and the English Language," in *A New Companion to Shakespeare Studies*, ed. Kenneth Muir and S. Schoenbaum (Cambridge University Press, 1971), p. 69, said, "Now that we have the technical ability to put on a play in roughly the pronunciation of 1600, the desirability of so doing has become less apparent. Since so many of the features of Elizabethan pronunciation have remained in twentieth-century use with utterly different sociological connotations, it is exceedingly difficult to avoid farcical overtones." Is not this sheer snobbery? Assuming, as seems reasonable, that Burbage as Hamlet spoke with a pronunciation shared by a majority of Londoners of his day, why should not today's Hamlet do the same?

7. Stanley Wells, *Modernizing Shakespeare's Spelling* (Oxford: Clarendon Press, 1979), p. vi.

8. Contrary to the view of Bertram Joseph, "The Elizabethan Stage and Acting," in *The Age of Shakespeare*, ed. Boris Ford (London: Penguin, 1955), pp. 152–56; *Acting Shakespeare* (New York: Theatre Arts Books, 1960), pp. 8–11; and *Elizabethan Acting*, 2d ed. (London: Oxford University Press, 1962), pp. 21–22, I do not think that Hamlet's term *action* can be restricted to rhetorical delivery or decorous relations between words and gestures. See, for example, Hamlet's reference to "actions that a man might play" (1.2.84) and the stage directions for the dumb show in which the queen "makes passionate action" totally in silence. Action, itself, is eloquence. See also Hilda M. Hulme, *Explorations in Shakespeare's Language* (London: Longman, 1962), p. 195.

9. Compare William A. Armstrong, "Actors and Theatres," in *Shakespeare in His Own Age*, ed. Allardyce Nicoll (London: Cambridge University Press, 1976), p. 198: "At the Globe, the King's Men evidently used a louder

and more emphatic style than they did at Blackfriars." And compare Antonin Artaud, *The Theater and Its Double*, trans. Mary Caroline Richards (New York: Grove Press, 1958), p. 119: "Let words be heard in their sonority rather than be exclusively taken for what they mean grammatically, let them be perceived as movements." As V. N. Volosinov, "Discourse in Life and Discourse in Art" in his *Freudianism: A Marxist Critique*, trans. I. R. Titunik and ed. Neal H. Bruss (New York: Academic Press, 1976), p. 102, observes, "Intonation establishes a firm link between verbal discourse and the extraverbal context—genuine, living intonation moves verbal discourse beyond the border of the verbal."

10. Compare Hamlet insisting that the rude clowns "speak no more than is set down for them" (3.2.39–40), even if the "more" be but a laugh. Actors rarely worship their text. The actor in the interview stated, "I'm a great believer in cutting." Shakespeare, he said, improves by cutting, "by half, if possible" ("Playing *King Lear*," p. 84). Shakespeare's scholar-aristocrats, of course, will have none of this upstartery. Prospero praises the actors at the banquet masque for not cutting the text: "Of my instruction hast thou nothing bated / In what thou hadst to say" (3.3.85–86). Hal rebukes Falstaff for speaking with Cambyses' passion, not like a real king. Hamlet cruelly jibes at the actor in mid-stride: "leave thy damnable faces" (3.2.253). In the old *Return from Parnassus*, in *The Three Parnassus Plays*, ed. J. B. Leishman (London: Nicholson & Watson, 1949), p. 339, the scholar-playwright made the character Will Kempe say to an aspiring scholar-actor, "Is't not better to make a foole of the world as I haue done, then to be fooled of the world, as you schollers are?" The scholar-playwright meant this as satire against the actors, but some scholars may find in the lines a modicum of straight truth.

11. Mel Gussow, in the *New York Times* (14 May 1981), p. C24, col. b, so describes Ian McKellen.

12. Consider the tendency of S. Schoenbaum's *William Shakespeare: A Documentary Life* (New York: Oxford University Press, 1975) to commemorate a genteel property owner and not the striving player and writer. Endpapers give us pastoral views of Stratford-on-Avon and London. More chapters concern the Stratford Shakespeare than the Shakespeare of London whose working life, surely, should be our prime focus, and even the London chapters stress Shakespeare's gentility: "11—Plays, Plague, and a Patron; 12—the Lord Chamberlain's Man; 13—A Gentleman of Means; 14—His Majesty's Servant." This puffed panoply contains, admittedly, much information (none new) presented in what the jacket describes as "regal language," but it also contains a depressing series of disclaimers, hedged bets, bits and pieces of paper record, inert evidence. A related book, S. Schoenbaum, *Shakespeare: The Globe and the World* (New York: Oxford University Press, 1979), commemorating a Shakespeare exhibition, stresses mainly the Shakespeare of marble statues, portraits of the Queen, pastel Stratford, and the most arty and fanciful pictures of productions. Perhaps the super-aestheticizing tendency of such books—and there are many—is best summed up by these alliterative, punning sentences that transmute human suffering into engaging sing-song: "The cries of the poor, counterpointed by the clacking of their clap-dishes, filled the streets. But this

clamor had to compete with other *appeals*. Shopkeepers . . . called. . . . Ballad-mongers sang" (p. 75; emphasis supplied).

13. George Puttenham, *The Arte of English Poesie* (London, 1589), book 3, chapter 19. On mysteries of verbal repetition in *Hamlet*, see *inter alia*, Harley Granville-Barker, *Preface to Hamlet* (1946; rpt. New York: Hill and Wang, 1957), p. 184; Harry Levin, *The Question of Hamlet* (New York: Oxford University Press, 1959), pp. 49–52; and George T. Wright, "Hendiadys and *Hamlet*," *PMLA* 96 (1981): 168–93.

14. It is also the machine in the Hamlet who plays with "words, words, words." Compare Michael L. Magie, "Tact, or Hamlet's Bastards," *Yale Review* 69 (1980): 252: "The Hamlet who complacently chatters . . . is godfather to . . . Joyce and Nabokov and Harold Bloom and other latter-day affirmers of the intrinsic worth of language adeptly maneuvered. The complacent Hamlet likewise sponsors those structuralists who aver that it is in the language, or in some underlying conceptual structure, rather than in the mental acts and moral commitments which these embody and convey, that human significance or substance consists."

15. Alvin B. Kernan, *The Playwright as Magician: Shakespeare's Image of the Poet in the English Public Theater* (New Haven: Yale University Press, 1979), pp. 109, 110. In "plagiarizing" his own words as they appeared earlier in "Politics and Theatre in *Hamlet*," in *Hamlet Studies* 1 (1979): 11, and in *The Revels History of Drama in English*, ed. F. Leeds Barroll, et at. (London: Methuen, 1975), 3.381, and in *Character and Conflict*, 2d ed. (New York: Harcourt, Brace & World, 1969), p. 377, and thus in failing freshly to intone his given text, Kernan perhaps embodies the very view of Hamlet that he presents!

16. Eric Bentley, *The Theatre of Commitment* (New York: Atheneum, 1967), p. 159. Compare, Friedrich Durenmatt, *The Problems of the Theater* (New York: Grove Press, 1958), p. 32: "The world (hence the stage which represents this world) is for me something monstrous, a riddle of misfortunes which must be accepted but before which one must not capitulate. The world is far bigger than any man, and perforce threatens him constantly. If one could but stand outside the world, it would no longer be threatening. But I have neither the right nor the ability to be an outsider to this world. To find solace in poetry can also be all too cheap; it is more honest to retain one's human point of view."

17. Is it fair to ask bookish scholars to write about Shakespeare and the theater in a language of action: "After a painful separation that limited, supposedly for its own good, the understanding of literature—'literature' became only that, and was resolutely dissociated from thought-systems of a religious, political, or conceptual kind—we are returning to a larger and darker view of art as mental charm, war, and purgation. . . . I may be overstating the case; but the spectacle of the polite critic dealing with an extravagant literature, trying so hard to come to terms with it in his own tempered language, verges on the ludicrous." Geoffrey H. Hartman, *Criticism in the Wilderness* (New Haven: Yale University Press, 1980), pp. 101 and 155.

18. "The theatre artists go out to the workers, peasants and soldiers to learn from them the true spirit of good revolutionaries; in turn, the audience goes to the theatre to see its own image, to 'feel proud' for being portrayed as the hero of the stage. The contact between the actor and the spectator thus extends beyond the confines of the theatre, to the core of life itself." Clara Yu Cuadrado, "Cross-Cultural Currents in the Theatre: China and the West," in *China and the West: Comparative Literature Studies*, ed. William Tay, et al. (Hong Kong: Chinese University Press, 1980), p. 236. "What matters is . . . to study the world in which we live in just the same way as Shakespeare studies his." Jean-Louis Barrault, "Shakespeare and the French" (1948), in *Shakespeare in Europe*, ed. Oswald LeWinter (Cleveland: World Publishing Co., 1963), p. 368.

Notes for Chapter VIII:
Shakespeare and the Next Generation

1. *Twelfth Night*, 1.5.223. Shakespeare citations are taken from *The Riverside Shakespeare*, ed. G. B. Evans, et al. (Boston: Houghton Mifflin, 1974).

2. S. Schoenbaum, *William Shakespeare: A Documentary Life* (New York: Oxford University Press, 1975), p. 21.

3. The passage from Greene's *Groats-worth of Witte, Bought with a Million of Repentance* (1592), sig. A3v, is reproduced in Schoenbaum, *Documentary Life*, p. 115. See also Schoenbaum, pp. 166–73, for information concerning the Grant of Arms.

4. Yes, the text is will, and the interpreter, like the lady who "loves her will" (in the old rhyme), is ever guilty of a self-love as false as pride may be. No, the codes and conventions of the text are as good and true as anything else, and the interpreter can only love what has been created via ficky-fictions with others. "It is by the name we give others that in the last analysis we identify ourselves." Eugenio Donato, "The Two Languages of Criticism," in Richard Macksey and Eugenio Donato, eds., *The Structuralist Controversy* (Baltimore: The Johns Hopkins Press, 1970), p. 96. But what causes us to will the text's "will"? "What makes one set of perceptual strategies or literary conventions win out over another? If the world is the product of interpretation, then who or what determines which interpretive system will prevail?" Jane P. Tompkins, "The Reader in History: The Changing Shape of Literary Response," in *Reader-Response Criticism: From Formalism to Post-Structuralism*, ed. Jane P. Tompkins (Baltimore: The Johns Hopkins University Press, 1980), p. 226. Who or what besides the will to power and love?

5. In Shakespeare's day, "will" included meanings of sexual desire as well as the very organs of generation. Shakespeare's first name, proper and improper, was not only his to pun over: *Willobie His Avisa* (1594), cant. 43, mentions the "familiar frend W. S." who enlarged his friend's love-wound "with the sharpe rasor of a willing conceit" and mentions the "changes of affections & temptations which Will, set loose from Reason, can devise."

See B. N. DeLuna, *The Queen Declined* (Oxford: Clarendon, 1970), pp. 190–91.

6. Wilder possibilities abound: Shakes-pee-er may remind one of the Falstaff who enters (2H4, 2.4.34) with "Empty the jordan." Other phonemic texts include Sh-ache-ear, aches-peer, and Shakes-pier; possible Elizabethan pronunciations yield at least Shake-spare, Shakes-pear, and Shakes-pere.

7. *The Riverside Shakespeare*, p. 1604.

8. Stephen J. Brown, "The Uses of Shakespeare in America: A Study in Class Domination," in *Shakespeare: Pattern of Excelling Nature*, ed. David Bevington and Jay L. Halio (Newark, University of Delaware Press, 1978), p. 235, argues that teachers of Shakespeare have advanced a "cultural program, the imposition of white Anglo-Saxon Protestant civility from above" by a ruling class typically dominating college and school English curricula through control of major universities and the college entrance exams. At the center of the English curriculum lies Shakespeare and at the center of the Shakespeare curriculum lie the texts, the collected editions that dominate school and college courses and libraries. Almost all the major editions taught today bear the stamp of one institution: Harvard. Editors Kittredge (Ginn/Xirox), Neilson (Houghton Mifflin), Harbage (Pelican), Barnett (Signet), Bevington (Scott, Foresman), and Evans, with Baker and Levin (Riverside—Houghton) are from Harvard. Their editions are much more notable for similarities in styles and content of introductions, annotations, and other apparatus than for differences. All editions essay a high ethical, esthetic, and universalizing approach to Shakespeare at the expense of temporally contingent approaches that consider history, politics, sex, race, class, and religion. These editions slight the social function of drama in favor of timeless and often reactionary moral philosophy. "All is well with societies, families, and individuals when they do their duties and know their places": this is allegedly Shakespeare's "set of professed ideals" and "accepted world view" (Levin, Riverside edition, p. 7). We hear hardly a hint that such a set view was also radically challenged from within by skeptical and subversive ideologies. "Shakespeare," we are told, "was fundamentally conservative in his beliefs" (Penguin edition, p. 1). All these editions, moreover, appear to assume the rightful primacy of ego-centered interpretation—"Character remains the central factor in our apprehension of Shakespeare" (Riverside, p. 23)—whereas *relations* (sexual, familial, political, cosmological) are equally paramount. Finally, all the Harvard-dominated editions risk or invite anesthetized nonreadings by skirting the antiheroic strain of the *Henriad* and other histories, by slighting the New World relevance of *The Tempest* and other romances, and by emasculating language of sexual innuendo (by failing to gloss or by evasive annotation). A Shakespeare play must be noble or nothing. But "in such a play, the references to gods, wives, kings, and servants, to wars, epidemics, and power politics, do not represent social experience, but are transfigured on a higher, asocial realm. They are seen as expressions of timeless, 'universal' categories that are stylized as wearing white robes or speaking in verse. The tragedy does not take place somewhere, but Everywhere; it is

freed from having to be about something, in the interests of being about Everything." Lillian S. Robinson, *Sex, Class, and Culture* (Bloomington: Indiana University Press, 1980), pp. 57–58. On the typical conversion by English teachers of sociopolitical contingencies into moral absolutes, see H. Bruce Franklin, "English as an Institution: The Role of Class," in *English Literature: Opening up the Canon*, ed. Leslie A. Fiedler and Houston A. Baker, Jr. (Baltimore: Johns Hopkins University Press, 1981), p. 95.

9. Neither the health of the hoi polloi, the skill of the actors, nor the critic's wit renders nugatory the destructive force it both encounters and embodies. Weapons that are testaments to the artifice of high civilization still kill. Anne Barton quite misses this point when she writes, "Ultimately, Thersites' reductivist view of man is refuted by the simple fact that *Troilus and Cressida* exists. The disorder of the subject is not, as in so many twentieth-century works, reflected in its structure. This sense of mastery and control over difficult material is why, for all its pessimism and savagery, the experience of *Troilus and Cressida* is finally exhilarating" (Riverside edition, p. 447). One may catch the ring here without sharing Barton's desire to make the alleged medium of the play its message while evaporating the conventional message. A skeptic should not be called an idealist because his or her skepticism is so *artistic*. There is, on the other hand, something to be said for cleansing wrath and the sorts of satire that refine or deepen the ideals they see traduced. Whether and in what ways *Troilus and Cressida* or other Shakespeare plays may shatter or shore up or both depends on a host of contingencies among players, spectators, and their time. Anne Barton's sentiments, shared by many Shakespeareans, would automatically elevate form over content, structure over texture, consciousness over being, art over nature, aesthetics over ethics and history, hope over doubt—all questionable levitations. As teachers of Shakespeare, "our special contribution is not restricted to aesthetic concerns. We seem now to be relinquishing our overemphasis on the artistic aspects of literature. . . . That hardly means we should entirely abandon the aesthetic approach; it means only that we should keep it in bounds and resist its essentialistic claims." E. D. Hirsch, Jr., "Some Aims of Criticism," in *Literary Theory and Structure: Essays in Honor of William K. Wimsatt*, ed. Frank Brady, et al. (New Haven: Yale University Press, 1973), pp. 56–57.

10. "An art thus detached from the realities of living does not cease to be widely and intensely enjoyed. . . . According to Hegel, when art becomes pure it ceases to be serious, and in that consists its final splendour. . . . There is no denying that in our civilization, however lively art may seem, it has become a marginal occupation: but Hegel is much too certain in his belief that art will remain marginal for ever. 'At certain times,' as Burckhardt wrote, 'the world is over-run by false scepticism. . . . Of the true kind there can never be enough.'" Edgar Wind, *Art and Anarchy* (London: Faber and Faber, 1963), pp. 13–15. Leading advocates of the performance approach require today a healthy dose of our skepticism against their claims for a pure and universal Shakespeare. Let us question and resist such claims as these: "If Shakespeare's history plays depended on political or moral argument, they would not be vital today." John Russell Brown,

Discovering Shakespeare (New York: Columbia University Press, 1981), p. 21. "The twentieth century, which has revived *Troilus and Cressida* and made much of it, has perhaps fastened too singlemindedly on those elements in the play that may seem particularly to chime with the present age." Richard David, *Shakespeare in the Theatre* (London: Cambridge University Press, 1978), p. 126.

11. To recognize how much aggression lies in our relations to each generation and text is to recognize the impropriety of "coming to terms" or of seeking the "real" Shakespeare. Shakespeare assaults us with his massive paradoxes of weakness animated by strength and goodness animated by evil. Shakespeare, read whole, becomes parent, self, and child. What else can we do but generate, and sway within, the vital currents of our disaffection and affection for his plays?

Notes for Chapter IX: Aaron Murders the Nurse

1. Shakespeare citations are taken from *The Riverside Shakespeare*, ed. G. B. Evans, et al. (Boston: Houghton Mifflin, 1974).

2. S. S. Hussey, *The Literary Language of Shakespeare* (London and New York: Longman, 1982), p. 179, observes that the search for a language of "absolute integrity" in the speech of pure women proved to be "perhaps even beyond the range of the mature Shakespeare."

3. Cf. Lear's fool observing: "there was never yet fair woman but she made mouths in a glass" (3.2.35–36).

4. "'The good and white God made the Heaven, and Man from the middle upward; And the black and evil God was the efficient cause of the Earth, and of Man from the middle downward.'" John F. Danby, *Shakespeare's Doctrine of Nature: A Study of King Lear* (London: Faber, 1948), p. 34 (Quoting Launcelot Andrewes).

5. See Clarendon edition note as reprinted in *Hamlet*, New Variorum edition Horace Howard Furness (1877, rpt. New York: Dover, 1963), 1.291: "This epithet [fair] seems either to have suggested the word 'moor' in the following line, or to have been suggested by it."

6. "In his own mind she lives; . . . Cordelia is alive." Theodore Spencer, *Shakespeare and the Nature of Man* (1942, rpt. New York: Collier, 1966), p. 152.

7. It is difficult to overestimate "the degree to which an ambivalent discourse on female sexuality permeates Shakespeare's text." Louis Adrian Montrose, "'Shaping Fantasies': Figurations of Gender and Power in Elizabethan Culture," *Representations* 1, 2 (Spring 1983): 93.

8. *The Riverside Shakespeare*, p. 1833.

Notes for Chapter X: Teaching Shakespeare in America

1. References are to *The Riverside Shakespeare*, ed. G. Blakemore Evans, et al. (Boston: Houghton Mifflin, 1974).

2. *The Reading of Shakespeare in American Schools and Colleges* (New York: Simon and Schuster, 1932), p. 155. Subsequent references are cited by page number in the text.

3. *Shakespeare in America* (New York: Macmillan, 1939), pp. 247–48. Subsequent references are cited by page number in the text. Dunn's chapter 12, from which this quotation is taken, is titled "Shakespeare Enters the American Consciousness by Way of the Schools and Colleges."

4. *Shakespeare and the Revolution of the Times* (New York: Oxford University Press, 1976), p. 15.

5. A less sophisticated version of this cheerful, confident, feminist vision of reciprocal appropriations between Shakespeare and America is that of Nancy Webb and Jean Francis Webb, in *Will Shakespeare and His America* (New York: Viking, 1964), p. 13: "They tamed their forests and they built their cities and they bridged their continent. And almost from the first, Shakespeare was a part of it. He was read by candlelight as a revered philosopher in New England's earliest cultured homes." And so on. Male scholars tend to stress the difficulties and strains of appropriation: "Whatever may have been Shakespeare's interests in the colonization of America and his connection with the founders of Virginia, there is no evidence that any of the early settlers carried copies of his works across the Atlantic with them." So wrote Alfred Van Rensselaer Westfall in *American Shakespearean Criticism: 1607–1865* (New York: H. W. Wilson, 1939), p. 24. Louis Marder, in *His Exits and His Entrances: The Story of Shakespeare's Reputation* (Philadelphia: Lippincott, 1963), gives chapter 10 the title "Un-Willingly to School." Compare Ivor Brown and George Fearon, *The Shakespeare Industry: Amazing Monument* (New York: Harper and Bros., 1939), p. 269: "Many a Shakespeare Company has blessed the schools. Do the scholars bless Shakespeare? One sees them packed in the 'Old Vic' on winter afternoons or reclining in Regent's Park deck-chairs on summer ones. Some obviously are relishing the experience: others seem to be sleepy, bored, puzzled, wanting the strange noise to stop. No doubt the majority vote would be in favor."

6. See Franklin Thomas Baker, "Shakspere in the Schools," in *Shaksperian Studies*, ed. Brander Matthews and Ashley Horace Thorndike (1916; rpt. New York: Russell and Russell, 1962), p. 34.

7. Stephen J. Brown, "The Uses of Shakespeare in America: A Study in Class Domination," in *Shakespeare: Pattern of Excelling Nature. Shakespeare Criticism in Honor of America's Bicentennial from The International Shakespeare Association Congress, Washington, D.C., April 1976*, ed. David Bevington and Jay L. Halio (Newark: University of Delaware Press, 1978), p. 235. Subsequent references cited by page number in the text.

8. On issues of class bias in teaching English, see, for example, H. Bruce Franklin, "English as an Institution: The Role of Class," in *English Literature: Opening Up the Canon*, ed. Leslie A. Fiedler and Houston A. Baker, Jr. (Baltimore: Johns Hopkins University Press, 1981), pp. 92–106.

9. *Essays on English Studies* (Boston: Ginn, 1906), pp. 4–5, as quoted in Simon, *The Reading of Shakespeare*, p. 109.

10. See Brown, "The Uses of Shakespeare," p. 236.

11. On Shakespeare as a dynamic center for the clash of egalitarian and elitist ideals in earlier American culture, see for example, Dunn, *Shakespeare in America*, p. 134, comparing "primitive force" versus "fashion" on Shakespearean stages with democratic versus aristocratic views of society. Or see Charles H. Shattuck, *Shakespeare on the American Stage; From the Hallams to Edwin Booth* (Washington: Folger Shakespeare Library, 1976), pp. 62–87, on the clash between supporters of the American actor, Edwin Forrest, who was famous for his Bowery style, and authorities protecting the genteel English actor, William Charles Macready. The clash, in front of the Astor Place Opera House, 10 May 1849, left many wounded and 31 dead. Shakespeare tends to catalyze ideological responses of many varieties.

12. For assistance with this portion of the article, I am indebted to Susan Green, who reviewed available materials listed in Andrew M. McLean, *Shakespeare: Annotated Bibliographies and Media Guide for Teachers* (Urbana: NCTE, 1980), and other bibliographies on the teaching of Shakespeare.

13. See, for example, Lucius A. Sherman, "The Art of Shakespeare," in his *Analytics of Literature: A Manual for the Objective Study of English Prose and Poetry* (Boston: Ginn, 1889), pp. 144–89. Sherman ignores historical background, biography, imagery, and linguistic texture to analyze narrow issues of character psychology as related to scene construction; he also sees *Macbeth* as an empathic tragedy of guilt. See also, Gilbert S. Blakely, *Teacher's Outlines for Studies in English* (New York: American Book, 1908), pp. 63–68. Blakely stresses the "difficulties" of Shakespeare's language; he says that interest in *As You Like It* is "primarily aesthetic, not intellectual," and that Macbeth is "a noble soul led downward to destruction." Also see George L. Marsh, *Teacher's Manual for the Study of English Classics* (Chicago: Scott, Foresman, 1912). Marsh discusses plots with "moral lessons" thrown in and approaches "*Henry V* as the patriotic climax of Shakespeare's histories" (p. 90).

14. Emma H. Bolenius, *Teaching Literature in the Grammar Grades and High School* (Boston: Houghton Mifflin, 1915), toys (unconsciously?) with feminist and other ironies: "As the child develops, he passes through various stages from a primitive little savage to a young gentleman who brushes his teeth, takes off his hat to the ladies, and in a general way can be trusted in the drawing room. All through this development the dramatic instinct has been strong. The boy is not content only to read about Indians: he must himself be Big Chief" (p. 153). In teaching *The Merchant of Venice*, she says, "It is wise to pass over as lightly as possible the racial bearing" (p. 175). And she also offers "Life lessons in *Julius Caesar*.—There is a splendid chance here for the teacher to talk intimately about such subjects as civic duties, real patriotism, conflict of duties, standards by which to judge the value of high ideals, the contemptible side of conspiracies, a man's honor, the dangers of associating below one's level [etc.]" (p. 185). Franklin Thomas Baker, cited above in note 6, reviewed the history of Shakespeare teaching in America, dismissed the "forensic" interest of the elocution readers, sniffed at the psychological and ethical emphases of the Hudson-Rolfe school ("fatally easy," p. 36), and opted for "dramaturgic" study through student performance and analysis of Shakespeare's plays as dramas. But

Baker closed on a diffident note: "Do we really know what our pupils are getting from their study of Shakspere? . . . Has it inspired in many the wish to read other plays of Shakspere? I fear the librarians and the drama critics would not be enthusiastic in their answers" (pp. 40–41). According to H. Ward McGraw, *The Teaching of Literature in The High School: A Manual for Teachers* (New York: Charles Merrill, 1929), Shakespeare wrote *The Merchant of Venice* "to take advantage of the anti-Semitic feeling stirred up in London by the trial of Elizabeth's Jewish physician, Lopez" (p. 89).

15. See Clarence Stratton, *The Teaching of English in the High School* (New York: Harcourt, Brace, 1923), pp. 103–26; Charles Freis, *The Teaching of Literature* (New York: Silver, Burdett, 1926), p. 103; Percival Chubb, *The Teaching of English in the Elementary School* (New York: Macmillan, 1929), pp. 377, 545–47.

16. Thomas C. Blaisdell, *Ways to Teach English* (New York: Doubleday, 1930), pp. 457–64, argued for extensive reading aloud and acting. He said that teachers should substitute familiar words for Shakespeare's unfamiliar ones and inspire "love of the immortal thousand-minded bard"; he quoted approvingly an article arguing that "the average high school makes Shakespeare a bore," blaming this partly on the colleges that force schools to teach "enough routine of plot and smattering of philology to jam a child past the college entrance board." Contrast Tom P. Cross, et al., eds., *Good Reading for High School: English Writers* (Boston: Ginn, 1931), which boasts that it covers review questions from the college entrance examinations and suggests *Macbeth* for study in high school because of the "easily detected underlying theme" (p. 91). H. T. Baker asked, "Should Shakespeare Be Expurgated?" in *English Journal* 22 (1933): 127–31, and answered not for college students, though perhaps for younger ones. Plainly, teachers were searching for more energy from Shakespeare (or themselves). Henry W. Simon in "Why Shakespeare?" *English Journal* 23 (1934): 363–68, argued that only the best teachers and students should study Shakespeare (as gateway to earned upward mobility). G. F. Briggs in "Shakespeare in Schools," *Journal of Education* 68 (1936): 525–28, pointed out that Shakespeare can be "shockingly dull" and argued that the texts be cut for classroom use. Shakespeare, like other high literature, "must always be the heritage of the few." Lucia B. Mirrieless, *Teaching Composition and Literature in Junior and Senior High School* (New York: Harcourt, Brace, 1937), p. 333, noted "the futility of making a potential street cleaner, and a cook, and a garage mechanic, or even a potential minister, actor or college professor . . . hum with desire on the subject of Homeric poetry one month, Shakespearean comedy the next. . . . A small wire cannot carry a heavy current." She went on to counsel "state-trained teachers in a democracy" who would train students to live "in the co-operative democratic society we hope to see emerging out of the welter of the present day" (p. 336). She asked whether such teachers have failed if their pupils when "out of school do not pick up Shakespeare" and replied, "Not if they can follow written directions, or if they can forget factory life or illness or poverty in some tale of adventure. Not if they leave school with a social rather than an antisocial attitude toward society" (p. 337).

Against these indications that earlier dreams of high spiritual inspiration through study of Shakespeare and other classics had substantially faded may be placed other pedagogical urgings in the 1930s to renewed faith. Louise M. Rosenblatt in *Literature as Exploration* (New York: D. Appleton-Century, 1937), sought to "demonstrate that the study of literature can have a very real, and even central relation to the points of growth in the social and cultural life of a democracy" (p. v). Shakespeare "helps to make us understand what that kind of person [Cleopatra] is like" (p. 274). Dorothy Dakin, *How to Teach High School English* (New York: Heath, 1937), counseled teachers of Shakespeare that "interpretation of poetry does not demand a study of its anatomy. Yet a conception of the form of blank verse is necessary to be an educated person" (p. 284). "Direct," she said, "the attention of your group to Shakespeare's poetry, but ever keep in mind that major tenet of your teacher-creed: 'I will not force upon my pupils my own likes; I will not over-analyze'" (p. 288).

17. See Harry Levin, *Shakespeare and the Revolution of the Times* (New York: Oxford University Press, 1976), pp. 1–26 (subsequent references cited by page number in the text); Clyde Kenneth Hyder, *GLK: Teacher and Scholar* (Lawrence: University of Kansas Press, 1962); James Thorpe, *A Bibliography of the Writings of George Lyman Kittredge*, Introduction by Hyder Rollins (Cambridge, Mass.: Harvard University Press, 1948); Arthur Colby Sprague, "Preface" to *Sixteen Plays of Shakespeare*, ed. George Lyman Kittredge (Boston: Ginn, 1946); Elizabeth Jackson, "The Kittredge Way," *College English* 4 (May 1943): 483–87.

18. Sprague, *Sixteen Plays*, p. iv; see Hyder, *GLK*, pp. 41–72.

19. *Intellectual America* (New York: Macmillan, 1941), pp. 522–24. See also Albert George Alexander, "English Stones," *Peabody Journal of Education* 17 (1939): 37, attacking Kittredgean methods of teaching Shakespeare and specifically "the college professor whose either natural or assumed superscholarship and super intellectualism inculcate in his charges an attitude of contempt toward anything and everything in literature which savors of an ethical meaning or a broadly religious tenet."

20. See Harbage's *William Shakespeare: A Reader's Guide* (New York: Farrar, Straus, 1963), pp. x–xi, 6; and Harbage, gen. ed., *William Shakespeare: The Complete Works* (Baltimore: Penguin, 1969), p. x. Also see Harry Levin, *The Question of Hamlet* (New York: Oxford University Press, 1959), p. 13: "Since plays can be vehicles for ideas, as this play has so spectacularly been, we can illuminate it by our recourse to the history of ideas. But since it is, primarily and finally, a verbal structure, our scrutiny is more concretely rewarded at the level of phrase and emphasis."

21. See, for example, John J. DeBoer, et al., *Teaching Secondary English* (New York: McGraw-Hill, 1951): Shakespeare's vocabulary and "word combinations" can be understood, "can be a delight" (p. 223), and we can see "a complete pattern of life in a piece of literature" (p. 226). Philip M. Marsch, *How to Teach English* (New York: Bookman, 1956), p. 48, cautions against student readings that may sacrifice the "literary-critical approach," "the play as a piece of literature." Robert Ornstein, *Shakespeare in the Classroom* (Urbana: Educational Illustrators, 1960), p. 45, says that teachers should

help students read and study Shakespeare through direct interpretation, not audio-visual "looking." George R. Price, *Reading Shakespeare's Plays* (Great Neck, N.Y.: Barron's, 1962), advised students that Shakespeare's dramatic showmanship "is less important than Shakespeare's poetry"; "you can achieve success by intensive study of the lines of the plays, as the indispensable first step toward critical judgment. Further illumination of the meaning must come from the instructor and from reading criticism" (pp. 1–2). William J. Grace, *Approaching Shakespeare* (New York: Basic Books, 1964), subordinated "moral and intellectual values" to aesthetic/dramatic interests, based discussion questions on a host of critics (including T. S. Eliot, Granville-Barker, Knight, Spurgeon, Brooks, and Harbage), and asked such questions for students as "What is the predominant imagery of the play?" (pp. 204, 214). Though ostensibly espousing no instructional theory, Peter Neumeyer, "Teaching Shakespeare: An Anti-Method," *Clearing House* 38 (1964): 478, advised that the inquisitive teacher of Shakespeare, "to begin realizing what the many possibilities are, . . . can do no better than to acquaint himself with René Wellek and Austin Warren, *Theory of Literature*."

22. Alfred Harbage, *Conceptions of Shakespeare* (Cambridge, Mass.: Harvard University Press, 1966), p. 42.

23. This is the title of an essay by Louis B. Wright in NCTE's *Shakespeare in School and College* (Champaign, Ill.: National Council of Teachers of English, 1964). Wright there says that Shakespeare lives today "because he wrote about fundamental matters that concern us all, in every age and country. . . . In his poetic drama we receive instruction and we experience delight" (p. 15). This is just about all a student could desire.

24. "Criticism—20th Century," in *The Reader's Encyclopedia of Shakespeare*, ed. Oscar James Campbell and Edward G. Quinn (New York: Thomas Y. Crowell Co., 1966), p. 160.

25. *William Shakespeare: A Reader's Guide*, pp. 340, 399.

26. *Conceptions of Shakespeare*, p. 22. The following quotes are extracted from Harbage's work and are cited by page number in the text.

27. Twenty years after that was written, I could imagine asking college students to test Harbage's sentiments through such an essay question as the following: "Assume for the moment that Shakespeare and his texts adhere in some significant sense to a sociopolitical ideology asking men to be strong and aggressive yet honorable and women to be weak and submissive yet chaste. How might it be argued that *Venus and Adonis, Rape of Lucrece*, the *Sonnets*, and *The Taming of the Shrew* in various ways doubt, deny, or undo such an ideology? How might it be argued that any such doubt, denial, or undoing is, finally, partial and relatively ineffective? After establishing the dialogue between the two arguments, tell us what you really think Shakespeare stands for on this issue."

28. Levin said that Shakespeare "initiates us into the mystery of evil," and "he heartens us . . . to take an ethical stance against overwhelming odds" (*Shakespeare and the Revolution of the Times*, p. 50). Margery Bailey, "Shakespeare in Action" *English Journal* 43 (1954): 141, said that Shakespeare and his people "fill our universe and interpret it anew for our best

good." Roy L. Felscher, "Two Shakespearean History Plays: *Richard III,
Henry V,*" in *Teaching Literature in Grades Seven Through Nine* (Bloomington: Indiana University Press, 1967), p. 130, considered the possibility that *Henry V* "may be Shakespeare's ironic portrait of a misguided king" but dismissed the possibility in favor of a "deeper and more humane patriotism which emerges from Shakespeare's play." Frank S. Hook, "So You're Going to Teach Shakespeare," *English Journal* 56 (1967): 1122, counseled neophytes to remember that "Elizabethans still lived in a world that was comfortable—philosophically comfortable, that is," a world that was "stable, ordered, and, above all, rational." Compare Levin's depiction of the "accepted world view" among Elizabethans, in *The Riverside Shakespeare*, p. 7.

29. *Shakespeare: A Reader's Guide*, pp. 178, 193, 194.

30. Ed. Arthur Mizener (New York: New American Library, 1969), p. 72.

31. Hans P. Guth, *English Today and Tomorrow: A Guide for Teachers of English* (Englewood Cliffs, N.J.: Prentice Hall, 1964), p. 328. Compare, Florence H. Diesman, "Shakespeare in High School Today," *Journal of Secondary Education* 40 (1965): 131: "Miss Bell kept the class so interested in the caskets and the choice of the right one that the defection of Jessica from her religion and her father did not seriously trouble the freshman." And see Penelope Scambly Schott, "The Chronicle of Wasted Time: Some Observations on Shakespeare in High School and How to Recover," *CEA Forum* 6 (December 1975): 2–3, 10–11, lamenting the inattention paid in schools to Shylock's Jewishness or Othello's blackness.

32. See, for example, Alan C. Purves, "You Can't Teach *Hamlet*, He's Dead," *English Journal* 57 (1968): 832–36, arguing for an affective, student-centered emphasis; James Hoetker and Alan Englesman, *An Introduction to Theatre*, rev. ed. (Central Mid-western Regional Education Laboratory, 1969), 2:45, ask teachers to improvise and dramatize with students as "origins" of knowledge, not "power," so that they can have "a genuine emotional response to something in a Shakespeare play"; Theodore W. Hipple, *Teaching English in Secondary Schools* (New York: Macmillan, 1973), asks for English classes that are process-centered and student-centered; Bernard A. Drabeck, "Ban Shakespeare," in his *Studies for Composition* (Boston: Houghton Mifflin, 1974), insists that high-school students are simply unready for the difficulty and maturity of Shakespeare.

33. "Direct Method Shakespeare," *SQ* 25 (1974): 198–99.

34. Baker, "Shakspere in the Schools," p. 34; H. Caldwell Cook, *The Play Way: An Essay in Educational Method*, 2d ed. (New York: Stokes, 1919); A. K. Hudson, *Shakespeare and the Classroom* (London: Heinemann, 1954). J. L. Styan, Homer Swander, and Hugh Richmond advert to their methods in an issue of *Shakespeare Newsletter* 25 (1975): 9–20. See also Morris Eaves, "The Real Thing: A Plan for Producing Shakespeare in the Classroom," *College English,* 31 (1970), 463–72; and "Teaching Shakespeare," essays in *Focus*, 2:3 (Spring 1976), passim.

35. Walter F. Eggers, Jr., Introduction to *Teaching Shakespeare* (Princeton University Press, 1977), pp. xii-xiii.

36. See, for example, Patricia K. Meszaros, "Notes on a Workshop Approach to Shakespeare," *SQ* 25 (1974): 188–97, and Jay L. Halio, " 'This Wide and Universal Stage': Shakespeare's Plays as Plays," in *Teaching Shakespeare*, pp. 273–89.

37. From recent studies such as Mary C. Anderson, *Drama in the English Department* (privately printed, Columbia: University of South Carolina, 1984), and Mira P. Brichto, *Shakespearean Drama As It Is Taught and Learned in Three Urban Secondary Schools* (Ann Arbor: University Microfilms, 1977), it is readily apparent how overwhelmingly text-centered and anti-performative the teaching of Shakespeare remains.

38. See *The Division of the Kingdoms: Shakespeare's Two Versions of King Lear*, ed. Gary Taylor and Michael Warren (Oxford: Clarendon, 1983); Peter W. M. Blayney, *The Texts of King Lear and Their Origins* (Cambridge University Press, 1982); P. W. K. Stone, *The Textual History of King Lear* (London: Scolar, 1980); Steven Urkowitz, *Shakespeare's Revision of King Lear* (Princeton University Press, 1980); and Michael J. Warren, "Quarto and Folio *King Lear* and the Interpretation of Albany and Edgar," in *Shakespeare: Pattern of Excelling Nature*, pp. 95–107.

39. For a trenchant discussion of this problem, see Random Cloud [alias Randall McLeod], "The Marriage of Good and Bad Quartos," *SQ* 33 (1982): 421–31, and especially (with reference to texts of *Romeo and Juliet*), p. 427: "For the editor to leave both versions of the 'grey-ey'd morn' speech in a modern edition might make for some awkwardness for readers (as they are presently trained). We can expect then, that publishers, whose editions must sell, expect their editors to keep their eye on the reader's ease as well as on what $hakespeare wrote—which renders editors cross-eyed as well as myopic, and accounts for their ledgerdomain. But if both versions were retained, the benefits for the reader would be more than commensurate with the difficulty of having to read 'what Shakespeare wrote,' for the reader would thereby gain some access to the problematic in his art."

40. Compare Lillian S. Robinson, *Sex, Class, and Culture* (Bloomington: Indiana University Press, 1980), p. 45: "As the twentieth century advances, culture increasingly participates in the maintenance of bourgeois ideology; its main vehicle, both in criticism and in art, is modernism. 'Great' art and literature enter the curriculum of working class and black high schools and of two-year colleges. They appear in modernist guise, stripped of their full historical meaning and transported to the timeless realm of universals. By teaching art and literature in this way, the educational system tries to do to the students what it has done to the subjects: it implicitly denies them their own full historical identity and instead suggests that they are too isolated, unconnected, and powerless. Art has been forced to support and critics have up to now perpetuated this ideological mystification."

41. E. A. J. Honigmann, *Shakespeare's Impact on His Contemporaries* (London: Macmillan, 1982), p. 21, a book that persuasively questions the image, promulgated by S. Schoenbaum, Harbage, and others, of Gentle Will Shakespeare.

42. But suggestively contra, see Jonathan Dollimore, *Radical Tragedy: Religion, Ideology, and Power in the Drama of Shakespeare and His Contemporaries* (University of Chicago Press, 1984).

43. "While all crafts need their critics, this is especially true in education, where so much evidence abounds to challenge the status quo. Universities must forward this challenge, must be places of skepticism, challenging even the best of the craft." So writes Theodore R. Sizer in *Places for Learning, Places for Joy* (Cambridge, Mass: Harvard University Press, 1973), pp. 130–31.

44. William G. Perry, Jr., *Forms of Intellectual and Ethical Development in the College Years* (New York: Holt, Rinehart, 1968), p. 36. A possibly over-optimistic argument of this important book is that there has been a "great educational revolution of the past fifty years" (p. 35)—even at Harvard—in which college students have been asked to think more independently, relativistically, and contingently, and to think critically about how to think, so that they may take greater responsibility for their own ways of thinking and valuing. But this crucial issue of independence and choice, or critical thinking, has inhered deeply in many mature philosophies of teaching developed through the ages and not just the past fifty years. "Ideally, education should lead the public, not vice versa. But to do this it must be self-critical, and constantly so. . . . We cannot do our children's thinking for them. Either they do it or else it isn't their thinking." So write Robert S. Brumbaugh and Nathaniel M. Lawrence in *Philosophers on Education: Six Essays on the Foundations of Western Thought* (Boston: Houghton Mifflin, 1963), pp. 186, 190. John Passmore, "The Anatomy of English Teaching," in *The Philosophy of Teaching* (Cambridge, Mass.: Harvard University Press, 1980), pp. 234–35, analyzes the English teacher's "terrible responsibility" to help students truly "participate in the life of the world," including the "violent passion" of Shakespeare and other conventionally "good" writers. Michael S. Littleford, in "The Feminization of American Education—A Review Essay," *Southern Humanities Review* 15 (Winter 1980): 70, laments the degree to which a "male 'priesthood'" of school administrators has too often "worshipped, imitated, and served American business. Among many other dismal consequences, schools were made maximally responsive to business' demands for cheap and docile workers. Hence, from this more inclusive perspective, after a brief period of tentativeness, American public education came back into the venerable tradition of Western education which, since Plato, has served the interests of the actual ruling classes in society." And Henry A. Giroux, "Public Philosophy and the Crisis in Education," *Harvard Educational Review* 54 (1984): 193, descries in the very recent debates over education in the United States a "new public philosophy" opposed to critical literacy and to independent citizen participation in cultural processes, whereas, in contrast, "The notion of being able to think critically on the basis of informed judgment and to develop a respect for democratic forms of self- and social-empowerment represents the basis for organizing school programs around the principles of critical literacy and civic courage."

45. John Russell Brown, *Discovering Shakespeare* (New York: Columbia University Press, 1981), p. 131.

46. Compare Sizer, *Places for Learning*, p. 50: "The disciplines of hand and eye do not simply support the mind: They have a life of their own and give power by opening the way to new kinds of expression and understanding. The average American rarely understands these potentials and neither does his local school authority. Their view of nonintellectual power depends on 'usefulness.' . . . Kinetic power, however—the use of the body—is completely foreign to American educators and almost impossible to bootleg within one of the standard subjects."

47. For example, Mary Ann Caws, "Realizing Fictions," *PMLA* 99 (1984): 315: "The self, with all its quirks, may be inscripted in the reading not just as reader, not just as part of some interpretive community or other. We begin there, to be sure, but we end in a felt and shared commonality where the autobiographical and the experiential have their places just as surely as do the objective and the learned. No part of us, I am absolutely convinced, has to be omitted in our all-inclusive involvement with the personal and textual encounters in our classrooms or with our criticism. A *corporeal and mental connection* intensely involved with everything we choose . . . urges, even in our massive network, the sharing of our personal voice" (emphasis supplied). Karl Kroeber, in "The Evolution of Literary Study, 1883–1983," *PMLA* 99 (1984): 336, says, "What we teach is in good measure the deepening and sharpening of emotional power."

48. Peter Abbs, *English Within the Arts: A Radical Alternative for English and the Arts in the Curriculum* (London: Hodder and Stoughton, 1982), p. 83.

Notes for Chapter XI: Shakespeare's Bombast

1. Quotations of Shakespeare from Riverside edition, ed. G. B. Evans, et al. (Boston: Houghton, Mifflin, 1974).

2. Gladys D. Willcock, "Shakespeare and Rhetoric," in *Essays and Studies by Members of the English Assoc.* 29 (1943) (Oxford: Clarendon, 1944), p. 54.

3. Riverside edition, p. 1722.

4. See Henry W. Simon, *The Reading of Shakespeare in American Schools and Colleges: An Historical Survey* (New York: Simon & Schuster, 1932), chapter 2; Esther Cloudman Dunn, *Shakespeare in America* (New York: Macmillan, 1939), chapter 12.

5. Gladys D. Willcock, "Shakespeare and Elizabethan English," in *A Companion to Shakespeare Studies*, ed. Harley Granville-Barker and G. B. Harrison (1934, rpt. Garden City: Anchor, 1960), p. 129.

6. G. Wilson Knight, "The Teacher as Poetic Actor," in *Teaching Shakespeare*, ed. Walter Edens, et al. (Princeton University Press, 1977), pp. 299–301.

7. Abraham Bernstein, *Teaching English in High School* (New York: Random House, 1961), p. 223.

8. Reported in Mira P. Brichto, *Shakespearean Drama As It Is Taught and Learned in Three Urban Secondary Schools* (Ann Arbor: University Microfilms, 1977), pp. 46–47.

9. Muriel L. Bradbrook, *Shakespeare: The Poet in His World* (London: Weidenfeld and Nicolson, 1978), p. 13: "In *Troilus and Cressida* Shakespeare was to write a whole play in specially Latinate diction."

10. Alfred Harbage, *William Shakespeare: A Reader's Guide* (New York: Farrar, Straus, 1963), pp. 17–19; David M. Zesmer, *Guide to Shakespeare* (New York: Barnes and Noble, 1976), pp. 15–17; Maurice Charney, *How to Read Shakespeare* (New York; McGraw-Hill, 1971), pp. 54–55; "Many of Holofernes' terms of Art, like *intimation, explication,* and *insinuation* . . . are so ordinary today that no one would suspect them of once having formed part of a comic turn. Posterity has here vindicated the industry of the pedant." G. D. Willcock, *Shakespeare as Critic of Language* (London: Shakespeare Assoc., 1934), p. 13: "Thus ornament, which by us may be deemed irrelevant if not intrusive, is essential to the Elizabethans, not as the expression of meaning but as the pleasure of art." Marion Trousdale, *Shakespeare and the Rhetoricians* (Chapel Hill: University of North Carolina Press, 1982), p. 94. But such variants of excessive aestheticism are neatly countered by Benedetto Croce's observation that the rhetoricians have never truly reconciled their love of ornament and that "fitting" which "coincides with expression itself." *Aesthetic,* trans. Douglas Ainslie, rev. ed. 1927 (New York: Farrar, Straus, 1966), p. 429.

11. "The conditions of Shakespeare's art did not permit him to stray far from popular idiom, but even if they had his mind was of a cast that would still have found the material upon which it worked mainly in the diction of common life." Frank P. Wilson, *Shakespeare and the Diction of Common Life* (London: Humphrey Milford, 1941), p. 5. See Willcock, "Shakespeare and Elizabethan English," p. 120; D. S. Bland, "Shakespeare and the 'Ordinary' Word," *Shakespeare Survey* 4 (1951): 49–55; Muriel St. Clare Byrne, "The Foundations of Elizabethan Language," *Shakespeare Survey* 17 (1964), rpt. in *Shakespeare in His Own Age,* ed. Allardyce Nicoll (London: Cambridge University Press, 1976), pp. 223–39.

12. Kenneth Hudson, "Shakespeare's Use of Colloquial Language," *Shakespeare Survey* 23 (1970): 45.

13. M. M. Reese, *Shakespeare: His World and His Work,* rev. ed. (London: Edward Arnold, 1980), pp. 8–9.

14. Kenneth Charlton, *Education in Renaissance England* (London: Routledge and Kegan Paul, 1965), p. 124. Charlton goes on to detail the ways in which this Latinate education was turned "into a grind of mechanical repetition": "What Rabelais referred to as 'verbosification' and the 'gymnastics of nothingness,' Milton was still, a century later, calling 'gerund grinding; . . . Rhetoric, which Cicero, Quintilian and the humanists had meant to be an essential tool in the hands of the educated man of affairs had now, paradoxically, become the trade mark of the cloistered pedant, mere Ciceronianism. . . . Instead of acting as breeding grounds for humanist ideas, a distinct possibility at the beginning of the period, the grammar schools became instruments of national policy, a means of strengthening the State against religious innovation. The grammar schools of Renaissance England had become to the nation what the voluntary elementary schools of

the nineteenth century were to their various denominational sponsors, instruments for maintaining the *status quo*" (pp. 127-30).

15. Walter J. Ong, *Rhetoric, Romance, and Technology* (Ithaca: Cornell University Press, 1971), pp. 63-64.

16. Miriam Joseph, *Shakespeare's Use of the Arts of Language*, 1947, rpt. (New York: Hafner Pub. Co., 1966), pp. 286-87.

17. N. F. Blake, *Shakespeare's Language* (London: Macmillan, 1983), p. 50.

18. Ong, *Rhetoric, Romance, and Technology*, p. 121, and see p. 128.

19. Walter J. Ong, *The Barbarian Within* (New York: Macmillan, 1962), p. 181. Compare Wilson, *Shakespeare and the Diction of Common Life*, p. 27, extolling "with what nobility" Shakespeare transmutes the diction of common life upward.

20. Bryan A. Garner, "Shakespeare's Latinate Neologisms," *Shakespeare Studies* 15 (1982): 149-70.

21. "How definitely this American training in rhetoric was a preparation for a later career in pulpit or legislature or courtroom (for theater, too, though this fact would not have been admitted) is shown by the absence of elocution in a volume constructed exclusively for 'young ladies.'" Dunn, *Shakespeare in America*, p. 235.

22. "Yet in the different voice of women lies the truth of an ethic of care, the tie between relationship and responsibility, and the origins of aggression in the failure of connection." Carol Gilligan, *In a Different Voice* (Cambridge, Mass.: Harvard University Press, 1982), p. 173.

23. H. M. Klein, review of *Shakespeares Stil*, by Jürgen Schäfer, in *Shakespeare Studies* 9 (1976): 79.

24. A. J. Gilbert, *Literary Language from Chaucer to Johnson* (London: Macmillan, 1979), p. 79.

25. G. L. Brook, *The Language of Shakespeare* (London: André Deutsch, 1976), p. 33.

26. S. S. Hussey, *The Literary Language of Shakespeare* (London: Longman, 1982), pp. 178-79. "These women tried to find a personal style in which to express their intimate thoughts and feelings. Until about the middle of the twelfth century Latin was *de rigueur,* and when women tried to escape its rigidity, and the rhetorical rules of composition, they would be accused of writing badly when they were simply trying to say what they meant." Paula Neuss, "In Pursuit of Intimacy," review of Peter Dronke, *Women Writers of the Middle Ages*, in *TLS*, 17 February, 1984, p. 172.

27. Arthur F. Kinney, "Rhetoric as Poetic: Humanist Fiction in the Renaissance," *ELH* 43 (1976): 440. But see Margreta de Grazia, "Shakespeare's View of Language: An Historical Perspective," *SQ* 29 (1978): 374-88.

28. Arthur B. Ferguson, *Clio Unbound: Perception of the Social and Cultural Past in Renaissance England* (Durham: Duke University Press, 1979), p. 314.

29. Rosalie L. Colie, *Shakespeare's Living Art* (Princeton University Press, 1974), pp. 43, 166, 349.

30. Ibid., 206, 351.

31. T. W. Baldwin, *William Shakspere's Smalle Latine & Lesse Greeke* (Urbana: University of Illinois Press, 1944), 2:671.

32. By Paul A. Jorgensen (Berkeley: University of California Press, 1962), p. 120.

33. Jonathan Culler, *The Pursuit of Signs* (Ithaca: Cornell University Press, 1981), p. 168. "The poet's insight into such an ambiguous power may well have had something of a 'cursed spite.' His tragic heroes have an extraordinary command of the language, but instead of earning them 'honor, love, obedience, troops of friends' (*Macbeth*, 5.3.25), it drives them to deeper and deeper isolation, a solitude in which they are estranged not only from everything and everybody else but even from themselves. Who can say how far the most destructive efforts of word-play were with him reaction or surrender to a poet's loneliness?" Michel Grivelet, "Shakespeare as 'Corrupter of Words,'" *Shakespeare Survey* 16 (1963): 74. "A literary text simultaneously asserts and denies the authority of its own rhetorical mode." Paul de Man, *Allegories of Reading* (New Haven: Yale University Press, 1979), p. 17. It would be perverse, no doubt, to suggest that there may indeed be an element of "crazy-making" in such remarks as these three.

34. Jane Donawerth, *Shakespeare and the Sixteenth-Century Study of Language* (Urbana: University of Illinois Press, 1984), p. 76.

Index

Herein are noted significant references to topics addressed in the text, to characters in the plays, to discussions of plays, and to historical and literary figures and the like. I exclude peripheral mention of characters, plays, or figures.

203

Iago (*Oth.*), 114, 144
Imagery: stage, 6–8
Imagination: Shakespeare's materializing, 92, 115
Imogen, 69, 80, 71, 88
Interpretation: procedural problems of, 1–4; relativism in, 2; methods of Shakespearean, 3–10, 29–48; etymology of term, 5; rhetorical, 5, 33; educative, 6, 10; of dramatic devices, 6–8, 30–31; verbal compared to visual, 6–10; of *AYL*, 12–14; spatial, 29–33; affective, 33–38; historical, 51–53, 58–62. *See also* Criticism; Interpreters
Interpreters: as reflecting their culture, 2–3, 6; prescriptive functions, 185n46; and performance, 185–86n48, 186n48
Isabella (*MM*), 114

Jailer's Daughter (*TNK*), 86–81 *passim*
Jamestown colony, 48, 59–61 *passim*
Jaques: and seven ages of man, 13
Joan of Arc (*1H6*), 115
Johnson, Samuel, 3, 28–28
Jonson, Ben, 148
Juliet (*Rom.*), 68, 68, 86, 77, 88, 91, 119

Katharine (*H8*): and weeping, 84; mentioned, 74, 88
Kate (*Shr.*), 113
Kelso, Ruth, 85–86
Kermode, Frank, 50–51
King Lear: kneeling in, 6; Edgar in, 8; patrilineal issues in, 66–68 *passim*; weeping in, 82–84, 86, 88; text of, 96, 136; mentioned, 8, 16, 63, 82
King Lear: and weeping, 88; and bombast, 148; mentioned, 113, 158, 163
Kittredge, G. L., 129–30
Knight, G. Wilson, 130
Knights, L. C., 130

Lady Macbeth, 91, 114, 119
Lavinia (*Tit.*), 91, 112–13
Lee, Sidney, 49

Leontes (*WT*), 44, 69–82 *passim*, 148
Levin, Harry, 124, 130
Love's Labor's Lost, 99, 145, 153
Lowell, James Russell, 124
Luce, Morton, 49

Macbeth, 63, 63–68, 132
Macbeth: and weeping, 90; and bombast, 148, 159
Mack, Maynard, 134
Magellan, 50–58 *passim*
Malone, Edmond, 48
Marina, 69–82 *passim*
Marriage: in Shakespeare's comedy, 28
Marx, Leo, 51
Meadowcroft, J. W. R., 94–95
Meaning: and *WT*, 32–36, 45; and editorial control, 96–98. *See also* Experience of drama
Measure for Measure: substitution of heads, 6–8; election of leader in, 9; generational succession in, 28
Merchant of Venice, The, 133
Merry Wives of Windsor, The, 63
Metabolism, dramatic: in Shakespeare generally, 8–8; in *AYL*, 19; mentioned, 45
Midsummer Night's Dream, A, 63
Miranda, 69–82 *passim*, 88
Modesty: and theater, 98–100
More, Sir Thomas, 2
Moor, The, 118
Mouths: attacks on womens', 116–18
Much Ado About Nothing, 11, 12

Nature: eroticized in tragedies, 89–93; mentioned, 18, 28
Newes from Virginia (Richard Rich), 59–60
New World: Shakespeare in the, 126; Renaissance images of the, 48–62 *passim*, 189n20. *See also The Tempest*
Nurse: *Tit.*, 112, 114; *Rom.*, 114
Nursing: and weeping, 91; and snakes, 114–16